"In Whittock's excellent volume, we have a boo
the end times? Has there ever been an age wit.
wars,' as the Gospels warn? Whittock's first-class study helps us to reengage
with some of those central questions and concerns that are common to all
faiths: What time is it? Where are we going? And are we nearly there?"

—Martyn Percy, Dean of Christ Church, Oxford

"This is a nicely written, very readable, and thoroughgoing review of the centrality of 'end-times' thinking within the history of Christian thought from
the Hebrew scriptures to the present. The importance of Whittock's book lies
in his demonstration that eschatology is not the sole preserve of the modern political and religious right but is, and has always been, compatible with
many different religious, social, economic, and political agendas."

—Philip Almond, Professor emeritus, The University of Queensland, and author of
The Antichrist: A New Biography

"Whittock writes a highly accessible and abundantly helpful account
of how Christian writers through the ages have interpreted apocalyptic
scriptures. Such readings have often, but not always, led to culturally and
politically divisive movements. Whittock, however, offers a hopeful vision, reminding us that Christians can remain devoted to the Scriptures
and still embrace the world and its challenges."

—Glenn W. Shuck, author of *Marks of the Beast: The Left Behind Novels
and the Struggle for Evangelical Identity*

"*The End Times, Again?* is truly a book for our time. It is a wonderfully well-written survey of a vast sweep of Western history and the ways in which
interpretations of biblical prophecy have influenced culture, politics, religion, and even armed conflicts. . . . The book is particularly noteworthy
in that it includes our post-9/11 world, Trump's MAGA movement, and
the profound ways in which recent ways of recasting 'prophecy belief' are
shaping our society."

—James D. Tabor, Professor of Ancient Judaism and Early Christianity,
The University of North Carolina at Charlotte

The End Times, Again?

The End Times, *Again?*

2000 Years of the Use & Misuse of Biblical Prophecy

Martyn Whittock

CASCADE *Books* · Eugene, Oregon

THE END TIMES, AGAIN?
2000 Years of the Use & Misuse of Biblical Prophecy

Cascade Books
An Imprint of Wipf and Stock Publishers
199 W. 8th Ave., Suite 3
Eugene, OR 97401

www.wipfandstock.com

PAPERBACK ISBN: 978-1-7252-5844-0
HARDCOVER ISBN: 978-1-7252-5843-3
EBOOK ISBN: 978-1-7252-5845-7

Cataloguing-in-Publication data:

Names: Whittock, Martyn, author.

Title: The end times, again? : 2000 years of the use & misuse of biblical prophecy / by Martyn Whittock.

Description: Eugene, OR: Cascade Books, 2021 | Includes bibliographical references.

Identifiers: ISBN 978-1-7252-5844-0 (paperback) | ISBN 978-1-7252-5843-3 (hardcover) | ISBN 978-1-7252-5845-7 (ebook)

Subjects: LCSH: End of the world—Biblical teaching. | Eschatology—History of doctrines. | Millennium (Eschatology)—History of doctrines. | Bible—Prophecies—End of the world. | Bible—Prophecies—Second Advent.

Classification: BT819.5 W45 2021 (print) | LCC BT819.5 (ebook)

10/08/21

To John Worth, Heather Waldsax, and John Waldsax.

People of deep Christian faith.

Thank you for your friendship over many years.

Contents

Acknowledgments

I AM GRATEFUL TO a number of people who have assisted me in the writing of this book. Allan Coutts, Heather Waldsax, and David Bowater offered helpful insights regarding a number of areas of the text. Conversations regarding faith, theology, and history are a frequent part of discussions with my family. I thank them for their support and for always being willing to let me discuss my ideas with them. I also wish to thank my agent, Robert Dudley, for his friendship, advice, and encouragement over many years, and the team at Cascade Books (an imprint of Wipf and Stock) for their support.

The authorial views, interpretations, and assessments within this book are my own. All errors, of course, are also my own.

1

Setting the Scene

IN JUNE 2016, AS a preacher and church leader, I organized a meeting, under the banner of the local council of churches in a West Country town in the United Kingdom, to discuss issues relating to the forthcoming EU Referendum. The meeting was intended to provide an opportunity for airing Christian views on the subject. It was very well attended and drew in participants from across the wide denominational spectrum of churches.

The evening was lively. Many of my friends (regardless of whether they were Leave or Remain in the context of the EU Referendum) expressed astonishment afterwards at the way the discussion developed. They had expected the topics to include debates over things like: sovereignty and parliamentary accountability; jobs and economic prosperity; continent-wide cooperation in order to meet global challenges; peace and security in Europe.

What they got was: whether the EU parliament building in Strasburg was modelled on the Tower of Babel; the accusation that the statue of Europa and the Bull in the European district of Brussels reveals the pagan origins of the EU; the allegation that the seat 666 is kept empty in the European Parliament chamber in both Brussels and Strasbourg (it isn't); discussion over whether the EU represents the final political structure arising from the four beasts/kingdoms prophesied in Daniel,[1] and also referred to as the "beast rising out of the sea, having ten horns and seven heads" in Revelation;[2] whether it was a political tool of Antichrist in advance of the second coming of Christ.

My friends were astonished at this. I wasn't. That was because, for me, it was a return to what had *once been* familiar home ground. During the previous month I had contributed a guest blog for *Premier Christianity online*. It had been entitled: "I Believe in Prophecy. But the EU Is Not Babylon the Great." During that month (it went live on 25 May 2016) it had become, from my calculations, one of the most visited blogs on this website.[3] It can still be read online but, unfortunately, the huge string of comments and conversations under it can no longer be accessed. That is a pity because they would have provided interesting source material for future students of theology and the sociology of religion. Like the meeting I organized later, in June of that year, the online discussion got lively. In fact, it got *very lively indeed!*

However, when it comes to end-time speculation I "have a past," as they say. I was born in 1958 and, consequently, I was a child of the seventies, as these were my teenage years. While the swinging sixties may have been the decade for other young people to push the boundaries from fashion to pop music (and a lot in between), the seventies were a great decade to be a young millenarian. Millenarianism refers to the belief that the second coming of Christ will establish a literal kingdom on earth, leading to a millennium of peace, prior to the final judgement. There are different variations of this concept, as there are to all aspects of end-times belief.

Back to the future

Like many around me in the 1970s, I looked back to the ancient biblical prophecies in an attempt to predict the future. I grew up in an evangelical Methodist household that had friendly connections with local members of the Church of England, Baptists, and (especially) Elim Pentecostals. I counted members of all these churches among my friends. But for all our differences in churchmanship (which was largely irrelevant to us) one thing that united many of us was our fascination with the second coming of Christ. At that time, over forty years ago, it influenced our whole approach to the news. For example, a friend of a friend thought that Henry Kissinger might be the Antichrist. I was never entirely sure why this identification was made but seem to recall it was in some way connected to a set of Bible verses,

> For you yourselves know very well that the day of the Lord will come like a thief in the night. When they say, "There is peace and security," then sudden destruction will come upon them, as labor pains come upon a pregnant woman, and there will be no escape![4]

2

The connection with Kissinger seemed to be that his shuttle-diplomacy might lead to a peace deal that, somehow, was not one approved by God but would elevate Kissinger to unheard of heights of (malign) political influence, due to the impressiveness of the achievement. Even as a teenager, I was unconvinced by the persuasiveness of this as the basis for such a serious charge. This was especially so as Kissinger was attempting to broker Middle Eastern peace. However, looking back, I think that quite a lot of what was being published then (often originating in the USA) on the subject of the second coming almost willed forthcoming catastrophic conflict.

In retrospect I think, perhaps unfairly, that some of the authors would actually have been disappointed if lasting peace had been achieved in the Middle East, as their apocalyptic expectations would have been disappointed. That is because these predicted catastrophes were seen as the prelude to the second coming. That had a particular irony because all the authors professed profound affection for Israel; despite not really wanting peace in the Middle East.

The fascination with Israel influenced the thinking of many end-times writers at the time, who followed events in the Middle East with intense interest. Those who read their books were encouraged to see all the twists and turns of these events as fulfilments of prophecy indicating the imminent end times. I remember reading one writer who strongly suggested that this would occur within forty years of 1948. That put it as occurring by 1988, which certainly focused the minds of those reading their work! Somewhere I still have the scrapbook I compiled during the 1973 Yom Kippur War. Its compilation was assisted by the fact that I worked as a paperboy for a local newsagent. After finishing my round, I would scour the abandoned newspapers for the latest on events of the war.

In 1975, as an impressionable sixteen-year-old, I avidly devoured the book *The Late, Great Planet Earth*, written by Hal Lindsey, with Carole C. Carlson. It had been published in 1970, but took five years to cross my radar. It pulled together so many threads of thought, or so it seemed at the time. Guided by Lindsey and Carlson, I explored chapters of Daniel, Ezekiel, and Revelation that I had never read before; and had certainly never heard addressed by a preacher in my church. I became familiar with kingdoms with four phases and beasts with ten horns. I learned of the role of the communist USSR (and China) in end-times events; and I discovered tribes called Gog, Magog, Meshech, and Tubal and their apparent invasion of Israel in the last days and how they represented the (then-communist)

Warsaw Pact states. I was introduced to a future end-times battle at a place called Armageddon and its geographical location in northern Israel. Also, woven into these future events, was the hidden role of the papacy.

The book encouraged its readers to trace the way all these things were playing out in the world around them. It was not an isolated publication by any means. It alleged that the European EEC/EU was the prophesied successor to the fourth kingdom of Daniel and also represented the ten-headed beast of Revelation. Since 1973 its membership had stood at nine nations[5] and such books encouraged readers to expectantly look for the accession of its critical tenth state. Norwegian voters had thwarted this expected enlargement to ten states at the time of the UK's accession, but the day would come. I had no knowledge of the pros and cons of membership, other than the negative mood-music I picked up from some secular UK newspapers. But it was not that which motivated my suspicions in the 1970s. It was the end-times books that were attempting to influence the opinions of a significant amount of people, within certain areas of the church, in both the USA and the UK. Remarkably, *The New York Times* assessed Lindsey and Carlson's book as one of the bestselling nonfiction books of the 1970s! It had tremendous reach.

In 1976, I caused waves in my high school when I led a school assembly and shared my views of the world and the nearness of the apocalypse. The only reason I was allowed to do any other assemblies after that was because I was a senior prefect, a national champion 400m runner, and a speedy winger in the First Fifteen rugby team. All of which helped my teachers overlook my (then) rather-radicalized millenarian utterances. Plus, they could not get any other senior students to volunteer to lead assemblies.

In 1977, I even tried to join the Christian militia of the, so-called, Free Lebanon Army (FLA). I knew next to nothing about them, except that they were allies of Israel in the conflict occurring in the border zone of Israel and the disintegrating state of Lebanon. Looking back, I realize that I was exhibiting a form of radicalization. Fortunately, the depth of my radicalization was rather limited; there were no online platforms assisting such a move; and a simple rejection-letter was enough to put a stop to my plan to take part in, what I considered, the end-times conflicts shaking the Middle East. Instead, I went to university to read politics.

I was not alone in my end-times views, even if none of my contemporaries went as far as actually volunteering to fight for the allies of Israel. Nevertheless, many of those in my circle shared these views. In the town's Methodist, Anglican, and Baptist churches we did not find these views espoused by the leaders and preachers, but those of us who held them formed a radical minority operating below the radar of what was preached each Sunday. However, in the local Pentecostal church things were different and the end times greatly informed its outlook on life. But we millenarians were present across the denominations, just without a voice in the traditional ones.

Getting a wider perspective

All of that was a very long time ago. And lots of us have things about their teenage years that shock their more reflective older selves. For me personally what challenged the mindset that the 1970s literature had fostered was experience and historical study. The EEC/EU grew to its tenth member, yet Antichrist did not appear. It grew bigger still and the confident assertions of the 1970s, about this so-called ten-nation confederacy arising from the legacy of the Roman Empire, fell apart.

A further challenge to my earlier mindset arose from one of my degree special subjects at the UK's Bristol University: religion and politics. In 1980, I completed my dissertation on radical millenarians of the seventeenth century.[6] It examined the ideas of Christian radicals in the British Civil Wars of the seventeenth century in England and Wales, as they tried to impose godliness, as they saw it, and the rule of the saints, on a society dislocated by the upheaval of civil war and regicide. They were also convinced that they were living in the last days. I read their pamphlets, kept in the British Library in London, and explored their theology, politics, and their ambitions.

One group—the Fifth Monarchy Men—made use of the passages from Daniel and Revelation with which I was so familiar. But they enthusiastically applied them to Charles I; and then to Oliver Cromwell, after they fell out with him. I realized we had been here before. This accompanied the realization that, despite clear scriptural injunctions not to indulge in speculation regarding the timing of the second coming of Christ,[7] this theme had occurred again and again over two thousand years, with only the targets changing. Indeed, the church was, and is, something of a repeat-offender in this area. Yet nothing deters the next generation, in significant areas of the Christian community, from returning to the speculation. It also became increasingly clear that the way in which end-times prophecies were used often revealed more about the contemporary political and cultural preoccupations of some Christians than they did about eschatological events. We will explore the meaning and application of this term, along with the term apocalyptic, in the next chapter.

In my thirty-five-year career as a high school teacher I developed an interest in early medieval history and came upon the same familiar end-times viewpoints. However, this time it was not the EU, or the papacy, or Cromwell, but the Viking hordes of the tenth century who presaged the last days. Other contemporary chroniclers saw signs of it in the Magyar invasions of the same period.

The approach of the year 1000 only accelerated such end-times anxieties. It became clear that—despite New Testament warnings against predicting the date of the promised return of Christ and despite the church officially reading prophetic end-times verses as being symbolic and metaphorical from the fifth century onwards—the specific predictions and identifications kept occurring. This was especially so at times of social, economic, and political stress. Millenarian writings and preaching surfaced several times during the crusades; during times of intra-church conflict over the succession of popes; at the time of the fourteenth-century Black Death; then in the Hussite wars of the fifteenth century.

This phenomenon then exploded following the Reformation, as Christendom fractured, and the medieval Catholic allegorical view of biblical prophecy was replaced by a more literal, historical, and futuristic interpretation again. It could lead to, or accompany, violent revolution and political upheaval, such as convulsed Germany during the Peasant Wars of the 1520s and which led to the nightmare Anabaptist regime that terrorized the city of Münster in 1534–35. However, it also became part of the Protestant mainstream across Europe.

The confidence that the last days were at hand influenced vast numbers of Protestants at all social levels and provided the mood-music to accompany the parliamentary conflict with Charles I and the British Civil Wars and their republican aftermath in the 1650s. It was carried to North America in the 1620s and 1630s and influenced much of the thinking among early Puritan settlers there. As such, it entered into the cultural DNA of what would become the United States, even as its influence declined in Britain following the restoration of Charles II in 1660. In the USA it continues to be influential across huge areas of the evangelical church and greatly influences the outlook of the so-called "religious right" and literally millions of key voters.

This is particularly important, given the size of the Christian population in the USA. This is because the USA is currently the home of more Christians as a percentage of its population than any other nation on earth. In 2014 an extensive program of research, by Pew Research Center, revealed that 70.6 percent of Americans identified as Christians of some form.[8] And of the total US population, 25.4 percent identified as evangelicals.[9] About 81 percent of white evangelicals, or about 33.7 million people, voted for Donald Trump in 2016.[10] A similar number of these believers voted for him in November 2020. Such numbers have been game-changers in US national elections in the past and may be so again. That many of these people have an outlook deeply influenced by end-times beliefs is highly significant. Even with data, from March 2021, suggesting the number of Americans identifying as Christian has fallen to 65 percent, and data published in July 2021 indicating that the number of white evangelical Protestants has fallen to 14 percent, the numbers remain very large.[11]

Such outlooks were present in my own personal roots, as in the cultural roots of the modern USA. Approaching the subject from a different angle, my research into my family's history brought me to ancestors who had been executed in 1685 for taking part in the Monmouth Rebellion, in England's West Country, and I noticed that, among those marching alongside them against King James II and VII, were people expecting the second coming of Christ.[12] This expectant optimism was still held, despite the huge disappointments that had crushed the hopes of many Fifth Monarchists in 1660, with the restoration of the Stuart monarchy. Clearly, my interest during the 1970s was not the first time that such beliefs had affected my own family story.

In 2015, I co-wrote *Christ: The First 2000 Years*.[13] In researching the chapter entitled, "King Jesus and the heads upon the gates," I again came across these historical radical millenarians (both on the continent, in Britain, and in North America). In fact, the chapter title in question was taken from a battle cry of the Fifth Monarchy Men in London, during the failed uprising, called Venner's Revolt, in 1661. This was a group who had not accepted defeat at the Stuart restoration of 1660 and who were energized by the approach of the year 1666. I realized, once more, how intrigued I was by the ideas and actions of these theological and political radicals and the kind of society and life-experiences that produced them.

What I was less prepared for was the way that the beginning of the twenty-first century would see a revival of the influence of millenarian ideas, and the impact of end-times theology, in a way far in excess of what I had experienced in the 1970s. What had been, and remains, a relatively fringe interest in the UK has gone mainstream in the USA, via the impact of the evangelical right on US politics. And it is apparent once more in a significant number of UK evangelical churches. The end times are again on the agenda and, as in the past, often intimately linked with radicalized politics.

Ancient beliefs . . . modern impacts

In 2016, the EU Referendum in the UK made it very clear to me that end-times beliefs were still driving the ideas of many Christians, despite the fact that such opinions frequently operate beneath the radar of much institutional Christian thought and expression. Later that year, 81 percent of white US evangelicals voted for Donald Trump and, among them, specific schools of end-times beliefs were, and are, both highly prevalent and influencing modern geo-political outlooks—from attitudes towards Middle Eastern policies, to climate change.

In 2018, my book *When God Was King: Rebels and Radicals of the Civil War and Mayflower Generation* was published.[14] In it I once more returned to the seventeenth-century manifestations of the phenomenon. But around me, what had once seemed historic was fast becoming a part of the modern political landscape. History had caught up with us and was overtaking us.

As if to emphasize the fact that end-times preoccupation is not solely a Christian phenomenon, in 2014 so-called Islamic State (ISIS/*Daesh*) proclaimed its caliphate, accompanied by apocalyptic claims and threats; and explicit references to the imminent return of Prophet *Isa* (the Islamic name for Jesus). Western sources associated this with radicalization, both in the Middle East and at home, but the focus on such prophetic themes was, and is, also a feature of mainstream Islam too. A teacher at a UK high school remarked to me that, on days when the news was full of turbulence, some of the Muslim students would remark, "It's the end of days," clearly reflecting what they were hearing within their religious community. While the exploration in this book focuses on Christian millenarianism, it is important to remember that end-times beliefs also influence the outlooks of other religious communities in the increasingly fractious world of the twenty-first century.

It was after this that I decided that, at the first opportunity, I would seek to explore the history of these ideas and practices, which linked the earliest Christians to the events of the twenty-first century. For, throughout church history, passages from the Old and New Testament have been interpreted as referring to end-times events. Despite the scriptural warnings against predicting the second coming, many sincere Christians have done this, as a way of understanding and explaining their world (hence the more neutral word *Use* in this book's sub-title). On the other hand, some of these interpretations have so reflected contemporary political views and agendas that they arguably amount to a virtual quarrying of biblical passages in order to justify existing ideologies (hence the word *Misuse* in the sub-title). However, it is not written as an exposé, but as a serious attempt to understand the phenomenon. Given the fact that I am a self-identified evangelical, with a great respect for the Bible (but also having, I hope, the analytical outlook of an historian), my aim is to do so in a way which engages, explores, and explains, rather than mocks or shocks. I was brought up within Methodism and became a Methodist local preacher, but for over thirty years now I have attended what would be described as evangelical Anglican churches and am a licensed lay minister in the Church of England. I hope that this book will be of interest to those of Christian faith, other faiths, and no faith at all.

I personally believe that much of what passes as end-times speculation in the church amounts, in effect, to a misuse of Scripture, however sincerely done. Exploring this is a pressing issue. While many churches in the UK will never hear a sermon preached on the end times, for many other fellowships (especially in the USA and elsewhere) it is frequently referred to and supplies much of the spiritual tone of these communities' outlook. Furthermore, in the age of the internet and social media, ideas about it cross denominational boundaries and inform the thinking of many believers, regardless of what is preached about on Sunday. At times it can only be described as spiritual conspiracy theory. After all, someone somewhere started the online (untrue) accusation that seat 666 is kept free in the European Parliament; then others forwarded it. There is much like this on the internet.

However, the impact of end-times views is more significant and far-reaching than this. Within the USA, President Trump's decision to move the US embassy to Jerusalem (announced in 2018) and to support Israeli sovereignty over the Golan Heights (announced in 2019) was designed not to appeal to American Jews but to American evangelical Christians, whose outlook on the Middle East is, today, similar to mine in 1975. It is one of the areas explored in my recent co-authored book entitled *Trump and the Puritans* (2020).[15]

Whatever one thinks about these particular geo-political decisions, it is very important that we understand what is going on and why. Polling in the USA, in December 2017 by Lifeway, and reported in *The Washington Post*, 14 May 2018, revealed that 80 percent of evangelicals believe that the creation of Israel (in 1948) was a fulfilment of biblical prophecy that will bring about Christ's second coming.[16] That is somewhere in the region of thirty-three million voters. For many, this includes support for the expansion of Israeli territory at the expense of neighboring states. This data accords with earlier research, in 2003 by Pew Research Center, which suggested that about a third of all adult Americans (not just evangelicals) believed that the establishment of Israel was in line with biblical prophecy regarding the second coming.[17] This amounts to many more tens of millions of US voters. This belief is of great political, as well as theological, importance.

Predictably, the Covid-19 pandemic prompted eschatological speculation in some areas of the global church. In the run-up to Christmas 2020, John MacArthur, the senior pastor of Grace Community Church in Sun Valley, California declared that the global impact of the pandemic created the ideal situation for the appearance of the Antichrist, global government, and the persecution of all who will oppose Antichrist. In line with such an outlook, the church in question was one of a number of similar faith communities in the USA that opposed Covid-19 lockdown restrictions.[18] Such state and federal restrictions are frequently framed as infringements of religious liberty; and indicative of the kind of state power that will be utilized by Antichrist.

The "end times" are very much "now times" for many who are influential in modern US politics and, indeed, for many in the global Christian community. For today, as so often in the past, it is a matter of The End Times, Again?

2

The Jewish Roots of the End Times

THE MODERN CHRISTIAN CHURCH is heir to a prophetic legacy that stretches back through two millennia of Christian history and is deeply rooted in Judaism. It will help, at this stage, to briefly explore something of the role of prophecy within what Christians call the Old Testament (the Jewish *Tanakh*), the concepts of the end times found there, and how the first-century interpretations of it influenced the outlook of the emerging Christian community.

Before that, though, it should be noted that a number of terms have been coined to describe different approaches to the study of prophetic texts.

- The "preterist" approach views biblical prophecy as having been fulfilled in past events, and sometimes in events contemporary with the writing of the prophetic texts (particularly, in the New Testament case, of Revelation).

- The "historicist" approach views prophecy as referring to events or institutions across the broad sweep of history, and not solely as end-times events. However, this can include ones related to the end times.

- The "idealist" or "allegorical" approach views prophecy as symbolic in meaning and communicating essential truths, not tied to detailed specific events.

- The "futurist" approach views the majority of prophetic texts as referring to specific literal events that have yet to be fulfilled.

As we explore the different approaches to the study of prophecy, these schools of thought will become apparent, even when not referred to explicitly by these labels.

The role of the prophetic within the Jewish Scriptures

The name *Tanakh* is an acronym of the first Hebrew letter of the three traditional divisions of Jewish Scripture as they are found in the Masoretic Text (the form of these Scriptures as copied and edited by Jewish scholars between the seventh and tenth centuries AD). These three traditional divisions were and are: *Torah* (Teaching), which is also often referred to as the Five Books of Moses, the *Nevi'im* (Prophets), and the *Ketuvim* (Writings).

Among the books designated as prophetic are ones familiar to later Christians as examples of this genre, such as Isaiah, Jeremiah, Ezekiel (the Latter Prophets), and Joel, Jonah, Habakkuk, Malachi (examples from the Twelve Minor Prophets). Others might be less familiar to Christian readers as prophetic books, such as Joshua and Kings (these being from the collection called the Former Prophets). Some, that modern Christians would be familiar with and consider prophetic or containing prophetic references, such as Psalms and Daniel, were not included within this category of the Jewish canon. These being grouped within the section termed the *Ketuvim* (Writings).

This tripartite division makes it obvious that something termed prophetic was a core feature of Judaism, even if it was not accepted by all members of the religious community at the time of Jesus. The Sadducees, for example, did not accept the inspiration of the prophetic books. This was one of their points of difference with the Pharisees.[19]

From a study of the Old Testament, it is clear that there was no *one* group who believed that they had an empowered message from the God of Israel to the people of God and, at times, to a wider community too. Some of those associated with prophetic utterances lived in communities such as the "company of prophets who were in Bethel" (2 Kgs 2:3). The Hebrew at this point can also be translated as "sons of the prophets," which may imply families associated with ecstatic utterances or may be a reference to a group that was virtually a guild of prophets. Others were drawn from the early cult centers or the later temple community, and some were probably priests. Examples would be Samuel, Isaiah, Jeremiah, and Ezekiel. Others were drawn from different sections of society. Of the so-called Twelve Minor prophets, very little is known. Malachi's name, for example, is a transliteration of a Hebrew word meaning "my messenger" and was probably a pseudonym;[20] Obadiah's name means "servant (or worshiper) of Yahweh" and may also be a pseudonym, although it is known as a proper name elsewhere in the Old Testament.[21]

While we naturally emphasize the role of major figures who came to be ascribed significant status, closer reading of the Old Testament can give surprising insights into a much larger community than these, what we might call, "A-list" prophets. For example, at one point the king of Israel enquired of four hundred prophets whether the kingdoms of Israel and Judah should jointly go to war against Ramoth-gilead (1 Kgs 22:6). The prophets who stood out, and whose writings became enshrined in later collections of literature that were accorded divine authority, were those whose words became accepted as "normative revelation for future generations and a touchstone by which future prophecies might be tested."[22] However, there would have been many others who were considered prophets by their contemporary society but whose names are lost to us and whose words did not make it into canonical collections of writings.

However, it needs to be remembered that what was termed prophetic in this context was not understood in the simplistic way that the term is now often used in colloquial speech. The Hebrew verb meaning "to prophesy" (*naba*) referred to far more than predicting future events and the "prophet" (*nabi*) was not simply someone who foretold what was to come. In the Old Testament, the primary focus was on *forth-telling* rather than fore-telling. The prophet's first concern was to declare the message of God to their own generation and to recall the people to covenant faithfulness. There is frequently also a sense that the message of the prophet is "conditional, dependent upon the response of the people." It might even be asserted that "by their response to this word, the people determine in large part what the future holds."[23] This is an important qualification when reflecting on the predictive nature of prophetic messages in the Old Testament. In this sense, to interpret and communicate the law and its demands had a prophetic quality. Consequently, both those termed prophets and those classed as priests shared a common role in mediating what was considered to be God's word to the community; and the boundaries between the two groups could blur.

There could be tensions between those regarded as prophets, such as when Micaiah contradicted the mass of prophets who were predicting victory in a planned war (1 Kgs 22:13–23). This occasion also revealed how a prophet might be in conflict with the secular elites over their policy decisions. Another example of both conflicts in the career of one prophet would be Jeremiah (as revealed in Jeremiah 23, for instance). And these are not isolated examples. The prophet and the prophetic message could be, and often were, a source of turbulence and conflict with contemporary society, its norms, behavior, and strategies. From this, it is clear that what were considered prophetic utterances often had a strong contemporary resonance.

Nevertheless, the Old Testament also contains many passages that were clearly intended to connect present decisions to future consequences. Many others looked forward in an even more radical fashion. These are the ones that are crucial in the context of this study. This is because they could be interpreted as revealing aspects of future climactic events that would radically transform history. And some looked forward to a future cosmic transformation. These are the end-times prophecies that became scrutinized, both within Judaism and Christianity, as indicative of events that would reveal the hand of God and usher in a new order.

Old Testament end-times concepts

It is not possible to give a comprehensive list of end-times prophecies and themes, as found in the Old Testament. This is for a number of reasons. The first is a lack of scholarly consensus over whether a message was actually expressed as a coded contemporary comment or was intended to be futuristic in application. As a result, a wide range of viewpoints can be found in the literature, both the scholarly and that aimed at the general reader. The second is that a message that was intended to have immediate resonance might also contain features that were thought to point to future events and wider issues. Thus, some prophetic oracles could be understood to telescope "now" and "yet to come." The third reason is rooted in the heavily symbolic forms of expression often associated with prophetic writings. While this certainly underpins and informs the dramatic effect of such a genre, it can also give rise to a complex and conflicted afterlife of interpretation and speculation regarding the ultimate meaning or meanings. And finally, the way in which later believers (both Jews and Christians) understood and understand the concept is made complex by developments within the Old Testament itself. There is a case to be made that, while early Jewish prophetic traditions "looked for God to bring judgement and salvation within history," this developed over time so that God's decisive action became seen as "a final resolution of history" and the creation of a "transcendent world."[24] As a result, both perspectives can be found in the Old Testament and sometimes modern interpreters (particularly if they are not conversant with the complexity of these variations) can assume end-times implications within prophetic statements that were not originally regarded as carrying this meaning.

This whole area is made yet more complex by interpretations offered by later faith communities (both within Judaism and Christianity) designed to find prophetic aspects in areas of Scripture that might not, at first reading, be perceived as prophetic in the foretelling sense. Such interpretations can vary as a result of contemporary experiences throwing new light (in the view of the observer) on a particular passage and can, at times, resemble the quarrying of Scripture in order to buttress an existing contemporary outlook or opinion. These practices can produce layer upon layer of exegesis (scriptural interpretation), which then colors the way later generations approach these particular texts in Scripture. In short, the history of a faith community's interpretations over time can become the lens through which others see scriptural passages. This can produce an unconscious predisposition at any particular time that is so strong it appears as a given.

A striking example would be that of the prophecies found in the book of Daniel. Whether read as contemporary coded comments on second-century BC political upheavals connected to the anti-Jewish activities of Antiochus IV *Epiphanes* (the view of many modern critical academic scholars); as biblical apocalyptic literature which combines revelations of heavenly secrets with explanations of earthly experiences (the view of some academic scholars and shared by those believing in its continued, divinely inspired, relevance); or as futuristic, and as yet unfulfilled, end-times predictions (the view held within many traditional interpretations, both Jewish and Christian, and strongly represented among most modern evangelical communities) will have a huge impact on how Daniel's dramatic details are read and interpreted.[25] As we shall see in due course, the book of Daniel was quoted by both Jews and Christians in the first century of the Christian era as predicting imminent end-times events.

Despite these complications, certain characteristics can be discerned. And, once identified, they can be spotted as they surface and resurface in later writings; and in later attempts to identify their fulfilment in past and in current events.

The end-times will be a time of vindication for God's chosen people. Israel and Jerusalem are assured of being rescued and will finally experience peace, stability, and prosperity. There are many examples of this theme.

> The LORD has taken away the judgements against you,
>
> he has turned away your enemies.

The king of Israel, the LORD, is in your midst;

you shall fear disaster no more.

(Zeph 3:15)

Such vindication-prophecies may also be accompanied by very specific references to enemy nations and ethnic groups, such as Ezekiel's references to Gog, Magog, Meshech, and Tubal; Persia, Ethiopia and Put; Gomer and Beth-togarmah from the furthest north (Ezek 38:1–6). There are many similar examples. As one might imagine, these have given risen to intense later speculations regarding which nations will be involved in these end-times conflicts.

This vindication and rescue could also include references to an exalted (messianic) figure who would act as the representative of the God of Israel; or as an ideal anointed ruler,[26] in the royal line of David; or demonstrate attributes variously reminiscent of angelic beings or even of the divine presence. It was to such prophecies that later writers of the Christian Gospels would turn when stating that the life of Jesus fulfilled Old Testament prophecies, and when looking forward to his second coming in glory, at the close of the present age. The latter references constitute a key part of later Christian end-times interpretation, identification, and prediction.

The end times are also described as a time of judgement and the destruction of evil. Among a vast number of such prophecies, examples would include: "See, the day of the LORD comes, cruel, with wrath and fierce anger, to make the earth a desolation, and to destroy its sinners from it" (Isa 13:9). That this is accompanied by the darkening of sun, moon, and stars seems clearly to be a poetic expression of a shaken world order, but has also been interpreted as having a literal meaning by later commentators. The same sentiment informs other prophetic statements: "That day will be a day of wrath, a day of distress and anguish, a day of ruin and devastation, a day of darkness and gloom" (Zeph 1:15).

This concept of "the day of the LORD," as found in Zephaniah, accompanies the idea of a remnant of the people of Israel being saved through a purifying judgement. Whether this was originally understood as referring to an historical event or a future end-times transformation is open to debate. This in itself gave much scope for later varied interpretations and identifications. The same concept appears in the earlier writings of Amos and Isaiah, and of Zephaniah's younger contemporary, Jeremiah. It should be noted that references to "earlier," "later," and "contemporary" are all open to debate, depending on the dating of the biblical texts as we now have them. What is clear is that it was a shared prophetic concept over time.

These times will also see restoration, often described as cosmic transformation. This is often conveyed through a reordering of the natural world in order to remove death and conflict from it.

> The wolf and the lamb shall feed together,
>> the lion shall eat straw like the ox;
>> but the serpent—its food shall be dust!
> They shall not hurt or destroy
>> on all my holy mountain,
>> says the Lord.
> (Isa 65:25)

These famous verses are, arguably, poetic images that encapsulate the idea of a re-worked creation that will establish harmony among living beings. However, at times, later commentators have taken a more literal message from such verses.

End-times events are also revealed through a succession of periods of history, as found in Daniel chapter 7 with its detailed description of successive beasts (later said to be kingdoms) described as being like a lion with eagle's wings, a bear with three tusks, a leopard with four wings and four heads, and a terrible beast with ten horns. From this last beast a little horn is seen to grow, displacing three other horns, and speaking arrogant words. This final beast's power gives way before "one like a human being," who is seen coming with the clouds of heaven and who is presented to the "Ancient One" (clearly, God) and whose kingdom will last forever (Dan 7:13–14). Such powerful imagery is capable of carrying complex layers of meaning. Jesus at his trial explicitly quoted from this passage (Mark 14:62) as an expression of his own pre-ordained authority and future glory. The details of the successive kingdoms, and their identification, has occupied students of prophecy for two millennia.

A number of end-times prophecies refer to the restoration of Israel to "the land" and the exalted status of Zion. The latter originated as the name of a specific hill in Jerusalem but became a term synonymous with Jerusalem itself and was also used in a way that, at times, referred to its historic location and role and, at other times, as a reference to its future exalted and transformed status. In this sense, Zion is both now and future, temporal and everlasting, in one sense subject to earthly limitations and yet also eternal. In Micah, for example, it is at Zion that the God of Israel or his royal regent will reign over a kingdom of peace, and will be the center of the return from exile for both Israel and Judah.

Given the different possible composition dates of prophetic texts, these restoration-prophecies can be variously read as restoration from Babylonian exile, rescue from foreign oppression and invasion, or an idyllic future state that has both spiritual and physical characteristics. This has made the idea of restoration a rich seam for later prophecy-prospectors to mine. This has especially been the case since the establishment of the State of Israel in 1948.

We will return to these passages from Scripture over successive chapters, as we unravel the complex history of attempts to apply them to contemporary events and societies. However, this is not a new phenomenon as there is persuasive evidence that related debates were occurring in the first century of the Christian era, at the time of the ministry of Jesus and the later formation of the Christian church.

A heated conversation: end-times outlooks at the time of Jesus

In the first century AD, many of the features associated with end-times prophecy were discussed within Judaism. The Christian emphasis on resurrection, judgment, and the drawing to an end of the current world order can be understood as developments of this existing trend within Jewish religious thought.

The evidence from the Gospels reveals a strong belief in prophecy being fulfilled in the life, ministry, and death of Jesus. Time and again we are told that an event fulfils an earlier scripture. There is also a strong sense of an impending decisive act of God that will transform society. In total, about fifty of Jesus' sayings and parables concern the kingdom of God/heaven.[27] While complex, this term included end-times meanings, rooted in the Old Testament, focused on the revealing and establishing of God's rule on earth. Then there is the reference to the Son of Man, with its echoes of Daniel 7, and explicit connections made to that prophecy by Jesus at his trial. Jesus' teaching regarding the coming of the new kingdom confirms his desire for the kingly rule of God on earth; and his disciples clearly understood this as Jesus' proclamation of himself as the new king who would introduce this rule.[28] This understanding that he acted as God's agent as a prophet was consistent with Jesus' teachings and proclamations heralding God's end-times kingdom.[29] This is allied to a similar interpretation by some biblical scholars that Jesus saw the imminent destruction of all existing society, due to the action of God transforming the world and cosmic order.[30] In Matthew chapter 24 we find detailed end-times teaching that has a recurring theme of the future apocalyptic judgement of God. It includes specific reference to the prophecy in Daniel.

It should also be remembered that the teaching of John the Baptist is set in the context of a warning of impending judgement, which has strong echoes of the day of the LORD as found in the Old Testament.

Others in broadly contemporary society were also speaking in both messianic and end-times terms. The Jewish community at Qumran wrote about a "Teacher of Righteousness" who may have been their leader at some point or may always have been a future end-times figure. This complex mixture of historic and future characters adds great complexity to the study of such terms. At least one biblical scholar has suggested that Hyrcanus II was the figure known as the "Teacher of Righteousness," and that Antigonus II was the figure known as the "Wicked Priest," in the scrolls (*Pesher Habakkuk* or *ms.1QpHab* and *Pesher Nahum* or *ms.4QpNah*) found in the vicinity of Qumran.[31] Or this identification may have varied over time, with differing apocalyptic interpretations of changing contemporary events. This illustrates the mutable nature of such ideas.

Pharisees believed that when all Israel obeyed *Torah*, the rule of God would be established on earth in fulfilment of messianic prophecy and Scripture generally. Others took a more muscular and political stance with regard to such a transformation of society. The second-century AD Jewish nationalist leader, Simon *bar Kokhba*, appears to have adopted this name, meaning "Son of the Star," as a result of its messianic connection with Numbers 24:17. During the Jewish wars against the Roman occupation, the linked themes of messianic hope and end-times expectations seem to have been intermingled and widely understood.

What the Christian community took from this apocalyptic heritage

Christianity inherited from Judaism apocalyptic literature (and associated outlooks) and an eschatological mindset. Although deriving from Greek words, with their own rich history, apocalyptic and eschatology developed a particular and distinctive form in Judeo-Christianity.

The production of apocalyptic literature is often associated with times of crisis. In the face of contemporary suffering, this genre of literature focuses the readers' thoughts on the hope of future transformation brought about by the direct action of God. This is described as being the culmination of a preceding time of trauma and upheaval. The Greek word *apokalypsis* (English apocalypse) literally means "an uncovering"[32] and refers to the revelation of something previously hidden. This type of writing is, technically, only found in the Old Testament in the book of Daniel, but aspects of it have been identified in some earlier works, which have been labelled proto-apocalyptic.

The key characteristics of this kind of writing are: revelations of heavenly mysteries; unveiling of the divine plan for history; the end-times future of the world; and the cosmic order being revealed. In apocalyptic literature, the revelation is often experienced by a well-known figure, often drawn from the past. This has the effect of setting the experience in a time earlier than that of the actual composition of the book in question. In such literature, the revelations usually occur through dreams and/or visions in which dramatic symbolic imagery occurs. These symbolic representations are then often interpreted by an angelic being to the recipient of the vision/dream. These can also involve lengthy statements by the angelic being or presented as a dialogue between the angelic being and the one receiving the revelation. A visionary journey might also occur, which reveals aspects of heaven, the cosmos, or the unfolding of historic events. Often the throne-room of heaven itself is seen, as the source of the revealed information.

Of the different kinds of apocalyptic literature that existed from the second century BC to the second century AD, the type most relevant to this exploration is termed "historical-eschatological apocalypse." Daniel is the Old Testament example and Revelation the New Testament one. Revelation differs from the Jewish prototype in being associated with a living contemporary figure, the apostle John. Another (later than the New Testament) apocalypse, known as the Shepherd of Hermas, was thought by some to have been written by Hermas the brother of Pope Pius I (bishop of Rome c.140–55), though the text itself is anonymous. The word apocalypse is used eight times in the New Testament itself to describe the second coming of Christ.[33] Among early Christians the word became closely associated with this longed-for event. It has continued to do so.

Reading Revelation immediately brings the book of Daniel to mind and indicates the model for the later writing. Both books feature (and bequeathed to later history a fascination with) schemes of divinely ordained periods of history. These unfold according to God's plan by which the current world (and cosmic) order will be drawn to a close; the imminence of this (frequently cataclysmic) event is stressed; the defeat of evil and vindication of God's people is seen; this culminates in the establishment of a universal kingdom of goodness in which God's righteous reign will be triumphantly seen on earth and will last forever. This reordering of earth and heaven is accompanied by the resurrection of the dead and a final judgement. Eternal blessedness is the lot of the righteous and punishment is the lot of sinners. God's rule is established on earth, or a reordered creation.[34] Jesus himself also referred to Daniel at his trial when he declared "'you will see the Son of Man seated at the right hand of the Power,' and 'coming with the clouds of heaven'" (Mark 14:62) It is highly significant that Jesus' favorite self-identifier ("Son of Man") was drawn directly from this Jewish apocalyptic source.

From these beginnings, the word "apocalyptic" is now used both for revealed truths about the end times, and (more colloquially) of cataclysmic world-changing events generally. But it is usually associated with dramatic claims concerning the end of days and the remodeling of the current world order.

On the other hand, an eschatological outlook is rooted in the Greek word *eschatos* meaning "last things." While it is expressed in a Greek word, this concept (as understood by early Christians) was firmly rooted in the Old Testament idea of viewing "history as moving towards a future goal."[35]

For Christians, the person of Jesus fundamentally modified what they understood from the Old Testament. Jesus himself, as presented in the Gospels, spoke of the impending coming of the kingdom of God/heaven. He spoke of events that would precede "the sign of the Son of Man [that] will appear in heaven, and then all the tribes of the earth will mourn, and they will see 'the Son of Man coming on the clouds of heaven' with power and great glory" (Matt 24:30). (There will be more on this, and its implications, in the next chapter.) His teaching had an urgent note of preparation for this dramatic action of God. John the Baptist had earlier spoken of preparation for the judgement day of God when he preached: "Even now the axe is lying at the root of the trees; every tree therefore that does not bear good fruit is cut down and thrown into the fire" (Luke 3:9). Its impending nature is strikingly revealed in phrases of Jesus such as: "Therefore you also must be ready, for the Son of Man is coming at an unexpected hour" (Matt 24:44).

For early Christians, eschatology (things pertaining to "the end") had begun to be realized through the ministry of Jesus, his death and resurrection, and the gift of the Holy Spirit at Pentecost. Jesus himself had declared its immediacy at the start of his ministry: "The time is fulfilled, and the kingdom of God has come near; repent and believe in the good news" (Mark 1:15).

For Christians, the final age in the history of the world had dawned. The key question was: for how long would the final age last? Many early Christians, as we shall see, considered that they were living in the end times and that the apocalypse was soon to occur.

3

The Early Christian Perspective

EARLY CHRISTIANS WERE THE heirs of a complex legacy, as far as their view of history and the end times was concerned. On one hand, they drank from a deep well of Jewish history, which for centuries had contained varied apocalyptic scriptures that looked towards future decisive acts of God to vindicate his people, judge their enemies, and establish a new order of righteousness. Such a hope, in its varied forms, had sustained the Jewish community through centuries of calamity and turbulence. Rather like the historic hope of exiled Judaism to celebrate Passover, "Next year in Jerusalem," it was the ever-present hope that sustained a community, even as it got on with the day-to-day experience of living in a world order that seemed unlikely (on past experience) to end any time soon.

On the other hand, the new community that rose out of first-century Judaism had experienced a seismic event that, its members fervently believed, signaled the beginning of the final age in the history of the world, indeed of the cosmos. This was the life, death, resurrection, and ascension of Jesus. As well as having an incalculable impact on the personal and community lives of those who put their trust in Jesus, the new faith had repercussions for how future history and the end-times acts of God were understood. Jesus, they believed, was the culmination of Jewish apocalyptic hopes. We can see the fusion of old and new in the way in which, for example, prophecies from the book of Daniel can be traced through the New Testament.[36]

However, this was a complex matter and the early church reflections on it can be traced in the emerging documents that would become canonical as the New Testament, and in the writings and actions of early Christians. These included both believers who occupied what became the mainstream of orthodoxy and those who trod a heretical path. Indeed, the way in which the significance of Jesus to end-times beliefs was understood—and these beliefs themselves and how they were expressed (and their repercussions)—could become a point of deep division among believers.

The end-times in the emerging documents of the New Testament

One of the most challenging areas was, and is, how to assess the way the end times—and their timescale—were to be understood in the teachings of Jesus, as they were recorded and presented by the early church in those letters and gospels that became mainline canonical texts. This clearly was the subject of much discussion in the first and second centuries AD, as it is among modern Christians (both lay and academic) as they study and interpret these texts in the twenty-first century. As we shall see, the matter becomes more complex if we take into account the way Jesus' teachings were seen through the lens of first-century events occurring at the time of the compilation of these texts. This is not surprising. It would be strange if a US recorder of a conversation regarding war and terrorism that occurred in 1980, was not influenced in how they communicated that conversation if they wrote it down after 9/11. The matter becomes more contentious, of course, when New Testament experts disagree regarding the date of compilation of these texts in the form that we now have them. Nevertheless, we should expect (at the very least) some references (conscious or unconscious) to contemporary events as compilation occurred. The significance of this, though, will be contested by different readers.

In the same way, since the rise of critical biblical scholarship in the nineteenth century, there have been polarizing disagreements among modern believers over the extent to which these apocalyptic teachings represent the authentic words of Jesus or the views of later followers, who looked back on his ministry through the lens of contemporary events and expectations. Here the perspectives of more conservative, or more liberal, believers will have huge impacts on whether such words are considered "prophetic" in a predictive sense. It is not in the remit of this book to examine this huge area of New Testament exegesis. Suffice it to say that for the majority of Christian history these words of Jesus (as recorded in the Gospels) have been understood as authentic records of his teaching; and they remain so to huge numbers of twenty-first-century believers around the world. This traditional position, as we shall see in future chapters, does not mean that believers were, or are, of one mind regarding either the literal prophetic character of these words or their interpretation and their application. Nevertheless, it is acceptance of these words as divinely authoritative, and also future-predictive in some form, that has underpinned Christian views of the progress and end of history, even when the frameworks of such understandings have been (and are) heavily contested. So, what end-times perspectives do we get from the words of Jesus as recorded in the Gospels?

One modern interpretation sees his teaching as containing a claim that he himself was the apocalyptic Messiah who would destroy the current temple and institute a new one in a fulfilment of messianic expectations. It was the later church, it has been controversially suggested, that toned down this radicalism in favor of a concept of personal purification, as revealed in the Gospels.[37] This is allied to a similar interpretation that asserts that he saw the imminent destruction of all existing society, due to the end-times action of God to transform the world and cosmic order.[38] In Matthew's Gospel, Jesus' disciples question him regarding the signs of his (future) coming and the end of the age (Matt 24:3). This follows his prediction of the complete destruction of the Jerusalem temple (Matt 24:2). His answer includes prediction of future events in which: wars, rumors of wars, and famines will be the beginning of end-times events; persecution of his followers will occur; sacrilege in the holy place (clearly implying the Jerusalem temple) will fulfil the prophecy of Daniel; terrible suffering will occur in Judea; the shortening of this period of suffering will save the elect; false messiahs and false prophets will be active; there will be cosmic disturbance of the sun and moon; the Son of Man will appear on the clouds of heaven (another reference to the prophecy of Daniel); followed by the angelic gathering in of all the elect at the sound of a trumpet (Matt 24:4–31).

His concluding words, "Truly I tell you, this generation will not pass away until all these things have taken place" (Matt 24:34), could be taken to mean that this series of events would occur within the lifetime of those who had heard his original teaching.[39] Given a common assumption that a generation lasted forty years, this meant the culmination of these events in or around the year 70. Or it could be understood as coming within forty years of the destruction of Jerusalem.[40] This is why some modern commentators have considered that this passage, as it now stands, was heavily influenced by the later Jewish-Roman War that occurred 66–73 and included the destruction of the Jerusalem temple. Others have understood it as predicting these events, rather than the end of the world.

On the other hand, these words have also been interpreted as referring to the Jewish people,[41] or human beings in general, rather than to a specific generational group. For this reason, the New International Version of Matthew's Gospel contains the marginal note that "generation" can be read as "race." Some commentators on the equivalent saying in Luke's Gospel, have concluded it should be understood as meaning "mankind."[42] In the Old Testament, a Hebrew form of the term "generation" was sometimes used to refer to a particular type of person (as in Psalm 14:5). On this basis, those who would continue to exist until Jesus' second coming could refer either to those who believed in him (the church) or those who rejected him and would continue to do so.[43] In which case, the whole series of events can then be read as stretching over a long period of time or be envisaged as being entirely set in a future period. As we shall see in due course, some modern students of biblical prophecy have suggested that these words have as their trigger the immediately preceding reference to a budding fig tree being a harbinger of summer (Matt 24:32) and that this is a reference to a specific event that will begin the final "generation." In short, the clock will start running as a result of that trigger. But what would constitute such a trigger? We shall examine the suggestions later in this study. Others subscribe to the concept of "multiple fulfilment," whereby a prophetic statement looks towards a number of fulfilments (for example the desecration of the temple under Antiochus Epiphanes, the destruction of Jerusalem by the Romans, a yet-to-occur final series of events).[44]

Given the destruction of the temple in the year 70 by the Romans, it would not be surprising if the compiler of Matthew and his readers thought these apocalyptic events were about to occur and this prophecy be imminently fulfilled. This could be construed as consistent with other teaching of Jesus as recorded in Matthew that, "Truly I tell you, there are some standing here who will not taste death before they see the Son of Man coming in his kingdom" (Matt 16:28). A similar statement is found in Mark (Mark 9:1) and Luke (Luke 9:27), associated with seeing the kingdom of God come with power (Mark), or simply seeing the kingdom of God (Luke). The key issue in these particular verses is what should be understood as the coming of the kingdom and this has prompted different interpretations, ranging from the post-Pentecost community of the church to the final end of the current world order.

Mark chapter 13 contains a similar (and usually considered earlier) version of this passage (the so-called "Little Apocalypse"), which is expanded on in Matthew's account. These passages are often considered to represent a belief in impending apocalyptic events and transformation of the current world order. However, as we have just seen, other interpretations that have an extended timescale are certainly possible.

On the other hand, and contrasting with this interpretation that his teaching envisaged imminent apocalyptic national and/or cosmic transformation, is the view that Jesus implicitly taught that existing Jewish nationalism was on a road to conflict with Rome that would destroy the Jewish community, the city of Jerusalem, and the temple in the resulting conflagration. In short: politically radical Judaism, fixated on revolutionary apocalyptic nationalist fervor, would not win. It had set its sights on national liberation, which would actually lead to death and destruction, rather than the community transformation that would come from embracing the good news being promulgated by Jesus.[45] In this view, the kingdom of God—as preached by Jesus—was about inner transformation that would flow out into community change, contrasted with revolutionary politico-military action. This kingdom was to be discovered within, rather than in external, and literal, apocalyptic changes.

This, it has been argued, finds corroboration in the words of Jesus to Pilate, as recorded in the later Gospel of John that: "My kingdom is not from this world" (John 18:36). By the time of the compilation of this gospel the expected apocalypse (as possibly reflected in Matthew's account) had not occurred and this text can be read as referring to an *other-worldly* kingdom, and not the literal millennial kingdom that we will address shortly.[46] A similarly spiritual, rather than literal, reference to the future kingdom can also be found in John 14:2–4, where Jesus reassures his disciples that he will prepare a place for them and come back and take them there. This can be variously read as occurring at the death of a disciple, at Christ's literal return (Greek *parousia*), at the resurrection of the dead, at the giving of the Holy Spirit at Pentecost, or as both a present experience and a future reality in heaven.[47]

The belief in an imminent second coming also had to be set alongside significant words (from within the same apocalyptic chapter of Matthew) that urged caution regarding speculation about timings. These included an explanation that the message would be preached throughout the world before the end occurred (Matt 24:14). First-century hearers knew that the known-world stretched far beyond the Mediterranean basin, and this alone indicated an extended time scale. Even more telling is the warning that concludes: "But about that day and hour no one knows, neither the angels of heaven, nor the Son, but only the Father" (Matt 24:36). This alone should have given pause for thought among believers then and since. The same tone underlies the mysterious wording that follows about some "taken" and some "left" (Matt 24:40–41), and his teaching about *nobody knowing* the hour of the Lord's return and its coming *like a thief* in the night, at an *unexpected* time (Matt 24:42–44). It is perhaps revealing that some early manuscripts of Matthew omit the words "nor the Son" from the earlier statement ("But about that day and hour no one knows, neither the angels of heaven, *nor the Son . . .*"). This variant reading may possibly have occurred as a product of a view that found this position of Jesus difficult to reconcile with some emerging christological perspectives. It may also have been prompted by an unwillingness, on the part of some early Christians, to accept a note of caution regarding the timetabling of events. If so, that was a tendency to sideline caution, which would run and run. Interestingly, the compiler of Acts added the same cautionary note to the account of the ascension, when the disciples ask Jesus if this is the time when he will restore the kingdom to Israel. He replies: *"It is not for you to know* [italics added] the times or periods that the Father has set by his own authority"* (Acts 1:7).

From this we may conclude that the early records of the teaching of Jesus contain an intense and dramatic focus on the future end-times culmination of the present age; but one tempered by warnings against timetabling it; and an emphasis on the pre-eminence of the transforming spiritual breaking-in of the kingdom now. This "realized eschatology" (happening now), needs to be set alongside the "future eschatology" (yet to come) with which early believers were familiar. That it included a belief that there would ultimately be transformation of the whole world order, of the kind envisaged in Matthew chapter 24, seems undeniable. The question was how soon such an event, or events, should be expected. It was this debate that occupied the minds of many early Christians. Clearly, many believers in the first century expected Christ's imminent return.[48] In 1 Thessalonians 4:13–18, Paul writes of Jesus' return with a commanding cry, the call of the archangel and the sound of God's trumpet. This is a literal return that will unite Christians, both those who have died and those alive at the time of his return. While it is not explicitly stated, the passage gives the impression that Paul expected some of those who read this letter to be alive when the event happened.

Some have interpreted this particular passage as implying that there will be two resurrections: one of the Christian dead, to allow their participation in a millennial kingdom, and a second one at the end of this period.[49] This, though, is unconvincing as the clear intention of the passage was to reassure believers of the uniting of all Christians (dead and alive) at the same event: the return of Jesus. However, there is a phased aspect of Paul's understanding of the sequence of events in 1 Corinthians, where he writes of the coming of Jesus, followed by him handing over "the kingdom to God the Father, after he has destroyed every ruler and every authority and power" (1 Cor 15:24). That this follows on from God having put all things under Jesus' feet can be read as indicating a period of time between Jesus' return and the culmination of the process of all being subjected to God.

Paul stresses that the day of the Lord will come like a thief in the night and will overturn expectations (1 Thess 5:2–3). It is an emphasis on the unpredictability of the event that echoes the message that was later found in the Gospels and in Acts. This association of the day of the Lord with shock and challenge to expectations echoes a sentiment found in the Old Testament in Amos 5:18.[50] The same note of the return coming as a surprise is found in 2 Peter, with the additional explanation that God is not being slow in bringing the events to pass but, instead, is being patient with people and acting on a different time-scale (2 Pet 3:8–10). It seems clear that the recipients of the letter were growing concerned that the return of Jesus had not yet occurred.

In contrast to the Gospels, the book of Revelation combines Jewish and Christian imagery and concepts in an apocalyptic series of visions. As such, it stands out from the rest of the literature that was eventually accepted into the New Testament canon. As in the Old Testament book of Daniel, Revelation chapter 13 describes a ten-horned beast that symbolizes the last world power, with a second beast demanding divine honors be paid to this ruler. References to the sea, animal imagery, and ten horns appear to link to Daniel chapter 7. It is not surprising that many then, and now, read this passage in Revelation as a reference to the persecuting Roman Empire. Modern students of prophecy see in the words something of the "multiple fulfilment" we referred to before, with earlier and later phases of this "last kingdom," which we will explore in a later chapter. The imagery is dramatic and goes on in later chapters to refer to a "great whore," riding a scarlet beast, which has seven heads and ten horns (chapter 17); the defeat of a force described as "Babylon" (chapter 18); followed by the destruction of the beast and its false prophet (chapter 19). This is then followed by the thousand-year reign of Christ (the millennium), the devil's imprisonment and eventual release, and the final judgement (chapter 20). After this a new heaven and earth are revealed, along with the New Jerusalem (chapter 21). The phased nature of this defeat of the devil is distinctive.[51] More will be said about this in the next chapter, but suffice it to say at this point that these vivid features of beasts(s), whore, Babylon, millennium, and creation reformed have had a huge impact on Christian thought and imagination over two thousand years. Although the millennium is hugely important in Christian thought, this thousand-year reign of Christ ("thousand" being *chilioi* in the original Greek, *mille* in later Latin translations and use) is only referred to in *one* passage in the New Testament, in Revelation chapter 20, where it is referred to six times.

This belief in the millennial rule of Christ is perhaps hinted at in the passage from 1 Corinthians we touched on earlier (1 Cor 15:23–28). Given the importance of this belief to later generations of Christians (and its continuing high profile) it is worth repeating that it only has one definite mention in the New Testament, in Revelation. That early Christians looked forward to the return of Christ and the reign of God is clear. However, there was no uniform view of how this would occur; whether it involved a literal thousand-year reign; the sequencing of these events; and the exact way in which this formed part of the eventual establishment of God's eternal kingdom.[52] What is now the familiar millennial framework emerged in the second and third centuries, as later generations reflected on Revelation 20 and refined their understanding of it and its significance.[53]

The figure of Antichrist

For later Christians these prophecies in Revelation became inextricably linked with the figure of "Antichrist" (capitalized). The actual term antichrist (usually uncapitalized) is found in the New Testament five times in the letters known as 1 John and 2 John, once in plural form and four times in the singular.[54] The wording of these particular references are such that they are often interpreted as marking out a certain category of persons, rather than an individual; but the individual identification has been made by many Christians. Later belief in an individual Antichrist figure also focuses on the letter known as 2 Thessalonians. Here the term "antichrist" is not actually used and the terms found here are "the lawless one," "the one destined for destruction" (2 Thess 2:3) and again "the lawless one" (2 Thess 2:8). The later conflation of this person with "Antichrist" and the fourth beast of Daniel 7 is understandable, given that he is described as one who "opposes and exalts himself above every so-called god or object of worship, so that he takes his seat in the temple of God, declaring himself to be God." (2 Thess 2:4)

The composite figure of the (singular) "Antichrist" has been, and is, often conflated by Christian writers with figures found in the New Testament book of Revelation, such as one of the beasts of Revelation 13. The enigmatic mark of the beast, which represents its name, is given in Revelation 13:18 as six hundred and sixty-six (666). The composite nature, in later Christian writings, of this evil figure who will be defeated by Christ, is such that the ideas of Antichrist, the blasphemous beasts, and the number 666 have become inextricably mixed. However, in the New Testament, the actual matter is much more complex and it is far from clear whether these distinct figures were regarded as being aspects of one end-times enemy of Christ and his elect.

This did not stop identifications of this composite figure from occurring. A document known as the *Ascension of Isaiah* (variously dated from the late first century AD to the beginning of the third century) thought Antichrist was Emperor Nero. Irenaeus (died c.202) suggested several possible candidates for Antichrist and thought that the ten horns of the beast represented the Roman Empire, which would eventually be divided into ten kingdoms. Tertullian (died c.240) thought something similar, as did Jerome (died 420). Athanasius of Alexandria (died 373) thought that the heretical theologian Arius of Alexandria was associated with the Antichrist. It was the beginning of a long history of (mis-)identifications. Irenaeus also sought to connect figures opposing God across Scripture by linking the 666 of Revelation to the age of Noah at the time of the flood (God's judgement on the wicked) and the dimensions of the golden statue mentioned in Daniel 3:1 (height sixty cubits, width six cubits). In this, he exemplified an interest in interpreting the symbolism of numbers, which was popular in his own day,[55] and has remained a preoccupation with many of those seeking to interpret prophecies containing numerical references.

The multiplicity of apocalyptic groups
in the early Christian era

The preoccupation with the (possibly imminent) end times was clearly a major issue for a number of groups prior to the destruction of Jerusalem by the Romans. It was not only an area for debate within the early church. The Jewish historian Josephus insisted that it was belief in the imminent appearance of a messianic king that launched many Jewish nationalists into the catastrophic war with Rome, which eventually culminated in the destruction of the Jerusalem temple in the year 70.[56] Such beliefs resurfaced during the anti-Roman Bar Kokhba Revolt that erupted in 131.[57] Clearly, the previous collapse of Jewish messianic hopes in 70 had not extinguished the flame of apocalyptic expectation. Indeed, the previous catastrophe may have fanned the embers into one final desperate conflagration.

Earlier, both John the Baptist and the inhabitants of Qumran held similar apocalyptic views, that were expressed in comparable terms. Both believed in the impending end of the current world order due to God's judgement. Both drew heavily on the prophetic language and imagery found in the Old Testament book of Isaiah. They were, as it were, on the same page. This is strikingly shown in the way that they both similarly interpreted Isaiah's "A voice cries out: 'In the wilderness prepare the way of the LORD, make straight in the desert a highway for our God'" (Isa 40:3), with the "wilderness" symbolizing a place of spiritual renewal and preparation for the end-times actions of God. Both also emphasized the role of ritual cleansing. It was the distinguishing mark of John's activity at the Jordan; a personal preparation for end-times testing and, eventually, salvation.

It has been suggested that John's group was one of a number operating in and around the valley of the Jordan preaching an end-times message. The later Jerusalem Talmud claims that twenty-four such sects were operating by the year 70.[58] In addition, John's followers did not disappear following the death of their leader. There is evidence that a complicated relationship between the emerging church and, what we might call, the "John the Baptist movement" ran on into the middle of the first century and even beyond that. Written perhaps as early as the year 70, the New Testament book of Acts (in Acts 18:25 and 19:1–7) refers to disciples of John active long after his death. In addition, as late as the third century, documents known today as the *Pseudo-Clementine Recognitions* and *Pseudo-Clementine Homilies* record garbled traditions suggesting the continuation of what it describes as a sect of "daily baptizers" active long after the death of John the Baptist. We know little more about this group, but it looks as if they continued to reference John as their founder. And they preached some kind of baptism-based ideology long after John had been executed. It may even have been seen as a potential rival to the Christian community.

This tension may also explain the emphasis in the Gospel of John (John 3:30) that, in the words of John the Baptist, "He [Jesus] must increase, but I [John the Baptist] must decrease." Recorded in a gospel written perhaps as late as the nineties and conscious of continued competition between the two groups of followers, it was determined to set out theological priorities clearly. The message was transparent: John was the honored but passing prophet; Jesus is the Messiah, the Savior, the revelation of the eternal nature of God.[59] We may assume that something of the end-times ideology, so prevalent in the preaching of the Baptist, survived within this rival movement. It was certainly a major feature of early Christianity, so this is a reasonable assumption.

Consequently, it is clear that end-times conversations were high on the agenda for a number of groups in the decades immediately following the ministry of Jesus. It was not solely a Christian preoccupation. However, it is to that Christian preoccupation that we will now return.

End-times beliefs from the late-first to the fourth century

Most leading Christians, in the first three centuries of church history, subscribed to a basically futurist "premillennialist" reading of prophecy: Christ would return and then he would initiate a literal thousand-year reign on earth. They clearly believed that this would happen soon. Clement of Rome (died 99) wrote: "Of a truth, soon and suddenly shall His will be accomplished, as the Scripture also bears witness, saying, 'Speedily will He come, and will not tarry.'" An additional statement—based on scriptural prophetic promises that "The Lord shall suddenly come to His temple, even the Holy One, for whom ye look"[60]—suggests a Jerusalem-focused expectation, even though the temple there had been destroyed by the Romans. His latter statement was based on a prophecy in the Old Testament book of Malachi that "the LORD whom you seek will suddenly come to his temple" (Mal 3:1). The *Second Epistle of Clement* (written c. 95–140) emphasized the immediacy of this hope: "Let us every hour expect the kingdom of God."[61] Despite the eponymous title, this was probably not written by Clement of Rome, but by a later and unknown author. It was a point expanded on in the *Epistle of Barnabas* (probably written sometime between 70 and 132): "The Lord has cut short the times and the days that His Beloved may hasten" and "the Lord is near [clearly meaning in terms of time]."[62]

The writer of the *Epistle of Barnabas* also assumed that the world would end six thousand years after the start of creation. This concept, known as the *sexta-septamillennial construct*, was modelled on the six days of creation followed by the seventh Sabbath-rest day of God, but with each day representing one thousand years.[63] It is also sometimes referred to as "sabbatical millenarianism."[64] Those who held the belief justified it by reference to Psalm 90:4, which states: "For a thousand years in your sight are like yesterday when it is past, or like a watch in the night"; and 2 Peter 3:8: "with the Lord one day is like a thousand years, and a thousand years are like one day." While neither of these were explicitly connected to the seven days of creation, and *that* had no connection whatsoever to a methodology by which the end-times might be calculated, the writer of the *Epistle of Barnabas* justified the connection with some ingenious and creative exegesis. Since Genesis stated that God finished his work in six days, this (the writer insisted) implied that "the Lord will finish all things in six thousand years."[65] The critical issue, with regard to this mode of thinking, lay in the calculation of the date of creation, from which the end-times countdown had started. None of the calculations common in the year 100 made it likely that the end of the six-thousand-year cycle was imminent. However, this did not diminish the sense of impending apocalypse that is found in the *Epistle of Barnabas*. We shall return to the *sexta-septamillennial construct* in chapter 5.

Papias of Hierapolis (died sometime after 100) recorded a millennial prophecy that he (mistakenly) attributed to Jesus. In fact, it is also known in a similar form in Jewish apocalyptic literature, such as the late-first-century *2 Baruch*, where the supernatural abundance of grapes on a vine is presented as a vivid picture of the future transformed creation (*2 Bar.* 29:5).[66] He also appears to have known and been influenced by the New Testament book of Revelation.[67]

In similar vein, Justin Martyr (died 165) in his *Dialogue with Trypho* maintained that most Christians believed in their gathering into a New Jerusalem, where they and the prophets and patriarchs would live for a thousand years.[68] This was regarded by many as a literal fulfilment of prophecy in which those living there would experience a miraculous age of abundance. Justin linked it to a prophecy in Micah 4:1–7, which spoke of the renewal of the world, and God's rule on earth.[69] Justin was familiar with Revelation and this was reflected in his writing.[70]

The apocalyptic influence of Revelation on the visionary text known as the *Shepherd*, by Hermas (first half of the second century and possibly earlier) can be seen in the references in the *Shepherd* to the coming tribulation, being transported by the Spirit, the church portrayed as a woman, and the beast.[71] While it may be that both drew independently on a common source of end-times ideas and imagery, it is likely that the *Shepherd* was dependent on Revelation.

The popularity of these and other similar prophecies is seen in the fact that when Irenaeus wrote his *Against Heresies* in the last decade of the second century, the culmination of the work was written as something of an anthology of existing messianic and millenarian prophecies, including that promulgated earlier by Papias. Like Papias and Justin, he was familiar with, and influenced by, the book of Revelation.[72]

In 156 or 157, in Phrygia (modern Turkey), a preacher named Montanus revealed how a belief in the literal fulfilment of the book of Revelation could be combined with heretical teachings to produce an explosive mix. He declared himself the incarnation of the Holy Spirit, with a mandate to lead followers into "truth." Gathering around him a group of ecstatic followers, their teachings even began to be described as a "Third Testament."[73] They proclaimed the imminent appearing of the New Jerusalem, which would descend from heaven to Phrygia. All Christians should gather there and await the second coming. Two settlements, Pepouza and Tymion, were designated as constituting "Jerusalem."[74] The early movement may have been influenced by aspects of the pagan cult of Cybele, with early sources maintaining that Montanus had been a priest of that cult.[75]

Occurring at a time of renewed persecution of Christians, Montanism spread throughout Asia Minor, south into Africa, and as far west as Gaul (roughly modern France). During this process, the focus on the descent of the holy city onto Phrygia was replaced by a less geographically stated hope of its appearance.[76] In this form, the movement drew in more mainstream believers, including the famous Western theologian Tertullian, who was clearly attracted to its end-times emphasis, while maintaining enough of an orthodox stance to prevent him being pulled into the more heretical aspects of the belief. He wrote that a walled city had been seen in the sky early in the morning in Judea and that this was a sure sign that the New Jerusalem would soon descend from heaven.[77]

This idea of Christ's literal return to the geographical location of Jerusalem helps explain the burial orientation that became something of a characteristic of Christian graves, as people converted from paganism during the Roman period and in the successor societies after the collapse of the Western Roman Empire. With feet due east, it was thought that the Christian dead would rise facing Jerusalem, where Christ had descended.[78]

Such beliefs in a literal thousand-year reign of Christ on earth, that would occur between his return (the *parousia*) and the last judgement, can be traced from this early period to modern times,[79] albeit with variations (some dramatic) in the timing and ordering of events. This millennialism (or *chiliasm*, from the Greek equivalent), giving rise to varied millenarian movements, became a core feature of Christian end-times beliefs, and remains a distinct aspect of these in the twenty-first century.

Such an intense atmosphere of expectation in the early period, which was not fulfilled, understandably led to disappointment. It also caused church authorities to regard apocalyptic literature with some suspicion and prompted a questioning of its authority. The book of Revelation was not the only example of Christian apocalyptic literature, but only it was officially accepted when others were rejected. Unlike them, its traditional association with the apostle John[80] had secured its place within the canon and with it the concept of the millennial rule of Christ.[81] By the early years of the third century, Revelation was widely accepted across the Western church (although Jerome, died 420, seems to have expressed some doubts), but in the East it faced sustained opposition. This opposition was based on doubts raised concerning its apostolic authorship, alongside anxieties over the impact of millenarian beliefs. As a consequence, it was not accepted as canonical at the Council of Laodicea (c. 360) and, in the fifth century, was omitted from the official Bible in Syriac-speaking churches (the *Peshitta*). Faced with the challenge of Montanism and its millenarian legacy, there was a tendency to deny the legitimacy of the one New Testament book that Montanists looked to in attempts to legitimize their beliefs. Its validity was also questioned because the age of Roman persecutions (persecution being a distinct theme in the book) had ended without the end-times prophecies being fulfilled. This led to questions over its authenticity. Later believers would maintain that the persecutions described in Revelation pointed to a *future* period of time, but to those who had felt this prophecy had imminent application, the fact that the second coming had not occurred was problematic. However, by the time of the Third Council of Constantinople (680) these earlier doubts had been overcome and the book became part of the official canon in the East, as in the West.[82]

Calculating the date of the second coming, despite the scriptural prohibitions, produced some striking timeframes. Theophilus of Antioch (flourishing c.180) devised a scheme based on the days of creation, which claimed Jesus had been born 5,500 years after this; the current world order would end five hundred years beyond that (six thousand years after the creation); Jesus' millennial kingdom would then last one thousand years, so that the final eternal heavenly kingdom would be established exactly seven thousand years after the creation.[83] This took its cue from similar calculations found in the *Epistle of Barnabas*, which itself echoed a similar approach found in the first-century Jewish text (with Christian interpolations) called *2 (Slavonic) Enoch*.[84]

The continued belief in the impending end-times can be found in a number of Christian writers in the Late Roman Empire. Lactantius (died 320) wrote how Christ would destroy the enemies of the righteous in torrents of blood. And, after Christ had judged the world, all heathen people would be subject to slavery under the righteous. The world itself would be transformed, with the stars and sun increasing in brightness, fruit growing without the need for labor, honey would drip from rocks, and fountains would flow with wine and milk. All wild animals would become tame.[85] This combined prophetic imagery of the Old Testament with the idea of the thousand-year-reign of Christ as found in Revelation.

A similar image of destruction of the wicked by an army—comprised not of angelic warriors, as found in some apocalyptic literature, but of the hidden elect—is found in the writings of Commodianus (probably third century, but sometimes assigned a fourth- or even fifth-century date). He believed the hidden elect were descended from the ten "lost tribes" of Israel. They would defeat the armies of Antichrist, represented by Gog and Magog (found in Ezekiel chapters 38 and 39, and in Revelation 20:8). We will come across these tribes at other points in this exploration. The holy elect would loot the cities of their opponents and enslave the captains of Antichrist and also the survivors of the Last Judgement.[86] As in the writings of Lactantius, we see a fervent desire for physical vindication by Christians over their enemies and the despoiling and enslaving of the latter by the former. It is a long way from the Sermon on the Mount.

Such violent enthusiastic attitudes would emerge again and again over the ensuing centuries, as more radical groups of believers would actually take it on themselves to implement the judgements of God, as active agents of the incoming millennial kingdom. But before that, the literal nature of the whole belief system would be questioned as Christianity became the official religion of the once-persecuting Roman Empire.

4

The "End-Times Toolkit"

Some Key Texts and Frameworks

A NUMBER OF KEY Bible passages appear again and again over two thousand years of end-times interpretations. In this chapter we examine what became key features of an "end-times toolkit." There are many passages of Scripture, from both the Old and New Testaments, that have been regarded as end-times prophetic texts over the centuries. It is not possible to list them all, but in this chapter we will identify a body of key texts that are referenced again and again by Christian writers. There are many other texts that speak of hope in God's intervention to overthrow injustice and wickedness, his actions to establish a situation of restored/transformed creation in which the righteous will be vindicated and God will dwell among people, and warnings of a coming day of judgement. However, the ones below are those frequently referenced due to their precise information, which is often perceived as identifying specific features, personages, geography, timetables, and frameworks of events relating to the end times.

It is not the purpose of this chapter to analyze whether these texts were all intended as prophecies of end-times events when they were originally written. Nor will we attempt a comprehensive exegesis of these texts. That lies outside the scope and purpose of this book. Here we simply accept that they have been used for the purpose of identifying key aspects of the future end-times by many Christians over the centuries. Whether that usage was/is correct is not the purpose of this exploration. Here we simply identify them and their content. How many Christians have engaged with these passages, and still do so, will be the subject of later chapters.

The methodology of end-time studies

As we explore the history of end-times reflection, identification and prediction, the different methods and approaches of different periods of history and of different practitioners will become apparent. However, a few are worth flagging up at this point since this may help us see the forest for the trees in the complexity of end times study.

The first key feature of many such studies is that of "multiple fulfilment." This is found across a wide range of mainstream traditions. It approaches scriptural passages with the understanding that one specific description or prediction can have a number of different applications over time. It may be assumed that the scripture passage was only ever intended to have a futuristic role, with a lesser impact on society contemporaneous with its compilation. However, it may also be assumed that it did have a contemporary impact, but can *also* be applied to a later event or even events in the plural. This approach can combine scholarly study of a text in its original context, alongside its future-predictive prophetic role. It is a very frequent feature of biblical study of such texts by people of faith.

The second key feature is an amalgamation of texts regardless of genre. Clearly, the Old and New Testaments contain a variety of different genres of literature. Some of these were arguably designed to be symbolic (although even here there will be disagreements among those studying them). Others appear more literal in their message. There is, though, no hard and fast rule for deciding between the two approaches and different interpreters will differ on how and where to strike this balance. Nevertheless, one of the noticeable features of much end-times analysis is to treat all Scripture as being fundamentally the same with regard to its application to specific religious, political, geographical, and social events; and to pay very little regard to the way genre might affect its use in this application. In this way, for instance, a verse predicting political crisis that is found in the Gospels will be combined with an allusive verse from Revelation or a poetic visionary statement from an Old Testament prophet. These diverse texts are all frequently cited and applied in a very similar, concrete and literal, sense. How this practice functions will become clearer once we see it in action.

The third key feature is extraction of information with limited or no regard to the context of compilation. One of the possible outcomes of the belief in canonical Scripture as being the authoritative "Word of God" is to assume that extracts can be understood as a message from God, and applied with little regard to their contextual information. This is usually unconsciously done and there is a long history of this use of Scripture. In this way, an individual believer will read a particular verse and feel that it resonates with their personal experience and context, in addition to any historic or wider application of that verse. In this way, there is a lively interaction between individual believers and specific scriptural verses and passages. It is not the intention of this study to question or disagree with the validity of this approach, which is the lived experience of many/most believers. However, in the field of end-times study this way of approaching Scripture can become problematic when a passage, verse, or even part of a verse is made to bear a weight of interpretation apart from its context. Corroboration is then sought from other scriptural texts, whose connection to the verse(s) being corroborated is, arguably, not at all obvious. One example would be the doctrine of "the rapture," where little (and mysterious) scriptural evidence has become the foundation for a highly complex and contentious set of beliefs, involving precise locations of this event within an end-times timeline, which itself has been constructed using a similar approach to, arguably disparate, scriptural passages. The resulting concept and its attendant future timeframe are now accepted by millions of Christians across the globe. Another example would be that of the figure of Antichrist, where the common historic and modern understanding is formed from an amalgamation of texts; and an assumption that these very different texts were intended to convey a related set of ideas about a specific future individual. At times, these connections may be more in the mind of the student of prophecy than in the actual texts themselves.

The fourth key feature is switching between literal and symbolic interpretation to suit one's needs. This shows itself in a number of areas. Highly specific interpretations of symbolic passages in Revelation, which are interpreted as referring to actual modern military hardware or technologies (the use of the identifier 666 in a microchip being an example of the latter), may be found at one point in an argument, but then the symbolic nature of another feature is accepted (such as the "beast" or the "whore") at another point (where clearly a literal animal is not in question, nor is a literal prostitute intended). This switching between literal and symbolic interpretation is usually done in order to advance a particular argument, which would fail if it was pursued via a wholly literal or a wholly symbolic methodology. The same applies to approaches to numbers, which are interpreted as specific numbers of years at times, but then as symbolic statements of time periods at others. Or interpretations of numbers may switch from them being regarded as days, to them being regarded as years, leading to widely differing applications of the resulting calculation. This inconsistency of approach will become apparent when we examine some interpretations of time periods referred to in Daniel and in Revelation and then applied to specific future events and time frames.

The fifth key feature is application of prophecy to contemporary society with no regard for the past history of misidentification. This might also be termed the ignorance of interpretative history or disregard for interpretative history. The theology of the end times is clearly not the only example of such cognitive dissonance. Human beings are very capable of holding contradictory views at the same time and separating them by a mental "fire wall," such that one idea/belief does not challenge or undermine another one. The more dearly a belief is held, the more impenetrable the "fire wall" becomes. We all do this at times, but are more keenly aware of it when we see it being practiced by others. In the field of end-times studies the figure of Antichrist has been confidently applied in the past to Emperor Nero, Holy Roman Emperor Frederick *Barbarossa*, numerous popes, King Charles I, Oliver Cromwell, Napoleon, Henry Kissinger, etc. One might think that this train wreck of past misidentification might make the next generation of end-times-orientated Christians pause when it comes to making identifications in their own time. Or, at least, that it might encourage caution. But it doesn't. The "fire wall" separates past mistakes from present dearly held speculations. At times, this is simply due to ignorance of the past. At other times it may not be so easily explained. Either way, it is a repeat phenomenon, as we shall see.

The sixth characteristic is the willingness to suspend critical study in order to buttress an interpretation of an end-times belief. This is particularly the case if the end-times belief resonates with a personal ideology or outlook. For example, Seat 666 is not kept free in the European Parliament buildings in Brussels and in Strasbourg. A quick online check can identify which members of the European Parliament use these seats (it differs between Brussels and Strasbourg). However, that it might be kept free for future use resonates with those who hold a deeply felt antipathy for the European Union and view it as a revived phase of the Roman Empire (related to interpretations of passages in Daniel and Revelation) and the seat (metaphorically and literally) of a modern-day antichrist figure. But it is *not* kept free. Nevertheless, in the age of social media and conspiracy theories, the claim that it is has legs and has travelled far.

These six methodologies need to be borne in mind as we examine the following key scriptural passages and, especially, as we later explore the use of these scriptures over the centuries. All the references below are followed by a precis of the content of these verses, as they have been understood to have end-times meaning.

Key end-times texts in the Old Testament

The Old Testament contains so many prophetic statements concerning future transformative acts of God and future events that it is not possible to cite all references to the "day of the LORD" or verses that might be included as such. These are some of the most frequently cited.

Deuteronomy 28:15–68

As a result of disobedience, the people of Israel will experience catastrophic destruction that will occur in many forms. This will include [a first?] exile to other nations. Then a nation from far away will sweep down like an eagle, lay horrific siege to the cities; few will survive this and these survivors will experience [a second?] exile, as they are scattered from one end of the world to the other. Life in this exile will be one of continuous fear and anxiety. The survivors will be returned to Egypt where they will wish for enslavement, but nobody will buy them.

Deuteronomy 30:1–6

As a punishment for sin, the people of Israel will be scattered to all the nations under heaven. However, as a result of the people's repentance, God will restore them to the land of their ancestors. There they will receive blessings and grow more prosperous and numerous than their ancestors. A new spiritual relationship with God will come from the resulting circumcision of their hearts.

Isaiah 11:1–16

A messianic figure will rise from the stump of Jesse (King David's family). He will bring judgement to the earth in favor of the poor. The wicked will be slain. A new world order will be established in which predator and prey will live in peace and harmony (e.g., the wolf with the lamb). From God's holy mountain (Jerusalem?) the knowledge of the Lord will flow out across the world. The exiles of the people of Israel will be gathered in by God's miraculous actions and they will subdue their historic enemies.

Jeremiah 23:7–8

The people of Israel will be brought by God out of the land of the north, and from all other lands of exile, and returned to their homeland again. (NOTE: Similar prophecies are found elsewhere and are often interpreted as referring to the Babylonian exile but are sometimes interpreted as having multiple meanings.)

Ezekiel 37:1–28

The dry bones of the people of Israel will be brought back to life. The exiles will be brought back to the land. There the people will live lives in harmony with God's holy will. They will be united under one ruler; the passage says that David himself will rule over the people. An everlasting covenant will be made with them by God. God will live among his people for ever.

Ezekiel 38:1–23

Gog of the land of Magog, the chief prince of Meshech and Tubal, will be drawn by God into a massive conflict with the restored people of Israel, who have been returned from exile. The invaders will be accompanied in this vast enterprise by armies from Persia, Cush, and Put, along with Gomer and Beth-togarmah from the far north. Their plundering of the land will be encouraged by Sheba and Dedan and the merchants of Tarshish. The mighty army that comes from the far north will be opposed by God. A great earthquake will rock the land; mountains will fall, as will walls; God will destroy the invaders with plague, rain, hail, and burning sulfur. Then the nations will know the might of the Lord.

Ezekiel 39:1–29

Gog, chief prince of Meshech, and Tubal will be brought by God from the far north in an invasion of Israel, which will result in Gog's destruction. God will rain fire down on Magog and those living in the coastlands and so they will know the Lord. God will make his holy name known to Israel and all the nations. For seven years the weapons of the defeated will be used as fuel. The burial place of the army of Gog will be so large it will block the route of travelers. It will take seven months to gather all the bodies of the defeated army. God will reveal his glory. He will restore the fortunes of the people of Israel. They will be returned from exile and will have a new spiritual union with God. (NOTE: See Rev 16:16 for a similar version of this colossal battle, but named as taking place at Armageddon; and Revelation 20:7–8 for a recounting of the devil being released after one thousand years and gathering Gog and Magog for battle.)

Daniel 2:31–45

King Nebuchadnezzar of Babylon has a dream of a statue with a head of pure gold, chest and arms of silver, belly and thighs of bronze, and legs of iron. The feet are made partly of iron and partly of clay. A rock (not quarried by human hands) hits the statue on its feet of iron and clay and shatters them. The statue then disintegrates and is blown away, but the rock remains and becomes a mountain that fills the earth. Daniel interprets the dream as revealing: Nebuchadnezzar's kingdom is the head of gold; an inferior successor (second) kingdom will arise (made from silver); then a third kingdom (of bronze) will rule the whole earth; a fourth kingdom (of iron) will arise and crush all opposition. However, it will be a divided kingdom, of mixed peoples, partly strong and partly brittle (the iron mixed with clay). In the time of these kings (presumably the rulers of the divided kingdom) God will shatter them and the whole statue (by the rock not quarried by human hands) and will establish a kingdom that will last forever.

Daniel 7:1–28

During the reign of Belshazzar king of Babylon, Daniel has a dream. In it he sees: four winds of heaven churning up the sea, from which comes four beasts; the first is like a lion with eagle's wings, its wings are torn off and it stands up like a man; the second is like a bear, with three ribs in its mouth; the third is like a leopard, with four wings and four heads; the fourth beast is powerful and terrifying and it has iron teeth, and it has ten horns; a little horn then grows up among them and uproots three horns and speaks boastful words. Following this, the throne of the Ancient of Days is set up and his court convened. The last beast is slain and burned, but the other three beasts continue to live for a period of time. Then, one described as like a son of man comes with the clouds of heaven and approaches the Ancient of Days. He is given power over all peoples and a kingdom that will last forever.

Daniel is told the meaning of the dream: the four beasts are four kingdoms but God's people will be given an eternal kingdom; the fourth beast will dominate the whole earth; ten kings will come out of that fourth kingdom; after them another king will rise, who will uproot three kings; this little horn will blaspheme God, oppress God's holy people, try to change the set times and the laws, and this time of oppression will last for an enigmatic period described as a time, times, and half a time. Then God will destroy this little horn oppressor and give rule to his holy people in a kingdom that will last forever.

Daniel 8:1–26

In a vision Daniel sees a ram with two horns (one horn grows after the first one and becomes longer). The ram charges to west, north, and south and none can stand against it. Then a goat with a single horn comes from the west and attacks the ram, shattering its two horns. Having defeated the ram, the goat becomes great, but its large horn is broken off and replaced with four horns. From one of these new horns another horn grows, which starts small but becomes powerful towards the south, east, and the Beautiful Land. It reaches the heavenly host and throws down and tramples some of the stars. It competes for power with the commander of the Lord's army, stops the daily sacrifice, and throws down the temple. This last act is possible because of rebellion against God, and it grows prosperous, and truth is thrown down. It is revealed to Daniel that the length of time of this situation (end of daily sacrifice, desolation-causing rebellion, subjugation of the temple and of God's people) will be 2,300 evenings and mornings. After this the temple will be restored.

The vision is explained to Daniel by Gabriel: the ram with two horns represents kings of Media and Persia; the goat is the king of Greece with the large horn representing its first king; the four horns replacing the broken one stand for four kingdoms that will emerge from this [Greek] nation. However, these kingdoms will not have comparable power. Then a fierce king will arise who will cause great devastation, including the defeat of God's people, the promotion of lies, and he will oppose God. But he will be defeated, though not by human agency. Daniel is specifically told that this vision of the evenings and mornings is true and will be fulfilled in the distant future.

Daniel 9:20–27

In this vision, Gabriel (described as a man, but clearly an angelic messenger) declares to Daniel that seventy sevens or weeks have been set for the Jewish people and Jerusalem to restrain wrongdoing and sinfulness, to make atonement for sinfulness, bring in eternal righteousness, seal up (complete?) prophetic understanding, and anoint the Most Holy Place or the Most Holy One. The timescale between the start of the rebuilding of Jerusalem and the coming of the Anointed One will be seven sevens (weeks), and sixty-two sevens (weeks). At the end of the sixty-two sevens (weeks), the Anointed One will be killed. An incoming ruler will destroy both Jerusalem and the temple. War and destruction will precede the end. This incoming ruler will establish a covenant with many people for one seven (week). In the middle of this seven (week) this ruler will stop temple sacrifice and, in its place, will set up an abomination that causes desolation. This will continue until he meets the end that is decreed for him.

Daniel 11:29–45

After a complex series of conflicts between the King of the North and the King of the South (in previous verses), the King of the North will invade the South. He will be opposed by ships from the western coastlands, which will cause him to fall back and take revenge on the Jewish people who are true to their holy covenant with God. He will desecrate the temple in Jerusalem and stop the daily sacrifice. He will set up the abomination that causes desolation. While some will accept his rule, he will be opposed by those who remain true to God. The wise will teach many but will suffer persecution and will undergo purification. The end will come at the appointed time. The terrible ruler will set himself up above every god and blaspheme the one true God. He will worship a god of fortresses. His attacks on opponents will be assisted by a foreign god and he will reward those who support him.

At the end time, the King of the South will attack him and the King of the North will respond with an army and a huge fleet. His armed forces will sweep through many lands, including through the Beautiful Land (the land of Israel), although Edom, Moab, and the rulers of Ammon will be rescued from him. He will conquer and loot the riches of Egypt, Libya, and Cush. Then worrying reports from the east and the north will cause him to react with an attempt to destroy those opposing him. He will establish his headquarters between the seas, at the place of the holy mountain (Jerusalem?). There, unaided by others, he will be destroyed.

Daniel 12:1–12

Michael the (angelic) protector of the Jewish people will arise. There will be a time of unprecedented suffering, but the true Jewish people will be saved. The dead will arise to face judgement and the vindication of the righteous. It is revealed to Daniel that the time until the fulfilment of the prophecy will be a time, times, and half a time (or a year, two years, and half a year). Daniel is told that the wise will understand the prophecies. Then additional information is revealed about the timeframe: the period of time between the stopping of the daily sacrifice at the temple and the setting up of the abomination that causes desolation and the end, will be 1,290 days. The one who continues until the end of the 1,335 days will be blessed.

Joel 2:20

God says he will remove the northern enemy from the land of Israel and drive it into a dry and barren land. The eastern part of the army will drown in the Dead Sea, while the western part will drown in the Mediterranean Sea. From it a great stench will rise upwards. God (?) has done great things.

Joel 3:2 and 14–18

God will gather all the nations in the Valley of Jehoshaphat for judgement for what they have done to Israel: scattering them among the nations and dividing up the land of Israel. Huge numbers will be gathered in this Valley of Decision, for the day of the Lord is near in the Valley of Decision.

This will be followed by the darkening of sun, moon, and stars, the Lord roaring from Jerusalem, the shaking of earth and the heavens, the Lord being a refuge for his people, and the establishment of his eternal rule in Jerusalem. It will be a kingdom of abundance, with mountains dripping new wine, hills flowing with milk, and valleys of running water. A fountain will flow from the Jerusalem temple, watering the land.

Zephaniah 1:14–18

As part of God's judgement on the world and the restoration of his people, these verses describe darkness and battle, then the whole earth and its inhabitants consumed by fire.

Zechariah

This book contains many references to the restoration of Jerusalem and the Jewish people to their land (from exile). Judgement is pronounced on their enemies. Within this there is a reference to a king riding humbly into Jerusalem (9:9), which New Testament writers quoted as being fulfilled by Jesus on Palm Sunday. It is interesting that this is set within verses that, otherwise, would be read as end-times prophecies.

Within the judgements on the nations are verses that describe a great future siege of Jerusalem culminating in God rescuing his people and empowering them (12:1–9; 14:1–5). The second siege account includes a dramatic description of the feet of the Lord standing on the Mount of Olives and splitting it in two. This is often interpreted as portraying the physical return of Christ to that spot. Then the land will be transformed; and the enemies of Jerusalem will be struck by plague sent by God (14:12) in which their flesh, eyes, and tongues will rot. The nations that survive will come to Jerusalem to worship God as the city is transformed in holiness.

Malachi 4:1.

God's judgement on the wicked will consumed them with fire.

Key end-times texts in the New Testament

Regarding passages from the book of Revelation, it needs to be noted that the use of this apocalyptic book in end-times studies is so extensive that those passages quoted below are only some of the most frequently cited.

Matthew 24:4–44

Jesus warns of wars and rumors of wars; famines and earthquakes; these are the birth pains of the end times. His followers will be persecuted. People will fall away from faith and false prophets will arise. The gospel will be preached across the whole world. The abomination that causes desolation, that is found in Daniel, will occur in the holy place of the Jerusalem temple. This will be a signal for those in Judea to flee to the mountains. This will be followed by unparalleled distress, a time of tribulation. Those days will be shortened, to save the elect. False messiahs and false prophets will perform great signs and wonders. People will falsely speak of the location of the coming of the Son of Man, but in reality he will come like lightning.

After the time of unparalleled suffering (tribulation), the sun and moon will be darkened; the stars will fall; the heavenly bodies will be shaken. The sign of the Son of Man will appear in heaven and he will come on the clouds of heaven with power and great glory. With a loud trumpet call he will send angels to gather the elect.

As these things begin to happen, they are pointers to the fulfilment of prophecy, just as the budding fig tree is a pointer to the nearness of summer. This generation will see it fulfilled before they die. Heaven and earth will pass away, but Jesus' words will not do so. Only the Father knows when these events will occur. Life will be going on as normal, as in the days of Noah. Of two men working in the field: one will be taken and one left. Of two women grinding corn: one will be taken and one left. The Son of Man will come at an unexpected hour.

(NOTE: A similar [slightly shorter] account of the events leading to the coming of the Son of Man can be found in Mark 13:5–37 [the so-called "Little Apocalypse"]. A version of the teaching found in Matthew's Gospel can also be found in Luke 21:8–36, but a little shorter and with an emphasis on Jerusalem besieged and then trampled by the gentiles until the times of the gentiles are fulfilled. Neither Mark nor Luke mention Jesus' mysterious comment about one taken/the other left, which has been built on as one of the key texts pointing to the rapture.)

1 Corinthians 15:20–28

When Christ returns his followers will be resurrected. Then the end will come when Christ hands the kingdom over to God the Father. This will be after Christ has destroyed all other authorities. He will reign until he has subdued all his enemies and put them under his feet. When this has been achieved, Christ will be made subject to God the Father who has put everything else under the feet of Christ.

1 Thessalonians 1:10

Christians wait for the second coming of Christ. He will rescue his followers from the coming wrath. (NOTE: This is sometimes taken as corroborative evidence connected to Matthew 24:40–41 [itself interpreted as the basis for the belief in the rapture]. However, the reference in 1 Thessalonians seems much more likely to be referring to protection from God's final judgement on the world in the future, rather than protection from a specific period of end-times tribulation prior to Christ's second coming. There seems nothing in the 1 Thessalonians passage to support such a specific interpretation.)

1 Thessalonians 4:13–18

Christ will return with a loud command and the voice of the archangel and the trumpet call of God. Then the Christian dead will rise. Then those Christians who are alive when Christ returns will join them in the clouds and, together, they will meet the Lord in the air. (NOTE: This is often quoted as key evidence in support of belief in the rapture.)

1 Thessalonians 5:1–3

The day of the Lord will come like a thief in the night. Destruction will come on people, even as they are saying "peace and safety."

2 Thessalonians 2:1–12

The day of the Lord will not happen until the rebellion occurs, which will reveal the man of lawlessness, who is doomed to destruction. He will oppose and exalt himself above everything called God or that is worshipped. He will proclaim himself God in God's temple. He is currently being held back so that he will be revealed at the proper time. The power of lawlessness is already at work, but the one holding this in check will continue to do this until taken out of the way. Then the lawless one will be revealed and will then be destroyed by Christ at his coming. The coming of the lawless one will be consistent with the way the devil works: signs and wonders will be used to uphold the lie and will deceive those who are perishing and who do not love the truth. A powerful delusion will be sent by God so that they will believe in the lie.

2 Peter 3:8–13

With God, a day is like a thousand years, and a thousand years are like a day. He is patient because he wishes for none to perish. The day of the Lord will come unexpectedly, like a thief. With a great sound the heavens will come to an end and fire will dissolve the elements and the earth. All will be disclosed (or destroyed) in this way. As a result, God's people should live holy lives in anticipation of this day; hastening (or earnestly desiring) this day, when the heavens and the elements will melt in fire. Believers wait for the fulfilment of God's promise of new heavens and a new earth characterized by righteousness.

1 John 2:18, 22; 4:3

This is the last hour and the antichrist is coming. Indeed, many antichrists have already come.

That is evidence that this is the last hour. The liar is whoever denies Jesus is the Christ. Such a one is the antichrist, denying the Father and the

Son. Every spirit that does not acknowledge Jesus, is not from God but is the spirit of the antichrist—which is coming and is already in the world. (NOTE: the term "antichrist" is usually not capitalized in the scriptural references since these do not uniformly refer to a specific figure, unlike later end-times studies, which do.)

2 John 7

Many deceivers who deny that Jesus came as a real human being have gone into the world and such a person is the deceiver and the antichrist.

Revelation 7:13–14

A huge crowd is seen, praising God. They are identified as those who have come out of the great tribulation and washed their robes in the blood of the Lamb (Jesus).

(NOTE: Before Revelation 7:1–8, 144,000 from the tribes of Israel receive God's seal. This same number will later appear in Revelation 14:1–3 [see below]. These seem different to the great crowd in white robes who have come out of the great tribulation. The phrase "great tribulation," which appears here, is frequently used (capitalized) by later students of prophecy to describe the persecution of God's people by the beast that is described later in the book of Revelation; and sometimes generally for the immense end-times suffering prior to the victory of Christ. The phrase [Greek: *thlipsis megale*] that appears here, echoes words of Jesus in Matthew 24:21 and 29 and Mark 13:19 and 24, referring to a specific time of suffering (tribulation) preceding his second coming. Some modern students of prophecy believe that the church will not be present during this tribulation. However, that is difficult to square with Revelation 7 and Matthew 24, which clearly refer to believers suffering during this time. In the case of the latter reference, the time [tribulation] will be cut short in order to spare the elect.)

Revelation 12:1–17

A woman appears, clothed with the sun and with the moon under her feet and wearing a crown made up of twelve stars. She begins to give birth, but this child is threatened with being consumed by a red dragon with seven crowned heads and ten horns. A third of the stars are brought to earth by its tail. However, the child—who is to rule the nations with an iron rod—is rescued and taken to God. The woman escapes to a place in the wilderness, prepared for her by God, for 1,260 days.

During a war in heaven, Michael and his angels defeat the dragon (who is the devil) and his angels and they are thrown down to the earth.

This victory heralds the triumph of God and his Messiah (Christ) and of his people. This brings rejoicing to the heavens but distress to the earth and sea to which the devil (angry that his time is short) has been thrown down.

The dragon pursues the woman, but the woman is enabled to fly into the wilderness for a time, and times, and half a time. The dragon pours out a flood to overwhelm the woman, but the earth swallows the water. After this the dragon wages war against the people of God.

Revelation 13:1–18

A beast rises out of the sea. It has ten crowned horns; and seven heads on which blasphemous names are written. This beast is like a leopard, but it has feet like a bear and a mouth like a lion. It is empowered by the dragon (the devil) and given authority. One of its heads appears to have received a death-wound, but it has healed. The whole earth follows this beast and worships the dragon, who has given the beast authority. People consider the beast without parallel and unconquerable.

The arrogant and blasphemous rule of this beast lasts for forty-two months. It blasphemes against God and against the citizens of heaven. It makes war on the people of God (and some manuscripts add: it conquers them). The beast has power over all the world and is worshipped by all those who do not believe in Jesus (the Lamb that was slain). God's people are instructed to endure and hold onto faith.

Then a second beast emerges, but this time out of the earth. Speaking like a dragon, it has two horns like those of a lamb. It exercises authority on behalf of the first beast. This second beast deceives the people of the world with astonishing signs. It also sets up an image of the first beast; an image able to speak and cause the deaths of any who will not worship it. This beast has a mark placed on all the people of the earth, which represents its name or the number of its name: 666. Without this mark, no one can buy or sell.

Revelation 14:8–11

After a revelation of 144,000 redeemed from the earth and standing with the Lamb (Jesus) on Mount Zion (Jerusalem), an angel cries that Babylon the great—with whom the nations committed fornication—has fallen. Another angel then declares God's judgement on all who had worshipped the beast (see Revelation 13).

Revelation 16:1–21

This chapter reveals seven angels sent by God to pour seven judgements (from seven bowls) onto the earth. These seven judgements or plagues are: a terrible sore on those with the mark of the beast, who had worshipped the beast; all creatures living in the sea die as the water turns to blood; rivers and springs turn to blood too; the sun scorches people; the kingdom of the beast is plunged into darkness and its citizens are in agony; the river Euphrates is dried up to allow the passage of the kings from the east; judgement is poured into the air and, amid thunder and lightning, the earth is torn by an unprecedented earthquake.

Following the drying up of the Euphrates, three frog-like evil spirits come out of the mouth of the dragon, the mouth of the beast, and the mouth of the false prophet. (NOTE: this is the first mention of this figure and may be intended as a reference to the beast that arose from the earth in Revelation 13:11, who caused people to worship the beast that rose out of the sea, whose mortal wound had healed, and also set up the talking image of the first beast). The evil spirits summon the kings of the earth to do battle with God at the place called Armageddon.

Also, as a result of the seventh bowl of wrath, the great city (Babylon/Rome?) is split into three parts and destruction occurs at all the cities of the world. God punishes Babylon (Rome?). Islands and mountains vanish, and great hailstones fall on the earth; due to this hail people curse God.

Revelation 17:1–17

The judgement of a woman described as the great whore is announced. She is depicted as sitting on a blasphemous scarlet beast that has seven heads and ten horns. On the woman's head a name is written, which is described as a mystery and is that of Babylon the great, mother of all whores and of abominable deeds. These include the killing of the followers of Jesus. The great whore is drunk on the blood of these martyrs.

This is followed by an enigmatic statement that the scarlet beast exists and yet does not exist and is yet to be revealed. It comes from the bottomless pit, and it will be destroyed. The seven heads are seven mountains on which the great whore sits (Rome?). These are also seven kings. Of these seven kings: five have already fallen, one is currently ruling, the seventh is yet to come. When this seventh one appears, he will rule for only a short time. The scarlet beast is an eighth king, but it belongs to the seven kings. The ten horns of the scarlet beast represent ten kings who have not yet begun to reign and, when they do so, their reign will last just one hour and they will rule with the beast (presumably the scarlet beast), to whom they will give authority. These kings will make war on the Lamb (Jesus) and will be defeated by him.

The waters, on which the whore sits, represent the peoples of the world. The ten horns (kings) and the beast (the scarlet beast) will hate the whore and they will destroy her. God has willed that these kings will give their kingdom to the beast (the scarlet beast) until God's words are fulfilled (presumably: the prophecies come to pass). The woman (the great whore) is the city that rules over the whole earth (Rome?).

(NOTE: the whole of Revelation chapter 18 then goes into detail concerning the destruction of the great whore, Babylon the great, who is referred to in chapter 17. God's people are commanded to flee from Babylon; and God's judgement falls on the kings and merchants of the earth who have committed fornication with the great whore and shared in luxuries with her. Sailors and ship owners who gained wealth from her existence will look with shock at the smoke rising from her destruction.)

Revelation 19:19–21

The beast and the kings of the earth make war on the rider on a white horse who, earlier in the chapter, has been described as "King of kings and Lord of lords." The beast is captured, as is the false prophet who had deceived those who had received the mark of the beast (666) and had worshipped the image of the beast. They are both thrown into a lake of fire. Their armies are destroyed by the rider on the white horse.

Revelation 20:1–13

The dragon (the devil) is bound by an angel for one thousand years. After that he will be released for a short time. Those who had remained true to Jesus and, consequently had been martyred during the reign of the beast (they had not worshipped the image of the beast nor received his mark), come back to life and rule with Christ for one thousand years. This is described as the first resurrection and the rest of the dead are not yet raised to life.

After one thousand years, the devil is released and deceives the nations and gathers Gog and Magog for battle. They besiege the saints and the much-loved city (Jerusalem?), but are destroyed by fire from heaven. The devil is thrown into the same lake of fire as the beast and the false prophet. There they will be tormented forever.

After this, comes the judgement of the dead by God. Heaven and earth flee away from him. This is the final judgement. After this (in chapter 21) a new heaven and a new earth appear and a new Jerusalem comes down from heaven.

5

A Shift in End-Times Theology

EARLY CHRISTIANS IDENTIFIED CONTEMPORARY events as fulfilments of end-times prophecies and this continued during the first three centuries of church history. However, the theological mood was changing, as leading church thinkers increasingly argued that the prophecies should not be interpreted literally. When Christianity became the official religion of the Roman Empire, futurism was steadily pushed to the margins of acceptable Christian thought.

The development of the "idealist" or "allegorical" approach

While many early Christians were unsure over exactly how to apply the scripture texts that they thought referred to end-times events, it is clear that most thought of them as pointers to literal events that would occur in the near future. While symbolic language was often used in these passages, it was decoded in order to identify concrete events. In other words, the prophecies were considered to be precise predictors of geo-politics.

This formed part of precise timeframes that looked forward to a visible return of Christ, who would then initiate a literal thousand-year reign on earth. While the Montanists initially looked to the establishment of the center of this millennial rule in Phrygia[87] most Christians thought it would be in Jerusalem.[88] (After the failure of the first-century Jewish revolt against Roman rule, Jerusalem was no longer a Jewish city.) After the millennium would come the general resurrection of the dead, the final judgement, and the creation of the new heaven and new earth, then the New Jerusalem would descend from heaven. Millennialist, or millenarian, believers are also sometimes known as *chiliasts* (from the Greek word for "thousand"), a term first coined in the seventeenth century, but less commonly used today than the alternative ones. Consequently, it is these alternative terms that are used in this book.

The literal and imminent approach fitted well with a milieu in which Christians were subject to official sanctions and, at times, lethal persecution. The fact that the original text of Revelation had been written against the background of persecution and martyrdom meant that those who thought this way felt very much in line with the enigmatic words that they found there. There was a kindred spirit of being victims of persecution that united those later believers speculating on Revelation (and the similar words in Daniel) with its original audience and enabled the ideas found in the book to resonate with such audiences.

Speculation could become quite inventive. In the late third century, Victorinus of Pettau (died c.304), in his *Commentary on the Apocalypse*, elaborated a pre-existing idea that the Emperor Nero (who died in the year 68) was not in fact dead but would return, and, more than that, was the fulfilment of the antichrist prophecies in the New Testament. This was the concept known as Nero *Redivivus*.[89] This proposal built on the idea that Nero was Antichrist but the second coming had not occurred during his reign. The idea of the return of Nero allowed for acceptance of this identification but accorded it flexibility so as to be redeployed when the earlier identification had proved to be wrong. In this, though, writers such as Victorinus sowed the seeds of the eventual rejection of a literal futurist approach to prophecy. Errors in identification undermined confidence in literal interpretations. This was especially so among the leadership of the church. This was even more so when it was associated with radical movements that both challenged church structures and risked bringing down trouble from governing authorities—who were quick to suppress radical movements that challenged the social order.

That Victorinus wrote as he did—about a revived Nero-Antichrist who would bring in a period of intense persecution—was not surprising since he himself experienced persecution, leading to his eventual martyrdom during the persecutions initiated by the Emperor Diocletian. Such active persecutions encouraged literal interpretations of the suffering (the tribulation) found in the book of Revelation.

It is clear that Victorinus was a confident exponent of beliefs in the millennium.[90] However, the repetition of such persecution—unaccompanied by the last days—caused interpretation to become more elastic and inventive. This is seen in his writing. He himself did not offer a commentary on the entire text of Revelation but, instead, focused on particular passages and did so in ways that were becoming more allegorical with a particular interest in arithmology.[91] Numbers would dominate significant areas of end-times analysis from then until the present day. The work of Victorinus also involved paraphrasing key passages in order to assess their meaning.[92] He developed an idea that the prophecies found in Revelation did not constitute a continuous sequence of events but were, at times, running parallel but using different imagery. This is sometimes described as "recapitulation" and examples, in the view of Victorinus, were the references to bowls and trumpets (in a number of chapters) in which he saw parallel expressions concerning the same events, rather than an unfolding continuous sequence.[93] This highlights the challenge of interpreting these poetic texts, with their powerful imagery. The problem, of course, is that the different ways in which such texts can be interpreted has given rise to endless permutations. This, in turn, means they can be utilized to point to a wide range of contemporary cultural and political features as alleged fulfilments of prophecy. Victorinus was not the first to adopt his own particular methodology (with its implications for interpretation). He would certainly not be the last.

In a similar way, he interpreted Revelation's seven churches (in chapter 1) as representing seven groups or classes of Christians within the wider church, instead of specific geographically locatable Christian communities. The seven seals (in chapters 5–8) were interpreted as revealing the spread of the gospel rather than seven particular events. The crowned rider of the white horse, among the four horsemen, was viewed as the victorious church and the red horseman was interpreted as indicating impending wars, rather than representing specific identifiable conflicts (all from chapter 6). Despite this, he still looked for actual wars, diseases, and periods of persecution as presaging the second coming. In this way, he mixed specific with more general perspectives in a way that would become very common among later students of prophecy. It is not surprising, given his own subsequent martyrdom, that he viewed the Roman Empire (still persecuting Christians in his day) as being referred to in the description of the red dragon with seven crowned heads and ten horns, in Revelation chapter 12. The great whore, Babylon the great, of Revelation chapter 17, he identified as Rome (as the writer of Revelation probably intended) with the seven heads of the scarlet beast representing both the seven hills of Rome and (very specifically) seven emperors. The sixth he specifically identified as being Domitian (died in the year 96), and the scarlet beast—who is an eighth king but belongs to the seven kings—he identified as Nero. Hence his assertion that Nero would come again. When it came to the millennium, he adopted a line that was in stark contrast to earlier interpretations and saw this as the years unfolding from the birth of Christ, with the references to the first resurrection of the dead being understood as referring to those martyred Christians who were already reigning with Christ in the heavenly realm. As a result, Victorinus can be described as adopting an amillennialist eschatology.

The kind of approach adopted by Victorinus came to be particularly associated with the church center at Alexandria in Egypt. Here the influence of existing Greek thought, the passage of centuries without the second coming taking place, and the unrest associated with Montanism, encouraged an increasingly spiritual interpretation of the prophetic scriptures. The roots of some of this could be discerned as early as the writings of Justin Martyr (died 165), when he spiritualized the study of the Old Testament in order to both see more of Christian beliefs in its persons and events, and in order to refute gnostic denials of the place of the Old Testament in God's revelation. However, a non-literal, non-historically predictive, and more allegorical approach to prophecy accelerated in the third century.

The allegorical approach (or the "allegorical hermeneutic") was closely associated with the work of Origen (died 254). Origen was heavily influenced by Greek philosophical thought, with its deep distrust of matter and its promotion of the non-physical. The idea of a literal, earthly, millennial kingdom was unacceptable to such a perspective. Instead, the idea of a non-physical and spiritual future kingdom was a push-back against what had become a widespread approach within the church towards prophecy and the future state that it looked forward to.[94] Origen saw prophetic scripture texts as giving an insight into the heavenly realms, and the inner discovery of eternal truths, rather than earthbound events. In his approach to the end times, he envisaged the appearance of Christ everywhere, with human beings finding themselves before his throne. This was in stark contrast to the concrete outlook of places, battles, and movements of armies so deeply engrained in many other eschatological frameworks. Origen robustly rejected the idea of a millennial rule of Christ from a physical, earthly Jerusalem; even if a transformed one. This meant an abandonment of much millennial speculation and expectation. In the same way, he rejected the literalism of ideas about eternal punishment and, instead, envisaged a situation of interior anguish, in which sinners were acutely aware of their separation from God, who should have been their supreme good. There was even a hint in his writings that such punishment would not be eternal but would, rather, eventually come to an end, when all things are restored to their original order. This he described through the doctrine of *apokatastasis* (restoration).[95] This came close to a doctrine of universal salvation, as his critics were quick to point out. Without getting further into his thoughts on such areas, the key thing to note is that it was a long way from the concrete eschatological debates that had occupied the minds of many others before him.

This non-literal approach was accelerated by Tyconius (died c.390), who took no account of historical settings, but instead saw all the prophecies in Revelation through a spiritual and mystical lens. For Tyconius, the figures, numbers, and events found there "symbolize abstract concepts, or theological teachings."[96] In this way, he identified deep and profound meanings in the book, but not ones that predicted specific future end-times geo-political events. On the other hand, he was not solely allegorical in his understanding, since he believed that the things referred to in Revelation had actual historical meaning but were "not a linear series of events that will happen at some future time but rather a mystical grouping of symbols that the faithful will see at work in their own contexts and that repeat in all places and at all times."[97]

This approach was followed by Augustine of Hippo (in North Africa), whose rejection of end-times speculation was to dominate the official outlook of the Catholic Church for the next thousand years. For Augustine, at its simplest, nobody could identify when it would happen, nor how it would occur, nor who would be saved. In key areas this was adopted directly from the view of history and the future that had been expressed by his fellow North African, Tyrconius. Around Augustine, fellow Christians were predictably speculating that the invading barbarian tribes of the Goths and Visigoths represented Gog and Magog of the prophecies. Others insisted that the Christianized Roman Empire was an expression of God's theocratic rule; although this was hard to maintain in the West after the fall of Rome to barbarian invaders in the year 410. At the same time, millenarianism was associated (as it had been for some time and still often is) with populist, turbulent, grassroots movements intent on overturning government and the social order. In one go, Augustine removed the detonator from all these potentially explosive, and influential, approaches to prophetic scriptures. For Augustine, the millennium represented the existence of the church and its counterpart in the heavenly city (since only God knew exactly who the citizens of the "city of God" were). Augustine did not look to an imminent intervention in history by God. In contrast, the millennium was immanent or "realized." The end-times battles had already occurred since God, in Christ, had defeated the devil. For now, the "city of the world" and the "city of God" coexisted. But, in time, that of God would triumph. For Augustine, Christians must be *always ready* for this, through the spiritual and moral qualities of their lives; but *always uncertain regarding when* the final moment will occur.

This Augustinian outlook became the norm in scriptural interpretation, with regard to Revelation in particular and prophetic scriptures generally. It was a seismic shift. The approach has been provocatively described as involving an interpretation of Revelation that "affirmed its historical realism while at the same time liberated it from the embarrassment of literalism."[98]

The Augustinian approach (as that of Tyconius) was also apparent in the writings of the North African bishop, Primasius (died 560), whose commentary on Revelation employed a general method of seeking out the universal meaning of the text rather than focusing on the particular aspects of the passage.[99] However, it took a while for the new orthodoxy to become commonplace.

Andreas (or Andrew) of Caesarea (writing in the early seventh century) took a similar approach to that which had been accelerating since the days of Origen, applying a threefold analysis of Scripture—literal or historical, figurative or tropological, and spiritual—and accorded primacy to the spiritual interpretation.[100] He never actually used the term allegory, as he was very concerned to avoid what he considered imaginative and fanciful interpretations, which were often (though not inevitably) associated with the allegorical method. Instead, he attempted to understand symbolic use of language and numbers (such as the use of seven or 666) by reference to their use elsewhere in the Bible or in church tradition.[101] With regard to the millennium, he was an amillennialist and believed that the thousand-year period was the time between the birth of Jesus and the eventual appearance of the Antichrist. In this, Andreas represented what had become the widespread outlook of his day. He also understood it symbolically rather than as an exact measurement of time. On the other hand, he believed that he was living in the time of the seventh kingdom

(Rev 17:9) and that the Antichrist would eventual appear from this king-dom as a future "king of the Romans."[102]

Andreas wrote the oldest Greek commentary on Revelation and ap-plied his method to understanding its meaning as he saw it. For Andreas, the figurative and symbolic images were to be understood as expressions of realities and of experiences that transcend human language. In other words, while they were not to be read as specific geo-political future events, they should not simply be read as imaginative either. He also as-serted the clear message of the New Testament—ignored by huge num-bers of Christians before and since—that nobody can predict or speculate regarding when the end of the world will occur. This revealed real self-discipline in Andreas, since the troubles of his own time (barbarian inva-sions, civil war, plague, famine, earthquakes, and extreme weather) had caused others to assume that the end was at hand. Throughout church history this has been a repeat phenomenon, of turbulence leading to end-times speculation, and it remains the case.

So influential was his work that some modern scholars have even (controversially) suggested that some of his glosses actually became in-corporated into the Greek text of Revelation as we now have it and add to some of its enigmatic passages. This view, however, is rejected by other scholars.[103] What is clear is that he played a major role in the Eastern Or-thodox church accepting Revelation in place of earlier reservations about the book (which had increased since the second century), due to its use by radical millenarians, schismatic movements, and others arguing for a literal interpretation of its contents.[104] In contrast, it had remained accepted in the West throughout this time period.

The impact of the conversion of the Roman Empire on end-times thinking

This movement from a futurist to a more-allegorical view of prophecy was not only prompted by the fact that the second coming had not occurred, concerns at extremist millenarian unrest, and the growth of Platonic philo-sophical thought within the church. It was also accelerated by the conver-sion of the Roman Empire to Christianity.

This occasioned a major shift from the premillennialism of the early church fathers, who had envisaged the second coming of Christ leading to a thousand-year reign on earth. In place of this, there developed an "amillennialism" or "postmillennialism" in the thinking of many theologians. The amillennial approach abandoned the idea of any earthly reign of a thousand years and came to understand the millennium in non-literal forms. The postmillennial approach envisaged Christ as returning to earth at the end of a thousand-year period in which the spread of the gospel, the influence of the godly, and the progress of holiness, had prepared the way for his coming. These later approaches would dominate much of the eschatological thinking from the fourth century to the middle part of the nineteenth century. Given the extent to which premillennialism is now deeply engrained in modern end-times thinking, this can come as something of a shock. What is now taken as normative in the way in which prophetic scriptures are interpreted across many Christian communities, has only become the settled position during the past century or so. For the previous millennium, some very different outlooks guided Christian understanding of prophecy across huge areas of the church. This was rooted in the paradigm shift that occurred in the Late Roman Empire.

The conversion of the Roman Empire in the fourth century had profound implications for how end-times prophecies were read. This was because the process of changing relations between empire and church—first of toleration of Christianity though the Edict of Milan (313) and then the official conversion of Constantine, followed by the increasingly prominent role of the church within the empire—made longstanding interpretations of prophecy, which had seen them as indicating a persecuting imperial power, unattractive. In itself, this did not mean that a literal interpretation of prophecy could not be followed. After all, the prophetic verses could still refer to a future empire or kingdoms deeply antagonistic to Christianity—just not the Roman one (and in time, such views would push back against the allegorizing position). Nevertheless, in the short term, the changes in imperial religious ideology defused much of the explosiveness inherent in traditional end-times interpretation. This was because, in the fourth century, few envisaged the end of the newly Christianized empire. Indeed, in the East, the Byzantine form of imperial rule would last (in an increasingly parlous state) until 1453. With no obvious successor state in view or imaginable, Late-Roman Christians were left with the experience of living in a state that was becoming increasingly Christianized and that seemed here to stay. Old views of emperors as Antichrist were no longer tenable when such rulers were the defenders of Christian orthodoxy. Both the church and the empire were now seen as "catholic, universal, ecumenical, orderly."[105]

Not surprisingly, this accelerated ways of reading the prophetic passages of Scripture that stood in marked contrast to the outlook that had once been strongly adhered to by large numbers of Christians, both clerical and lay. The road to reading prophecies as allegory, as spiritual, as symbolic, and (crucially) non-historically predictive, was being cleared.

This change was assisted by a related process, which increasingly saw the church as the inheritor of all the status and prophetic significance of Israel in Old Testament prophetic writings. This caused a radical re-reading of the pre-Christian prophetic scriptures, with their distinctive geo-political details and context. When re-read, these became loosened from their specific connections with place and ethnicity and became mutable. They were increasingly read as profound spiritual truths whose meaning was only understood through the new people of God, the church. In this process, these meanings became symbolic rather than concrete.

The approach that has just been outlined will have jarred on many modern readers. This is because, as we will see in later chapters, much of end-times study since the nineteenth century has been strongly influenced by a very different approach, termed "dispensationalism." This modern system is particularly known today as developed through, and from, the teachings of John Nelson Darby (died 1882), who is often considered to be the father of dispensationalism. His work and influence was consolidated by Cyrus Ingerson Scofield (died 1921). We shall hear a lot more about these thinkers and their continued influence on end-times interpretation in due course. To cut a long story short at this point, the key thing to note is that dispensationalism considers biblical history to have been divided by God into so-called "dispensations." These are clearly defined periods in which God wills particular revelations of himself and his nature to be experienced, and God decrees particular and distinctive organizational principles and roles to characterize these periods of time. While today some so-called "progressive dispensationalists" see some Old Testament promises as being developed within the New Testament to include the Christian church, the classic dispensationalist model views Israel (the Jewish people throughout history, and today also including the State of Israel) and the church as representing two distinct dispensations. In what has become the classic version of this way of reading Scripture and history, God has willed two distinct group-roles on earth: one for Israel and another one for the church. According to dispensationalism, the dispensation of God that applies to Israel (the Jews) has not ended, despite the rejection of

Jesus by the Jewish establishment and the rise of the Christian community. It remains that Israel/the Jews are still divinely called as a religious and ethnic group and the end-times prophecies still apply to them, literally and geo-politically. In the great sweep of providential history, the church and the Christian dispensation, since the first century, represents an age of grace (in contrast to Old Testament law) that constitutes "a parenthesis" (a pause/break) in the long-prophesied history of Israel. This amounts to an *earthly* kingdom program that applies to Israel/the Jews and a *spiritual* heavenly program for the Christian church. According to this outlook, the prophetic program for Israel was, in effect, paused after the dramatic events of the rejection of Christ and the fall of Jerusalem and the destruction of the temple in the year 70.

According to this methodology, there will come a future point of change (occasioned by the rapture) at which the church will be supernaturally removed from the earth. There are some minority positions among dispensationalists on the timing of this rapture event in the context of the period of terrible suffering known as the "great tribulation." Then the prophetic program for Israel, paused in the first century AD, will resume. Following this, there will occur a refocusing of attention on Israel/the Jews (who have never lost their providential role); the great tribulation; conflict with Antichrist; the conversion of the Jews to Christ; the return of Christ; his theocratic millennial rule on earth; then the final judgement and the establishment of the eternal new heaven and the new earth. This is the dominant outlook found within present-day premillennialism.

This whole aside on the modern outlook has itself been something of a parenthesis, but one worth making at this point in order to emphasize that the approach that was firmly in place by the end of the Roman Empire was something *very different* to this modern outlook. Given that dispensationalism is now widespread and mainstream among most modern students of the end times, it must be emphasized that *this was not the case for over a millennium and a half of Christian history*. Instead, what developed as the church became a distinct multi-ethnic group, distinct from Judaism, was a very different take on providential history. The outlook that developed rapidly over the first four centuries of the Christian era can broadly be described by the terms "covenant theology," "supersessionism," and "replacement theology." In short, the new covenant, based on faith in Jesus, has replaced (or superseded) the old covenant, between God and the Jews. According to this understanding, the Christian church has replaced the Jews as the people of God and inherited what was promised to them. Beliefs in line with this outlook can be found in the writings of Clement of Rome (died 99) in his *Epistle to the Corinthians*; much more clearly in the writings of Justin Martyr in his *Dialogue with Trypho*; expressed by Hippolytus of Rome (died 235) in his *Treatise Against the Jews*; in the ideas of Tertullian (died 240) in his *An Answer to the Jews*; and expressed by Augustine of Hippo in *The City of God.*

The destruction of Jerusalem in 70 led many early Christians to conclude that God had rejected the Jewish people. The expulsion of Christians from the synagogues, by the end of the first century, was accompanied by the realization that the wider Jewish community and the Jewish religious leadership were not going to accept Jesus as the Messiah. This realization occurred alongside the increasingly gentile nature of the Christian community. The Christian church and the Jewish community parted ways and, as they did so, the former concluded that God had called them out of the latter and had made them the new chosen people and heirs to the promises of the Old Testament.

This understanding largely dominated the outlook of the church from the second to the nineteenth century and is still influential today (though not in evangelical circles); although since the Holocaust some denominations have become wary of it, given its past (though by no means inevitable) association with antisemitism. In such a viewpoint, Israel and Jerusalem became synonymous with the church. The Old Testament was searched for typologies that threw light on the coming of Christ and could be used in Christian teaching. This was based on features of the Gospel accounts where Old Testament prophecies were stated to have been fulfilled in Christ and in the letters of the emerging New Testament where Old Testament events, features, and people were seen as spiritual parallels (types) of the new Christian faith and understanding. This "typological hermeneutic" became widespread among Christian writers.[106] It paved the way for a more extensive allegorical approach, developed by Clement of Alexandria (died 215) and applied in a systematically developed manner by Origen.

For a while, the literal belief in the coming millennium remained very strong within the Christian community, but it was one in which they, not the Jews, were to be vindicated and would rule with Christ on earth. They also assumed that the Old Testament saints would join them there. Over time though, as we have seen, a whole range of factors combined with the growth of allegorical interpretation to produce a non-literal understanding of Christian prophetic hope and a revising of interpretations of the Old Testament promises to the people of Israel. Since these were no longer considered to apply to a literal Israel, they were also thought not to apply to a literal Jerusalem, or indeed to any other geo-political feature found in the prophecies. Allegory and the search for "deeper meaning" had replaced the concrete expectations once applied to these texts.

By the end of the Roman Empire in the West, these two great streams—supersessionism and a non-historically predictive understanding of prophecy—had joined to form a powerful current with long-reaching influence on Christian thinking. With regard to allegory, this approach was not universally accepted in the fifth century. It has been argued that, at Antioch, something of an opposition developed to the Alexandrian method of allegorical explanation. Aspects of this can be traced in the writings of Theodore of Mopsuestia (died 428) and John Chrysostom (died 407) and even, some have suggested, in aspects of some later Augustinian thought. But this was insufficient to fundamentally challenge the growing influence of allegory and non-literal method across the wider church community, and Augustine certainly seems to have always adopted a more "spiritual approach" when assessing end-times prophecy.[107] By the end of the Roman Empire in the West, the end-times mood as represented in official statements had changed significantly. Literal and predictive interpretation of prophecy and attendant premillennialism—once the dominant orthodoxy in the church—increasingly became associated with fringe movements, even with heresy.[108]

However, one should not overstate this. Almost a decade after the sack of Rome in 410, Augustine was engaged in debate with the Dalmatian bishop, Hesychius, in 418–19, who openly promulgated apocalyptic end-times views. He was not alone in maintaining these views in turbulent times and using them to interpret contemporary events. Despite the views of Tyrconius, Andreas, Augustine, and the rest, it is clear that some bishops continued to preach the impending end times. In this, they encouraged the apocalyptic enthusiasm of their congregations and contributed to the view that the collapse of the Roman Empire in the West was an apocalyptic event. At the same time, while the time of the end might be unknown, Augustine had also "opened up the similarly radical existential mode in which action was necessary because Judgement could come at any time." This would drive a restless political energy, from Charlemagne (died 814) onwards.[109]

As with so much in the history of the end times, what was happening at one level of the church was not necessarily indicative of what was happening elsewhere. Even as the new amillennialist view became official policy, it was not accepted by all Christians. Any time of turbulence would stir this complex state of affairs and encourage a new intensity of belief in the impending fulfilment of prophecy. This was especially so for ordinary believers, but might be adopted by some leaders too. Older patterns of thinking were liable to revive at such times of stress.

6

Storm from the North

The Vikings as Fulfilment of End-Times Prophecy?

A SHIFT IN THE way prophecy was interpreted defused what otherwise might have been an intense time of apocalyptic speculation in the couple of centuries following the collapse of the Western Roman Empire in the fifth century. In many ways, the collapse of Rome could have become a hot spot of end-times speculation and anxiety. This was because earlier calculations had targeted this time as being one of eschatological significance.

Calculating the second coming as occurring six thousand years after the creation of the world (AM or *Anno Mundi*, "In the year of the world") depended on the assumed date of that creation, but a number of suggestions resonated with the end of the Roman Empire. Clement of Alexandria (died 215) suggested that Jesus had been born 5,600 years after creation and calculated that the end-times would occur around the year 400. Hippolytus of Rome (died 236) considered that the birth of Jesus had taken place 5,500 years after the creation. This indicated that the end of the current world order would occur in the year 500. Then, in around the year 303, Eusebius (died 339) had calculated that the start of Jesus' ministry (in contrast to calculations connected to his birth) had taken place 5,228 years after creation. It was traditionally thought that Jesus began his ministry when he was thirty years of age. Eusebius thought that there would be another five hundred years of church history until the end, which by his calculation would occur in about the year 800 (more on this particular date in due course).[110] With the exception of Eusebius, these speculative calculations were within a similar timescale due to their common adherence to the idea of *sexta-septamillennialism* or "sabbatical millenarianism"[111] and they shared similar calculations (usually based on Old Testament genealogies) concerning the date when it was thought that God had created the world.

Consequently, the period following the collapse of Rome *should* have been one in which there was intense focus on these earlier calculations. However, the changes that we explored in the last chapter meant that the expected widespread millenarian activity did not occur. While Augustine had once subscribed to the outlook of sabbatical millenarianism, he abandoned it for a symbolic interpretation of the critical one thousand years found in Revelation. The influence of this approach can be seen in the lack of documentary evidence regarding millenarian anxiety or agitation occurring around the year 500. This stands in stark contrast with later anxieties around the year 1000; and some modern anxieties and speculation associated with the year 2000.

Continued end-times anxieties

Despite these changes in church dogma, which dampened down end-times speculation, some anxieties in the years after 500 still affected those lower down the social and ecclesiastical scale. This was particularly so in the context of upheavals caused by barbarian invasions and by outbreaks of infectious disease. Gregory of Tours (died 594), in his *History of the Franks*, describes the activities of the so-called "False Christ of Bourges." In 591, following a terrible outbreak of disease in the old Roman province of Gaul, this peasant claimed to be the returned Christ. His claim was greeted by enthusiastic crowds. We may assume that they were desperate for the second coming to alleviate their current sufferings. Not everyone was so positive in their reaction to the news, as Gregory also refers to "those who despair at the coming end of the world."[112] The peasant preacher was eventually assassinated by killers in the pay of the bishop of Clermont. The woman travelling with him—who presented herself as Mary—was tortured into admitting her guilt of misleading people. Despite this, it took some time for the popular enthusiasm to die down. Gregory resorted to a version of the old *Anno Mundi* calculations when he stated that since the False Christ of Bourges arose in AM 5790, then he clearly was a false Christ.[113]

Other examples of anxieties over the possible approach of the end-times also occurred in the period following the collapse of the Western Roman Empire. This period saw barbarian invasions that caused the Western

Roman provinces to fall out of imperial control entirely; North Africa was contested between Roman authorities facing Berber tribes from the interior and Germanic invaders (the Vandals), who crossed the Mediterranean and temporarily seized control of most of the province; then huge swathes of once-imperial land in the Middle East and North Africa were permanently lost to Islamic rule between 632 and 750. Given the fact that many Christians had come to see Roman rule as a permanent fixture, these losses were deeply shocking. This was especially so when it became clear that Islam was a completely different religion and that it was not going to fade away. The heartland of Christianity in the Middle East had been lost. These political and cultural catastrophes were reflected in apocalyptic writings. One, later called the *Apocalypse of Pseudo-Methodius*, was written in the seventh century (c. 691), probably in Syria, but it purported to date from the fourth century. In it the armies of the "Ishmaelites" (the Muslims) conquer the land as a punishment for sin. Then a future emperor arises, defeats them, and establishes a Christian empire of peace and prosperity. But the armies of Gog and Magog devastate it until defeated by the heavenly host. However, the emperor dies and his empire falls under the control of Antichrist. Then Christ returns and destroys Antichrist and the last judgement follows.[114] As a response to the Islamic conquest of Syria, this text combined aspects of prophecies found in Revelation with the new concept of the "Last Emperor" that we will meet again in the next chapter.

A similar Syriac prophetic work that promised the impending destruction of Islam, but this time at the hands of the Byzantine emperor, is that known as the *Edessene Apocalypse*, written in about the year 700. Another Syriac document, with a comparable message, was *The Gospel of the Twelve Apostles*. It is likely that all three Syriac apocalypses were written as a response to the building of the Dome of the Rock Mosque on the Temple Mount in Jerusalem in 692, by the Umayyad Caliph, Abd al-Malik. Constructed in the middle of a war between the Islamic forces and the Christian Byzantines and their Syrian Christian allies, the mosque exemplified Islamic control of a city revered within Christianity and Judaism. That such a city—with its end-times importance—was now in the hands of a non-Christian conqueror seems to have prompted these three Syriac reworkings of Christian apocalyptic hopes.[115] In the *Edessene Apocalypse*, the Byzantine emperor was cast in the role of God's avenger on the Ishmaelites. According to it, once the Christian community had been sufficiently chastised for its sins, then the apocalyptic vision would be fulfilled, and

Christian Roman rule restored. This replaced an earlier outlook, associated with Monophysite Christians (at odds with Byzantine orthodoxy regarding the nature of Christ) that had seen the Arab conquests as a punishment on the Byzantine Christian community for its christological position.[116] The approach to the apocalypse was clearly malleable.

Other Christian responses to Islam, that developed between the seventh and the eleventh century, interpreted the new religion and its prophet as being the fulfilment of prophecies in Revelation regarding the beast and the composite figure of Antichrist, found in Revelation and in the New Testament letters.[117]

The official church view, though, remained the same: the prophecies should not be used to identify specific geo-political events. And it was not possible to predict the date of the second coming of Christ. This was the position that had been bequeathed by Augustine in the early fifth century.

Despite this, identifications of certain contemporary events as portents of the imminent second coming began to increase again as a response to raids, invasions, and turbulence, occasioned by a new phase of barbarian attacks that hammered Western Europe from the eighth century onwards. The Vikings were coming and, with them, came a new and urgent interest in end-times prophecies concerning enemies descending from "the north."

The end times, the Viking Wars and enemies from the north

Writers in Anglo-Saxon England in the late eighth, and then in the tenth and early eleventh centuries, attempted to make sense of Viking attacks by interpreting them as fulfilments of biblical prophecy. On the continent, others too reached similar conclusions. In the 950s, as we shall see, continental writers viewed the invasions of Magyar raiders as heralding the revealing of Antichrist and the events leading to the end of the world. The end times were back on the agenda.

In 847, a woman named Thiota came to Mainz and announced that the world would end in 848. She was originally from Alemannia, which was then part of East Francia. The unrest associated with her is recorded in the chronicle known as the *Annals of Fulda*, which refers to her "presumption." In a time of increasing turbulence, she attracted supporters, both among the clergy and lay people. Those clerics who opposed her had recourse to the old timeframes, which asserted that Jesus had been born five thousand years after creation and that the apocalypse would not occur before the year 1000. So, Thiota had proclaimed the end about 150 years too early. Gregory of Tours (who had used a similar approach, but with different mathematics, to oppose the False Christ of Bourges) would have approved. Augustine of Hippo would have been appalled. According to Thiota's critics, as exemplified by one cleric in Paris, the release of Antichrist would not occur until the year 1000. Only after that would the second coming and last judgement happen. Thiota was summoned to a synod in Mainz where she confessed that she had made up her prophecies, in the hope of financial reward from those to whom she preached. She was punished by public flogging.

However, Thiota's turbulence was as nothing compared to the shock that accompanied the beginning of Viking attacks in the late eighth century. In 793, the Anglo-Saxon monastery at Lindisfarne was sacked by a Viking raid. The event sent shockwaves across Western Christendom. Lindisfarne was a spiritual, cultural, and intellectual powerhouse. Not for nothing is it still known as Holy Island. Far away, in Aachen (in what is now Germany), at the court of the Frankish ruler Charlemagne, the Northumbrian churchman, scholar, and educationalist, Alcuin, penned the only contemporary account of the attack. The equally famous account in the *Anglo-Saxon Chronicle* was not penned until almost a century later, in the 880s. Alcuin wrote: "Behold, the church of St Cuthbert spattered with the blood of the priests of God, despoiled of all its ornaments; a place more venerable than all in Britain is given as a prey to pagan peoples."[118]

Many contemporary Christians saw the atrocity as the fulfilment of an Old Testament prophecy found in Jeremiah 1:14: "Then the LORD said to me: Out of the north disaster shall break out on all the inhabitants of the land." Clearly, the Scandinavian (northern) origins of the raiders had prompted this association. This geographical location almost certainly inspired Alcuin's reminder—in the same letter quoted earlier—of a bloody rain that had fallen from a clear sky on the *northern* side of the minster church in the Northumbrian town of York. To Alcuin, steeped in the church tradition of finding scriptural precedents for major events, this suggested that "from the north there will come upon our nation retribution of blood."[119] Alcuin then went on to attempt to explain why such a disaster had occurred to such a holy site. He identified sins that were as varied as hair fashions imitating those fashionable among the northern pagans, luxurious clothing, and the impoverishment of the common people as a result of the wealth that was enjoyed by their leaders.[120]

The first two might not seem the most obvious reasons for the unleashing of such terrible punishments, but Alcuin certainly thought they may have led to it. In this, he reflected an approach (seen before and since) of interpreting misfortune as a direct consequence of judgement visited on the one identified as the sinner. However, in his comments there was a hint of an end-times interpretation forming. Within Old Testament prophecy, the north was stated as being the source of calamities that would occur in the period before the day of the Lord (for example Joel 2:20). The words of Jeremiah clearly identified a northern source of the judgement about to come on the people of Israel in his day. But these northern origins also resonated with later students of prophecy, who saw great significance in disaster coming from that quarter. Indeed, Jeremiah's prophecy concerning all the tribes of the northern kingdoms coming against Jerusalem could be interpreted as having far-reaching apocalyptic meaning. Consequently, it is not surprising to discover that: "To these Christians it seemed like an End Time event. It sent shock waves across Britain and Western Europe. As established Christian centres suffered escalating destruction, the faith itself seemed under threat, and Vikings were identified as manifestations of Antichrist and their actions were read as apocalyptic signposts."[121]

The pagan nature of the attackers is reflected in the way that English sources refer to them, in Old English, as the *"heathen here"* (heathen army).[122] It did not take a lot of imagination to view such enemies as the agents of Antichrist and the years of the Viking Wars as heralding the last days. In addition, the sense of facing an enemy who did not follow the established conventions of warfare (violent though these were) further increased the stress and anxiety of those on the receiving end of Viking attacks.[123] The "alien other" had descended on the land, in ways reminiscent of the destructions mentioned in Revelation and in the Old Testament prophecies. Land charters of this period often note that the land was granted for "as long as the Christian faith should last in Britain," which suggests that some thought its continuation was in doubt. At the same time, many bishoprics vanished, and church land holding was also greatly reduced by the destruction.[124] It really did seem like the world was coming to an end.

The return of the Vikings

By the year 900, the most intense period of early Norse raiding and settlement was drawing to a close. Across Western Europe, those kingdoms that had survived the first onslaught adopted a range of polices in order to survive. Ranging from innovations in defense, to accommodations with Norse settlers they could not evict, a "new normal" began to emerge. However, in the later tenth century a fresh wave of raiders exploded out of Scandinavia. This time the fleets of ship were showing the results of kingdom-building in the north. The fleets were larger and better organized. They were manned by warriors drawn from across wider areas of Scandinavia than before. Emerging royal houses in Denmark (and to some extent in Norway) were driving this new phase of Viking expansion. While Christian missions to the north had increased since the first Viking waves, many of the warriors involved in the second phase were still pagan. Royal dynasties were moving towards conversion but generally this had either not yet occurred or had not fully taken hold. As result, paganism was still a characteristic of these invaders. In addition to this, the size and organization of the new armies meant that the destruction they caused was, at times, comparable to the earlier phase. In addition to the lives they destroyed, they drained huge levels of resources out of the economies of victim countries. Archaeologists have found vast numbers of Anglo-Saxon silver coins in Scandinavia that were paid to persuade raiders to go away. Damage escalated on both sides of the English Channel and around the Irish Sea. The Vikings had returned with a vengeance.

When the Viking raiders returned in the late tenth century more explicit references were made to them as harbingers of the second coming. Their unexpected return was a shock and prompted a lot of heart-searching by Anglo-Saxon Christians. One of these was Wulfstan (sometimes called Wulfstan II), who was the archbishop of York until his death in 1023. He is famous for a dramatic sermon that he preached in 1014. It may originally have been written in 1009 and there is evidence that it was reissued and updated several times as disaster unfolded.[125] Its title, "The Sermon of the Wolf to the English," was a play on his name, which meant: "wolf-stone." Wulfstan recorded a great catalogue of sins that stood against the English nation. These were religious, political, social, and sexual and all, in his opinion, stood in the scales against the people of Anglo-Saxon England. It seemed that, as well as bringing death and destruction, the Vikings were upturning the whole social order. Along with many contemporaries, Wulfstan oscillated between seeing the Vikings as the punishment sent by God as judgement on a sinful nation (which might be averted by repentance) and an inevitable accompaniment to the end of the world and the second coming of Christ.[126] However, the apocalyptic theme increasingly influenced his view of events. In this he reflects an interest in Antichrist that also appears in the West Frankish work, *Letter on the Place and Time of Antichrist* by Adso of Montier-en-Der (died 992). But, whereas Adso focused on the life of Antichrist, Wulfstan was more interested in the moral decay that indicated the nearness of the end times. He was not alone, as an anonymous Old English translation of Adso's work reveals a similar concern.[127] Other prominent English people at the time had similar interests and anxieties. One, named Ælfric, in his *First Series of Catholic Homilies* (c. 990), concluded that "people need good teaching most urgently in this time, which is the ending of the world."[128]

In 1005 the Anglo-Saxon king Æthelred II (often known as Æthelred the Unready) issued a land charter for the monastery at Eynsham in Oxfordshire. In a rare insight into perspectives on contemporary events, its introduction refers to the *tempora periculosa* ("dangerous times"). This phrase is a Latin parallel to the "distressing times," referred to in 2 Timothy 3:1 as characteristic of the last days.[129] A similar phrase appears in a letter written to Bishop Wulfsige of Sherborne, Dorset, by the archbishop of Canterbury. In case anyone had missed this significance, the Eynsham charter continues and explains that the contemporaries of the charter were those "upon whom the ends of the world are come." It conveyed, in Latin, the Greek words of 1 Corinthians 10:11. It was not a unique use of this verse in the charters.[130] Wulfsige of Sherborne used the same phrase when issuing a charter in 998, and the phrase also appears in other church documents. Other writers also pondered on the moral failings that would accompany the close of the age. Even more explicit is the preamble to the charter for Bradford on Avon, Wiltshire, of 1001. Quoting Luke 21:31, it warns "when you shall see these things come to pass, know that the kingdom of God is at hand."[131] A charter of 1002 quotes Matthew 4:17, where Jesus warns people to repent for the kingdom of heaven is near. In 1004 the same verse is found in the charter for Burton, Staffordshire. The end-times were on many people's minds. The worse the upheavals, the closer seemed the end.[132]

Gog and Magog: enemies from the east

Apocalyptic interpretations of the troubled years of the tenth and early eleventh centuries were not restricted to Anglo-Saxon England. On the continent, others too reached similar conclusions about raiders from

Scandinavia and also those from the east who threatened Central Europe-an society. Only a little earlier than Wulstan wrote about Vikings, writers on the continent, in the 950s, had viewed the invasions of Magyar raiders as heralding the imminent revealing of Antichrist and the unfolding of events leading to the end of the world.[133] In a Lotharingian source, the *Letter to the Hungarians*, these particular invaders were explicitly identi-fied as Gog and Magog, the terrible invaders referred to in Revelation as accompanying the devil.

Originally from western Siberia, by the late ninth century the migrat-ing Magyars (Hungarians) had reached the present location of Hungary. Over the next sixty years they raided into Western Europe as far as Bremen, Orléans, and even reached Constantinople to the south. Seeking booty and slaves, they terrified the communities that were the victims of these fero-cious raids. This occurred as the Vikings were similarly devastating north-western European coastal communities and the British Isles. So terrible was the reputation of the Magyars that the English word "ogre" is a corruption of the group identifier *Hungar*.

The identification with Gog and Magog was a reference to Ezekiel 38:2 and Revelation 20:8 in which Gog of the land of Magog (in the former) and Gog and Magog (in the latter) are named as end-times enemies of God and the elect. In Revelation they are referred to as being gathered for battle following the devil's release from his thousand-year-long imprisonment. The identification of the Magyars with them was prompted by three main factors. The first was the approaching end of the millennium (the year 1000). In some calculations, this was the end of the devil's imprisonment that had occurred at Jesus' incarnation. The second reason was the implica-tion in Revelation that they are pulled in from the edges of the world ("the four corners") to take part in the final battle. In the tenth century it was known that the Magyars had originated in lands understood as liminal and "other," as viewed from the perspective of writers in Western Europe. As such, they seemed to fit the bill of alien enemy invaders, who represented "movement from the margin to the center of the earth."[134] The final factor was that Gog Magog had become synonymous with evil forces, particularly those from beyond the borders of "civilization." The exact geographical lo-cation, considered to be the original homeland of these destructive forces, varied among medieval writers and cartographers. Their main role was as a general metaphorical reference to enemies of the Christian church and its communities.[135] In this way, the Gog Magog identification placed them in the general category of barbarian invaders of Europe.[136]

Nevertheless, the original eastern origins of the Magyars almost certainly played a part in the decision to name them as Gog and Magog in the particular case of the *Letter to the Hungarians*, as this gave them an origin beyond the center of Christendom. It was also a geographical direction from which many barbarian invasions had come over the preceding six hundred years. There may also have been an echo, in this identification, of the reference in Revelation 16:12–13 to kings from the east, and three evil spirits in the form of frogs appearing, when the sixth angel pours out a bowl of wrath. This again accompanies a description of the gathering of the enemies of God for the battle at Armageddon. The *Qur'an* also names Gog and Magog as enemies of Allah in connection with the end of days.

However, the Magyars were not the precursors to the rise of Antichrist. In 955 they were defeated at the Battle of Lechfeld, near Augsburg (Germany), by the German king (later emperor) Otto I. We will meet Otto I's grandson (Emperor Otto III) in the next chapter as we explore the harnessing of end-times beliefs in the ideology of imperial power. In 973 the Magyar ruler approached the German Emperor Otto II and, in 974, he and his whole family were baptized as Catholic Christians. The tribe once feared as the embodiment of Gog and Magog had joined the Christian community.

Vikings and the year 1000

What is clear is that the nature of these pagan invaders appears to be more important in the *Letter to the Hungarians* than the impending end of the first millennium. From England, there is less surviving evidence expressing anxiety about this date than about the nature of those causing havoc in Western Christendom. However, it did concern some. Wulfstan in England, for example, directly applied the words of Revelation to the year 1000 as representing the releasing of the devil after one thousand years. For Wulfstan, this referred to the end of the millennium following the birth of Christ. Some others too were counting down to the year 1000, as seen in surviving documents.

Sensitivities about the date may explain the convoluted way that three English charters describe it. One used the strange formula: "Since the incarnation of Christ 990 years, nine and thrice two."[137] The writer could have just written MV but seemed reluctant to refer to M (thousand). In contrast, others such as Byrhtferth of Ramsey (died 1020) and Abbo of Fleury (died 1004) maintained the scriptural line that forbade attempts to date the second coming.

However, as so often with regard to the end times, the scriptural prohibition on calculating the prophesied event did not stop people from speculating. Parallel to the events that we have described in this chapter, other processes of calculation and speculation continued to be at work in other parts of Christendom. It is to this that we will now turn, in order to explore the ways in which the end-times were harnessed as part of a post-Roman imperial project; first in the East and then in the West. It was a project that would be influential for centuries and would reverberate throughout the Middle Ages.

7

Harnessing End-Times Prophecy
for Imperial Causes

WE HAVE SEEN HOW some leading Roman Christians had advanced schemes for calculating the future date of the second coming, and the turbulence that would precede it, that were based on the seven days of creation in Genesis. According to this model, the world would last six thousand years from the creation. This would then be followed by the thousand-year reign of Christ on earth.

This calculation had lost ground in the face of the more allegorical and non-literal view of prophecy that had become the dominant outlook in church leadership by the late fifth century. However, it had never entirely gone away. Revisions to it occurred and these proved to be particularly potent in the surviving Eastern Roman Empire. From there the concept eventually flowed back into the church and politics of the successor states that had emerged from the wreckage of the western part of the Roman Empire. But first, it is necessary to explain a subtle but significant tweak that had occurred with regard to these *Anno Mundi* (Year of the World) calculations.

A new time frame: *Anno Mundi* II

In the fifth century new calculations—known as *Anno Mundi* II (AMII), and based on a version of the system proposed by Eusebius and, before him, Hippolytus of Rome—adjusted the supposed age of the world by about three hundred years. According to this adjustment, Jesus' incarnation had occurred 5,199 years after creation. Consequently, the crucial year AM 6000 would be in 801.[138] It would be *then* that the seventh millennium would begin. While this identified a potential future date of cosmic significance, it took the heat off the fall of Rome within apocalyptic speculations. For many, the year 500 was no longer of end-times importance. And the whole system of calculation was challenged by the non-literal view of prophecy expounded by Augustine in the fifth century.

There is, though, other evidence which suggests that the *Anno Mundi* method of calculating the end-times did not fall entirely out of favor (in this case, the revised *Anno Mundi* II version). In the year corresponding to *Anno Mundi* II 5999 (on Christmas Day 800) Pope Leo III crowned Charlemagne of the Franks emperor in Rome. This seems more than a coincidence. Instead, it seems far more likely to have been chosen as it was an auspicious year for an imperial ruler to begin a new political era. The point was not explicitly made, but the date is certainly thought provoking. Perhaps the significance of the date AMII 6000 had not been entirely forgotten. We will return to that. But first it is necessary to examine how not everyone was persuaded by the new *Anno Mundi* II approach to explaining providential history.

The growth of Byzantine imperial millenarianism

The shift in chronologies that *Anno Mundi* II implied was not reflected in the Greek church in the surviving Eastern Roman Empire (also termed the Byzantine Empire). There, church leaders continued to believe in the significance of the old reckoning of AM 6000 and prepared for the possible turbulence of its approach in the year 500. This occurred in a section of the old Roman Empire where a more theocratic approach to the—now Christian—political system was developing and which buttressed the ideology of Byzantine imperialism, despite the collapse of Roman authority in the West after the deposition of the last Western emperor (Romulus Augustulus) in 476. This led to the emergence of what was, in effect, a Christian imperial millenarianism. In this construct, the approaching millennium did not threaten the imperial system by asserting its character as the future base of Antichrist. In contrast, it was presented as representing Christ's reign on earth, albeit mediated through his supreme agent: the Eastern Roman emperor.

This was, in effect, "postmillennialism," but without the literal interpretations of Revelation to inform understanding of exactly what would be happening within that time period. It held that Christ would return *after* a thousand-year reign had occurred, during which his rule was increasingly seen on earth. The Byzantine Empire was viewed as the embodiment of that reign on earth. In many ways, this chimed with the more positive view of Roman rule that had been developing since the time of Origen in the mid third century. This was in stark contrast to the highly negative view of Roman rule that was found in the book of Revelation and the new view accompanied re-evaluation of the way that book should be read by Christians.[139] It is surely no coincidence that Revelation found the severest opponents to its acceptance as Scripture in the eastern half of the Roman Empire.[140] The first Greek commentaries on Revelation that appeared in the sixth century minimized the hostility towards the empire that is found in its apocalyptic verses.[141] Even when the timeframes and details of Old and New Testament prophecy were engaged with, they were given a new perspective that was favorable to the Eastern Roman state, which had survived the cataclysms that had befallen the western half of the empire.

This interpretative approach built on earlier work by Eusebius (died 339), Cyril of Jerusalem (died 386), John Chrysostom (died 407), Jerome (died 420), and Theodoret of Cyrrhus (died 457), who understood Rome as representing the fourth kingdom of iron (and clay) in Daniel 2 and the fourth beast of Daniel 7. But this outlook saw this fourth kingdom through a positive lens and presented Rome as the final kingdom that would endure almost until Christ's coming. Chrysostom and Jerome had even identified Rome as the force restraining the appearance of Antichrist that is found in 2 Thessalonians 2:6–7. As a force for good, within God's providential plan, it would only fall to Antichrist in the last days and this would then be rapidly followed by the final victory of Christ and the establishment of his eternal heavenly kingdom.[142] This glossed over the negative aspects of the fourth kingdom/beast as represented in Daniel and did this by assuming that these negative aspects described its very end, when it would fall to Antichrist, rather than being indicative of its fundamental nature. This now reads as a less-than-convincing view of this kingdom as found in Daniel and of the condemnatory way that Revelation describes the kingdom that will precede the return of Jesus. However, while this exalted view of the fourth kingdom/beast was a far cry from the impression of it found in the verses of Daniel and Revelation, it was grist to the mill for later Byzantine writers in the early Middle Ages.[143]

It is an intriguing insight into the way that the millennium could be reinterpreted. We will find aspects of postmillennialism influencing the outlook of Christians right through to the end of the nineteenth century. At that point it gave way to premillennialism again and this has become the current dominant outlook among students of the end-times into the twenty-first century. But it was not ever thus.

As a consequence of this imperial postmillennialism, the years immediately after 500 in the Eastern Roman Empire saw the emergence of some extraordinary assertions that the surviving Greek-speaking empire even represented the kingdom that will never be destroyed of Daniel 2:44. This claim, by Kosmas Indikopleustes of Alexandria (died 550), fused the idea of the Eastern Roman Empire with that of the eternal kingdom of Christ. For Kosmas, barbarian attacks might occur as chastisements for sin, but the permanence of this imperial theocracy was not in question.[144] He was not alone in such imperial eschatological confidence. This meant that the eternal kingdom, understood as being in association with the imperial regime, was "both imminent and immanent."[145] The Eastern Roman Empire could be described as a "New Israel" and Constantinople as a "New Jerusalem."[146] This was a heady mix of eschatology and imperial politics. It is a vivid insight into the way that prophecy can be quarried for political purposes and has echoes in the way that America was later seen, by both its Puritan founders and the evangelical/neocon alliance that became so influential in the decade after 9/11 in the USA.[147] There is much that repeats itself in the history of the end times. With regard to the earlier example, it would influence the way that the Byzantines regarded themselves for the next thousand years. As we shall later see, it would be Islam that was increasingly cast in the role of Antichrist, in opposition to the sanctified imperial rule from Constantinople/Byzantium (the "New Jerusalem").

This outlook influenced the development of a belief in the so-called future "Last (Roman) Emperor," which found its most lasting form in the prophetic work known as the *Tiburtine Sibyl*. This work was probably originally written in the late fourth century but redacted in the sixth century (that significant century again), sometime between the years 502 and 506. It was originally written in Greek, but its final form was in Latin. In this work it was envisaged that, in future times, a final Roman emperor would emerge. He would subdue the enemies of Christianity, before travelling to Jerusalem to lay down his imperial crown and rule, and yield sovereignty to God. This would immediately precede the second coming of Christ.[148] In the later Middle Ages, the *Tiburtine Sibyl* was as influential in molding apocalyptic outlooks as the book of Revelation itself. There is evidence to suggest that, for a time, it was even *more* influential in this respect than Revelation. We will come across it again.

As a result of this, the year 500 saw imperial millennialism in the Eastern (Byzantine) Empire overcome the once-popular—and anti-imperial outlook—that had underpinned "sabbatical millenarianism." In the West, though, things were more complex. There, despite some attempts to harness the same momentum in the service of the Germanic kingdoms (among the later Franks in particular) that had replaced Roman rule, what one might called "popular millennialism" remained more potent. This was undoubtedly due to the fact that almost four centuries separated the fall of the Western empire from the rise of the Frankish empire of Charlemagne. This was ample time for other influences to affect outlook. Consequently, nothing quite as systematic as the imperial Byzantine theocracy managed to eclipse the turbulent views of the end-times and the conflicts that would accompany them. This helps explain the recourse to this outlook that accompanied the Viking invasions, as we have seen in the previous chapter.

Limiting the impact of *Anno Mundi* calculations in Western Europe

Another factor further dampened down the calculations, based on the date of creation, in the societies that had once been part of the Western Roman Empire. This was the advent of the AD/BC method of calculating dates, which was based on the hinge-event of the birth of Jesus. Within the emerging kingdoms of Anglo-Saxon England this was promoted (though not devised) by Bede (died 735), who was writing in the northern Kingdom of Northumbria. His book, entitled *The Reckoning of Time*, concluded with a long quote from Augustine of Hippo on how eschatology should properly be considered. He clearly both agreed with Augustine on this and also realized that the new dating system undermined many older and rival eschatological timeframes. By the time that the revised AMII 6000—the year AD 801—approached in the West, Bede's new chronology and the use of it in Easter Tables (used to decide the date of Easter) was widely adopted. As a result, by AD 801, with very few exceptions, all the main historical chronicles and histories were dating events by the *Anno Domini* system.[149] Even though *Anno Mundi* II 6000 had not been entirely defused, the explosive force of its charge had been much reduced.

Having replaced earlier Christian dating systems that were based on the assumed creation of the world, dates that had once resonated with significance were no longer so redolent with meaning. This rather undermined some of the attraction of sabbatical millenarianism as a tool in end-times studies and calculations. So profound was the change that by the time that Charlemagne was crowned emperor in the West in the year 800, there is no record of anyone actually commenting on the significance of a date that had once loomed large in some earlier versions of the sabbatical millenarian approach. As we have seen, the AM II dating system *may* have influenced the date of the event, but it was certainly not emphasized. This particular method of calculating the start of the seventh millennium—and with it, the thousand-year reign of Christ on earth—seems to have partially fallen into abeyance as far as many Western writers were concerned.[150] However, the legend of the Last Emperor would return. And perhaps things were not quite so clear cut with regard to the lack of perceived significance of the year 801.

Western ambiguity

On Christmas Day, in the year 800, Charlemagne, the ruler of the Franks was crowned as Roman Emperor in the West. A little confusingly, the *Frankish Royal Annals* date the event as occurring on the first day of 801. However, most written sources, that appeared soon afterwards, pull it back to the end of 800. It seems likely that the Frankish compiler of these annals chose 801 due to a deliberate attempt to make it coincide exactly with AMII 6000. This was caused by a peculiarly Frankish error in combining the AD system (as devised by Dionysius Exiguus) and the AMII date for the incarnation (as devised by Eusebius), which ignored a two-year gap in the two dating systems.[151]

Charlemagne and his successors came to rule a complex of territories in Central Europe known as "the Empire" or "the Roman Empire." This revived the Roman title of emperor in Western Europe; although it gained a more stable and long-lasting foundation on the crowning of Otto I as emperor in 962. It is often referred to as the "Holy Roman Empire." However, it was not until 1157 that the term "Holy" was first used to describe it and it was only after 1254 that the formal title "Holy Roman Empire/Emperor" came into use. To avoid confusion with the imperial power in the East (ruled from Constantinople/Byzantium) we will henceforth refer to the Eastern Roman

Empire as the "Byzantine Empire/Emperor." This Eastern empire, shrinking in size, survived until its final defeat by Islamic forces in 1453. The Western (revived) empire survived until 1806, when the last Holy Roman Emperor abdicated, following military defeat by Napoleon.

The historic event of Charlemagne's coronation and the Western revival of the imperial title should have been a moment of unambiguous eschatological excitement. After all, this was just when AMII 6000 fell. In fact, some variations in ecclesiastical mathematics created a timespan for that momentous date ranging from 799 to 806.[152] Nevertheless, the juxtaposition of coronation and looked-for end-times date was extraordinary. However, as we have seen, something of the explosive nature of this date had been reduced by shifts in theology with regard to interpreting prophecy. Only one written source from the time (the *Annals of Augia*) linked the year AD 800 with AMII 6000; and having done so, it makes no mention of the coronation.[153]

It seems that, in the absence of an official theology of a literal millennial rule of Christ on earth (following its abandonment as doctrine in the early fifth century), "a number of other messianic figures were created to help keep alive Christendom's optimistic hopes for the future."[154] This helps explain the eventual adoption of the Last Emperor concept in the Catholic West (despite its origins in the Eastern Orthodox Church); and the Last Emperor's role as a proxy for the figure of Christ found in the earlier literal millennial beliefs. Despite this, the concept—for all its potency and popularity—never made it to the status of an official papal pronouncement.

This has left modern historians divided as to just how eschatologically significant this historic coronation was regarded by contemporaries of the event.[155] Given all the other issues leading to this momentous occasion, the surviving sources can be argued to show people as much motivated by other factors, as by the idea of the impending apocalypse in this period of time.[156] In addition, there is evidence to support the idea that when the apocalypse was referred to in ninth- and tenth-century sources, it did not necessarily imply a belief in its literal occurrence. Instead, it has been argued, it could be more revealing of the way contemporaries turned to traditional language and metaphors in order to frame their arguments in ways most likely to resonate with audiences.[157] However, this should not cause us to assume that all uses of eschatological language and terms at the time were simply for effect.[158] And we are left with a coincidence of dates that brought together eschatological calculations (however reduced in their impact) and an event that stands out as "among the most memorable dates in Western history."[159]

Furthermore, we should not assume that absence of evidence constitutes evidence of absence. While explicit connections between the coronation of Charlemagne and this momentous eschatological date may be lacking, there is plenty of other evidence that shows that the end of the sixth millennium (as it was then understood) was being tracked. So, why the documentary silence with regard to the significance of the date of Charlemagne's coronation in particular and the start of the long-awaited seventh millennium in general? After all, this was the beginning not just of a new millennium but *"the* millennium." The answer seems to be the same as that which had once caused church leaders to downplay the importance of the book of Revelation and which had driven much of the non-literal interpretation of scriptural prophecy in the past: "not a lack of interest but an acute consciousness of the suppressed dating system and its apocalyptic implications."[160]

This was almost certainly driven by a fear of the grassroots turbulence that might be encouraged by awareness of such a date. In the past, as in the future, an intense focus on the end-times tended to be accompanied by radical upheavals and the activities of "false prophets." The end-times could be religious, social, and political "dynamite" in the hands of the laity. Such a potent theological explosive had to be handled with great care and only by authorized "explosives" experts. So, it seems that this apparent silence was actually a deafening vindication of the powerful potential of apocalyptic beliefs.

Western imperial millennialism

In the West, as in the East, Christian elites recognized both the problems and the potential inherent in the manipulation of end-times beliefs. In the years after Charlemagne, we see this in royal politics in Western Europe, just as we have earlier seen it in the imperial millennialism in the Byzantine Empire.

The coronation of Charlemagne added two essential ingredients to European millennialism that would have long-lasting effects. The first was a relocation of much of the apocalyptic expectations concerning the Roman Empire, from the East (where it had been much emphasized by the Byzantines) to the West. From the ninth century to the twenty-first century this has influenced end-times speculation. The modern proponents of the view that the European Union is, in some way, an embodiment of a revived "Roman Empire" are the latest in a long line of those who can trace the origins of their belief to that event on Christmas Day in the year 800. It has been a long and winding road since then and we shall chart the journey and its milestones over later chapters. But it is a legacy of that coronation and a revival of the Roman Empire with its end-times connotations.

The most important legacy of that event was on what, one might call, the "mind map" of later students of the apocalypse. Until Charlemagne, that "map" was firmly centered on the Mediterranean basin, with twin poles located at Jerusalem and Rome. The interaction between these two dominated the way that Christians interpreted prophecy from the first to the ninth century. The emergence of Constantinople/Byzantium as being of millennial significance only constituted an adjustment of that geo-political model of how God would bring his providential plan to completion. After all, Constantinople/Byzantium was a stand-in for Rome and the overall focus on the Mediterranean world was not fundamentally altered by it. All of that changed with the coronation of Charlemagne. This act shifted the end-times center of gravity. Now its reach had moved north and west of the Alps. Central and Western Europe now shared with Jerusalem the apocalyptic focus. "He 'transferred' the empire, with all its apocalyptic and millennial freight, to the West, including the notion of the Last Emperor and the idea that the Carolingians were the new 'obstacle' to the Antichrist."[161]

What the *Edessene Apocalypse* and *The Gospel of the Twelve Apostles* had envisaged as a role for the Byzantine emperor in the decades around the year 700 had, in the space of a century, been appropriated by the newly revived Roman Empire of the Frankish and German lands. The atlas of the end-times would not be the same again. For that reason alone, the coronation that took place in the year 800 was highly significant.

Later imperial European rulers were ready to take on this sanctified mantle of being the Last Emperor, or related to his anticipated deeds. Otto III (died 1002) applied this outlook to defining his role as emperor. It was a thoroughly Byzantine one in which the dominant power in the state was embodied in the person of the sacred emperor, who would take precedence over the pope. A millennial imperialism of the Byzantine model was clearly on his mind. This idea would be further developed by Emperor Frederick I *Barbarossa* (died 1190) and Emperor Frederick II (died 1250). Like Otto III, they also pursued a policy of competition for power with the papacy that was, in part at least, rooted in their apocalyptic concept of the significance of their imperial office. We shall return to them in chapter 8.

Otto III expressed his confidence in his enhanced imperial role in projects that ranged from the conversion/subjugation of pagans in eastern European lands, to the commissioning of the south-German illuminated manuscript of Revelation, known as the *Bamberg Apocalypse* (completed sometime between the years 1000 and 1020, in the scriptorium at Reichenau, on Lake Constance). It is possible that it was commissioned by Emperor Henry II (died 1024), but this simply emphasizes the continuation of interest that had started under Otto III. Otto III further underlined his imperial millennialism when he visited Charlemagne's tomb, on the feast of Pentecost, in the year 1000. This was part of a project that harnessed both the significance of the year 801 and the year 1000 (with its millennial potency). That the two dates arose from competing eschatological timeframes did not prevent them from both being utilized. This latter date was both the end of the millennium, since the incarnation, and redolent with meaning in the outlook of many church thinkers who were still committed to the timeframe of sabbatical millenarianism.[162] When it came to the year 1000, the apocalyptic nature of the date could not be defused by debatable mathematics, as had occurred in the AM/AM II calculations. The millennium was the millennium. In fact, of course, it wasn't—because the AD/BC dating system was flawed and Jesus was actually born a few years earlier than it envisaged. However, this complication (which rather upended the simple millenarian calculation) was unknown at the time and so the calculation continued to be (erroneously) deployed.

This was all part of a project that has become known as the *renovatio imperii romani* (renewal of the Roman Empire). The phrase might have been taken directly from an earlier commentary on the second phase of the fourth kingdom, referred to in the prophecies of Daniel chapter 2; and the fourth beast with ten horns, of Daniel chapter 7 (and referenced in Revelation).

Otto III was certainly not alone in these exalted views of the imperial role in the tenth century. In about 950, Adso of Montier-en-Der (whom we met in the last chapter reflecting, in his *Letter on the Place and Time of Antichrist*, on the life of Antichrist) wrote a letter to the Frankish queen, Gerberga, regarding one whom he styled the "last World Emperor." This figure was providentially destined to conquer all non-Christians before the arrival of the Antichrist and the eventual second coming of Christ. What had once been a Byzantine preoccupation was now a preoccupation of the competing rulers north of the Alps.

As the year 1000 approached, the intensity of anticipation and anxiety increased. Church leaders might earlier have defused that association with the year 801, but the year 1000 was impossible to ignore. In France, the social upheavals accompanying the installation of a new ruling family (the Capetians), which replaced that of the Carolingians in 987, accompanied the arrival of the millennium. King Robert II, the Pious (died 1031), ruled a kingdom fragmented among rival warlords. The attendant in-fighting, upheaval, and suffering reminded many that the Carolingians had once been considered to be the force restraining the appearance of Antichrist, found in 2 Thessalonians 2:6–7. Now this restraining force had been removed. This led to a whole range of grassroots end-times movements across the lands of the king of France, as a way of expressing the rising tide of anxiety.

One of these movements was, arguably, the earliest grassroots religious movement of the Middle Ages. This was the so-called "Peace of God" initiative. Unlike many other popular (and populist) millenarian movements, this one met with official approval because it did not threaten the social order; quite the opposite, in fact. There is a strong argument that it arose from strong religious convictions, which saw the establishment of peace as "connected with the millennial anniversary of Christ's life on earth."[163] The Peace of God (*Pax Dei*) was proclaimed at the Synod of Charroux in 989. It aimed to protect non-combatants, specifically peasant farmers and members of the clergy, from elite-led violence. It included a prohibition on attacking churches. Children and women were later added to the groups of people to be protected from soldiers. Merchants and their goods were added in 1033. Huge, and enthusiastic, crowds supported the movement, often accompanied by holy relics and engaged in penitential behavior. In time, nobles swore oaths to maintain it and the practice spread down the social scale to include heads of households meeting and swearing to respect its restrictions and keep the common peace. While its effects were very limited, its importance lay in a postmillennialist enthusiasm to mark the period around the year 1000 by taking action to promote peace, justice, and good government. It was envisaged as an example of the kingdom of God being established on earth. Such postmillennialist beliefs held that the people of God, empowered by God, could affect such transformations of earthly society, rather than being dependent on his return for the transformations to occur (as envisaged in premillennialism). Indeed, it was these transformations, it was believed, that would prepare the way for the coming of Christ. A new age of millennial thinking was dawning that would inform much of the understanding regarding the end-times (and the timetable of events connected to them) throughout the Middle Ages.

In 1027, at the Council of Toulouges, similar sentiments led to the proclamation of the "Truce of God" (*Treuga Dei*). This was an attempt to limit the days of the week and the times of the year when warfare was carried out by the nobility. As with the Peace of God, its long-term effects were very limited, but it too revealed a socially positive outcome to millennial concerns.

When the second coming did not occur in 1000, attention shifted to the year 1033. This was made possible by an alternative belief that the thousand-year period should be dated from Christ's victory on the cross and his resurrection, rather than from the incarnation. This was one of many such shifts in calculations that have occurred over two thousand years, as a response to the failure of previous calculations. Rather than unsettling the sense of certainty driving such speculations, such revisions simply produce a new generation as committed to the new date as a previous generation was to the earlier erroneous calculation. Once again, the scriptural commandment not to calculate the expected date was and is ignored. It was part of a repeat pattern of behavior that is still with us.

It is clear that the period from 1000 to 1033 coincided with events that accelerated apocalyptic concerns. In the year 1009, the Fatimid caliph, Abu Ali Mansur, also known as al-Hakim bi-Amr Allah (The Ruler by the Order of God) destroyed the Church of the Holy Sepulcher in Jerusalem and forced Christians to convert to Islam (in his case, to the Shia Ismaili form). Convents and churches in the region were demolished. This sent shockwaves across Christendom. There is evidence that he later allowed Christians and Jews, who had been forced to convert, to return to their previous beliefs and to rebuild some of their holy sites. But by that time the damage had been done. Only in 1042 was the Byzantine emperor allowed to reconstruct the sacred place of the Church of the Holy Sepulcher, with the permission of al-Hakim's successor.

Across Western Christendom, the view that Islamic leaders were agents of Antichrist increased. Violent urges began to be channeled against those regarded at the time as enemies of the Christian faith. In France, where apocalyptic feelings had been running high for a generation, there was a wave of antisemitic violence, as Jews were targeted. They were the "alien other" on the doorstep. At the same time, in 1022, the first heretics were executed; this also occurred in France. This was the other side of the coin to the spiritually positive ideas associated with postmillennial attempts to reform society. For, when medieval Christians took to transforming the world in a thousand-year-long preparation for the eventual return of Christ, many of those believers would also, at times, take on themselves the role of purifying from society all those that they considered enemies of God and the faith. Puritanical "cleansing" could be as likely an outcome as social transformation and the pursuit of justice in the postmillennialist worldview.

In the millennially important year of 1033, another wave of Peace of God mass assemblies occurred across France. These accompanied renewed pilgrimages to Jerusalem. Many present at these Peace of God assemblies believed that they had made a covenant with God.[164] The stage was being set for the explosion of faith, violence, and end-times hopes that became intertwined in the crusading movement. The violent impulses, that had been partially contained by the Peace of God, were about to be channeled out of Western Christendom and in the direction of Jerusalem. At the same time, it would result in the mass murder of Jews closer to home. The preoccupation of many with building the millennial kingdom on earth was about to take an extremely violent turn.

8

Medieval Apocalypse?

THE TERM "MEDIEVAL," AND its equivalent "Middle Ages," as applied to
Europe and the Mediterranean world, is a fairly flexible one. It is now usually considered to cover a period of time from the emergence of successor
states to the Roman Empire, in the sixth and seventh centuries (now often
termed the "early medieval" period), to the early sixteenth century, when
its culture and society was dramatically fragmented by the Reformation
and the beginning of, what many historians now call, the "Early Modern"
period. In this chapter, we will be looking particularly at events from the
late eleventh to the late fifteenth century; and will end on the cusp of the
great Reformation changes.

The crusades as end-times events

The First Crusade was the beginning of a complex series of religious, military, and political activities that drew Europe and the Middle East together
in violent conflict, but also compromises and cooperation, over the span
of some two centuries. With its supreme focus on seizing back control of
the Christian holy places it tapped into a deep reservoir of spiritual fervor,
which often had millenarian aspects. After all, in the minds of many of
those taking part, they were engaged in warfare for God in a way reminiscent of the conflicts found in the verses of Revelation. And in the holy
places, and against opponents who, since the seventh century, had been
described as agents of the Antichrist. The crusades built on the popular
enthusiasm that had driven the Peace of God movement and that had also
stimulated renewed enthusiasm for pilgrimage to the Holy Land in the
1030s. But this time, the enthusiasm had a sharp military edge for those

who regarded themselves as soldiers of God in conflict with "the infidel" for possession of the holy places.

At their simplest, the crusades encompassed a series of military adventures usually described as the First Crusade (1096–99), Second Crusade (1147–49), Third Crusade (1189–92), Fourth Crusade (1202–4), Fifth Crusade (1217–21), Sixth Crusade (1228–29), Seventh Crusade (1248–54), and the Eighth Crusade (1270). As a result of this extraordinary movement, control of Jerusalem was temporarily wrested from its Islamic rulers and a Christian Kingdom of Jerusalem established, along with a series of other crusader states. The geo-politics of the Middle East appeared to have been profoundly changed.

The astonishing success of the First Crusade—a Western response to a call for assistance from the hard-pressed Byzantine emperor—made many of those involved feel that they were taking part in a divinely sanctioned activity that would accelerate the coming of Christ's kingdom on earth. This resonated with the enthusiasm that had been rising since the turn of the millennium in 1000 and also after 1033. It also struck a chord with the idea of the "Last Emperor"—who would lead Christian armies to Jerusalem— that had first been promulgated around the year 700, revived after 801, and continued to influence Western ideas throughout the Middle Ages. When Pope Urban II launched the crusading movement, at the Council of Clermont in November 1095, he was pushing on an open door as far as religious apocalyptic enthusiasm was concerned. Or, to change the metaphor, he was engaging with, and channeling, a powerful head of steam that had been building up for a generation. It also turned the violent inclinations of a troubled society outward against an external enemy. For many, the road to the "Last Battle" had been thrown open, to the cries of "*Deus le volt*" (God wills it) and the wearing of the cross.

Across many communities in France and Germany there were claims made regarding miraculous signs and portents appearing, which pointed to the apocalyptic nature of the events that were unfolding following the pope's declaration of the crusade. Those that had particular end-times resonance included beliefs that Charlemagne had risen from the dead to lead the crusaders to Jerusalem (a link to the belief in the Last Emperor) and that the conflict was the fulfilment of Jesus' prediction that "nation will rise against nation, and kingdom against kingdom, and there will be famines and earthquakes in various places" as the start of the birth pangs of the end (Matt 24:7). Ekkehard of Aura (died 1126) took part in a supporting crusade in 1101 and, following this, became abbot of Aura in Bavaria in 1108. He recorded events of the First Crusade. In his chronicle *Hierosolymita* (Of Jerusalem) he confidently stated that, "At that time the gospel trumpet sounded the arrival of the just judge and behold! Everywhere the universal church could see the world bringing forth portents and prophetic signs."[165]

The popular enthusiasm for the crusade was infused with this deeply-held belief that events of eternal significance were taking place. This was underscored by claims of a quite extraordinary kind, in terms of their drama and miraculous nature. Some of these claims linked directly to specific prophecies, which supporters of the crusading movement were convinced were now being fulfilled.

Sometime shortly before 1109, Bertulphe de Nangis—apparently basing his work on an early version of the *History of Jerusalem*, compiled by Fulcher of Chartres between 1101 and 1128—recorded a tradition that when the crusaders broke into Jerusalem in July 1099 they were preceded by a rider on a white horse who had galloped down from the Mount of Olives. The crusader leaders Godfrey and Tancred immediately spurred their horses to follow this warrior into the city, which fell to their armies as a consequence. It was a direct reference to Revelation 6:2: "I looked, and there was a white horse! Its rider had a bow; a crown was given to him, and he came out conquering and to conquer." That such intoxicating traditions were being recorded within ten years of the capture of Jerusalem is vivid testimony to the apocalyptic way that the event was understood by many Christians in Europe.

The loss of Jerusalem to Saladin (Salah al-Din Yusuf ibn Ayyub) in 1187 came as a terrible shock. The cry of "*Hierosolyma est Perdita!*" (Jerusalem is lost) expressed the profound depth of despair for those who had interpreted the earlier capture of the city by crusaders in 1099 as a clear sign of divine approval of the crusading movement and as vivid evidence of the eschatological significance of the crusade.

After two centuries of warfare, the capture of the Christian city of Acre in 1291, by Islamic forces, marked the end of the crusader states in the Middle East. By that time the nature of the crusading movement had radically changed, and the period had even seen Constantinople/Byzantium itself (the original object of crusader defensive enthusiasm) sacked by Western crusaders in 1204 at the culmination of the Fourth Crusade. The confident intolerance of Latin Catholic crusaders could not have been more vividly demonstrated. In this event, their violence was targeted against non-Catholic, Orthodox *Christians;* as earlier it had been targeted against Muslims and Jews. It also demonstrated how the crusader movement could be subverted by the ambitions of Mediterranean states, in this case the Venetians, who were rivals of the Byzantine Empire. Common membership of the Christian faith had been no barrier to this extreme act of violence against fellow believers. Relations between Catholic and Orthodox Christians were severely damaged for centuries and the long-term effects accelerated the collapse of Eastern Christendom in the face of continued expansion by Seljuk and Ottoman Islamic forces.

The crusading movement was not confined to the Middle East. In Spain, the so-called *Reconquista* (Reconquest) was fought against Islamic states in the Iberian peninsula. By the mid-thirteenth century only Granada remained. It finally fell to Christian forces in 1492. There were also smaller crusades launched against heretical Christian groups, such as the Albigensian Crusade or Cathar Crusade (1209–29) in Languedoc, in southern France. German crusaders waged wars against still-pagan communities as part of the eastward expansion of German cultural hegemony in the lands bordering the Baltic.

With regard to end-times studies, what is significant is the apocalyptic aspects of the crusading movement. There were a number of features of the initial call to crusade that carried an apocalyptic sub-text. The first was the idea of a march to Jerusalem, which called to mind prophetic verses concerning battles for the Holy City and the idea of confronting the armies of Antichrist (now identified as Muslims) in the Holy Land. The concept of such a colossal battle in the last days was found in Revelation as well as the Old Testament. It seemed, to many medieval Christians, that Gog and Magog had been loosed in the form of Islamic armies. What would follow would be a last stand of Christian armies at Jerusalem as they faced these forces of Antichrist. In such a battle, Christ himself would appear, to give the Christians victory, and his second coming would occur on the Mount of Olives.[166] It was a powerful message to those who heard it. The second was the millenarian excitement that had been building since the year 1000 and had inspired popular beliefs that had no basis in Scripture but which added to the mix of apocalyptic excitement. One of these was the belief that the second coming would occur on Easter Day in a year when the Feast of the Annunciation and Good Friday fell on the same day. This occurred in 1065 and again in 1076.[167] Both dates had come and gone by the time the First

Crusade was preached in 1095, but the belief illustrates the deep reservoir of millenarian ideas that a military venture could tap into.

As with so many millenarian movements, before and since, this was most vividly seen in the lower-class and popular expressions of crusader enthusiasm. These often involved poorly organized groups of lesser knights and peasant volunteers and contrasted with the official (and usually better organized) groups that coalesced around powerful nobles and royalty. The most famous of these, the so-called People's Crusade, started in 1096 and was led by Peter the Hermit. It occurred in response to Pope Urban II's call for the First Crusade.

In the early stages of this, and related movements at the time, the extreme excitement, and the desire to be avenged on so-called enemies of Christ, led to pogroms against Jews and forced baptisms in western German cities such as Mainz, Speyer, Worms, and Cologne, as expressions of fanatical enthusiasm for becoming part of God's end-times judgement. Peter himself was not directly involved in these atrocities, but he had played a major role in whipping up popular enthusiasm and encouraged the idea of avenging Christ's sufferings. He also was part of activities that put pressure on Jews to financially support the crusade. The threat was implied, but very real. And actual violence soon followed.

The extreme nature of this populist millenarianism can be glimpsed in the actions of those who claimed that a she-goat was filled by the Holy Spirit and would guide people to Jerusalem. Albert of Aix, in his early-twelfth-century chronicle *History of the Expedition to Jerusalem*, condemned this as a "detestable crime."[168] Then there was the case of a woman from Cambrai, France, who claimed that God had caused her goose to lead her to Jerusalem. Christian chroniclers, such as Guibert of Nogent in his early twelfth-century chronicle *The Deeds of God through the Franks*, dismissed the idea of this goose-led crusade as "detestable to the Lord" and only accepted by "stupid people."[169] He went on to say that it would have been better roasted than going crusading. However, there were many who embraced the idea of the divinely-led goose. The Jewish chronicler Solomon bar Simson, looking back from the middle of the twelfth century, noted that it was followers of the woman with the goose who launched the first attacks on the Jews in the Rhineland.[170] In this case, in the city of Mainz.[171] The association of the followers of these animals with the "cruel slaughter" of the Jews is also found in the chronicle of Albert of Aix,[172] who condemned the followers of the goose in the same terms as he had condemned those who believed in the she-goat. Such murderous attacks were also launched against Jewish communities at the beginning of the Second Crusade in 1147, and the Third Crusade in 1189–90. Popular millenarian enthusiasm for crusading and such murderous violence against Jews went hand in hand. The forced conversion of the Jews was believed by some to be a way of accelerating the arrival of the second coming.[173]

It should also be noted that the capture of Jerusalem, in 1099, was accompanied by the slaughter of many Muslims and Jews living there. The traditional figure of thirty thousand civilian casualties has been reduced to three thousand in more recent studies and the point made that such killings of non-combatants was, sadly, a common feature of medieval warfare.[174] Nevertheless, the violence was appalling and it is not hard to imagine that, in this case, it had the added impetus of those perpetrating it considering themselves to be agents of the judgement of God in an apocalyptic struggle.

In an extraordinary journey, the huge group that Peter inspired travelled through the Balkans to Constantinople and, from there, to Nicomedia (now Izmir, Turkey). In Anatolia discipline disintegrated and Peter returned to Constantinople. Those who remained in Anatolia were destroyed by the Turks. Eventually, Peter ended up as part of the princely expedition that captured Jerusalem in 1099. After the capture of the city, Peter returned to Europe in 1100. Once back, he became prior of the Augustinian monastery of Neufmoustier. "In an earlier age he would have been killed or imprisoned; in the late 11th century he managed to win approval from the church hierarchy for his millennial enthusiasm."[175]

His success at the time was testimony to the way that the contemporary church read events in a millennialist way. Peter's radical teaching was on-message in the 1090s in a way that it would not have been in previous centuries. This was helped by the fact that the response to his preaching directed the enthusiastic violence outwards and away from Western Christendom. The exception that proved this rule was in the form of the violence directed towards the Jews in the crusaders' homelands. But this was acceptable in the antisemitic world of the late eleventh century, so long as it did not do damage to the wider economy or social fabric.

Another example of lower-class crusading enthusiasm can be seen in the events of 1212 in which a number of poorly organized attempts to reach the Holy Land and convert or conquer the Muslims are now remembered as the "Children's Crusade." Closer analysis suggests that there were, in fact, two broad movements, one in France and one in Germany, and that these involved lower-class followers of various ages.[176] They centered on two young preachers—Nicholas of Cologne in Germany and Stephen of Cloyes in France—both of whom were shepherds. Nicholas claimed that God would part the sea to allow passage to Jerusalem; Stephen seems to have promised something similar. The followers sang "Lord God, exalt Christianity! Lord God, restore to us the True Cross!" The so-called "True Cross" had been captured from a crusader army by Islamic forces at the Battle of Hattin in 1187. It was never recaptured. Thousands were drawn to the two young preachers. There were claims of miracles occurring. The German group crossed the Alps to Genoa in Italy, with many dying on the way. The French group marched to Marseilles. The sea did not part and none of them reached the Holy Land. Its millenarian aspects lay in the actions of poor people (not just children) seeking an escape from the poverty of their lives as they formed part of God's plan to liberate Jerusalem.

In time this populist medieval millenarian enthusiasm would become harder to manage and, when not directed abroad, soon took on a hostile attitude towards targets closer to home. This usually included Jews, as in the past, but when it also encompassed church authorities, better-off citizens, and the educated, it was no longer acceptable to those in authority.

Emperors of the last days

Chroniclers who were the contemporaries of the early crusades did not always agree on exactly how these events fitted into an end-times program. For some, the First Crusade had initiated events that, in some form, constituted the start of the millennial rule of Christ. This was implied by the white-horseman event described by Bertulphe de Nangis. For others, it was an event that would lead to the appearance of the "Last Emperor" and it would be this ruler who would battle the forces of evil, before the appearance of Christ.[177] What almost everyone agreed on, though, was that events of cosmic significance were occurring. This was despite the official abandonment of belief in a literal Christ-led millennial rule, that had occurred in the fifth century. As we have already seen, this did not prevent apocalyptic speculation regarding proxies for Christ who would act as "rulers over the final age of peace and prosperity" and this serves to "demonstrate the ongoing vitality of the millenarian impetus in Catholic views of the end times."[178] This informed a great deal of the narrative at the time, and it could reveal itself in surprising ways.

Supporters of Count Thierry of Alsace (died 1168), in his ambition to rule the city of Damascus, during the Second Crusade, promulgated alleged prophecies that identified his family line as representing the final restraint on Antichrist. This claim was applied to many different people and institutions. During the same crusade, a French preacher quoted the sixth-century *Tiburtine Sibyl* to "prove" that King Louis VII of France (died 1180) was the embodiment of the Last Emperor. In this role, he would conquer the entire Middle East and would be a godly conqueror in the mold of the Old Testament king of Persia, Cyrus.

Other leaders too were acclaimed as the Last Emperor, or courted this role. During the First Crusade, Emicho of Flonheim, who led the pogroms against the Jews in the Rhineland, actually styled himself as the "Last World Emperor" and claimed that when he reached Constantinople, Christ would crown him. When he finally reached Jerusalem in victory (which he never succeeded in doing), he would lay down this crown. This was following the Last Emperor script. However, there was one notable difference when compared with earlier attempts to harness this concept. Along the way to that goal, his slaughtering of Jews was designed to finally resolve the long debate over the continuation of Jews into the age of the Christian church. They would convert or be destroyed and so would be removed from the scene.[179] The punishment and/or conversion of the Jews appeared as part of the preparation for the second coming in most, if not all, medieval prophetic traditions.[180]

While Emicho of Flonheim represented the most radicalized version of the Last Emperor tradition, its most famous examples were associated with those at the top of the medieval hierarchy. They, unlike Emicho, had a greater opportunity to put such eschatological imperial pretensions into practice. After the Emperor Frederick I Barbarossa died while on the Third Crusade, in 1190, rumors began to circulate that he was not truly dead but would return. This was clearly related to the fact that he had died far from home and so seemed to have vanished. This had happened while on a holy cause, the crusade, so his absence could be viewed as a kind of translation to another place. This was also clearly connected to the idea of the Last Emperor and particularly appropriate for a ruler who had tried (and ultimately failed) to enforce an exalted view of imperial authority in relation to the papacy. From the fourteenth century onwards, many Germans believed that he slept in the imperial castle of Kyffhäuser. Their hope for his return was akin to the belief in the sleeping Arthur in the Celtic lands of the west.

Also a member of the Third Crusade, Richard I Lionheart, of England, conversed with Joachim of Fiora (see below) regarding interpretations of Revelation chapter 12 and the idea that the seven heads of the dragon represented seven powers that would persecute the church. The sixth was identified as the Islamic leader Saladin and the seventh as Antichrist. This made Richard's role in the Third Crusade of great importance as it presaged the end of the world. It was expected that the Antichrist would appear soon after 1194, when it was predicted that Saladin would fall from power (he actually died in 1193).

Then, during the Fourth Crusade, William Aurifex (burned for heresy in 1210) announced that the world would end in five years and that Philip II Augustus, of France, was the Last Emperor. Who was the Antichrist? William identified him as Pope Innocent III. William may well have been an alchemist. He certainly pushed theological speculation well beyond its acceptable bounds, was revered by followers as a prophet, and died for it.[181] A contemporary of his, Rigord (died c. 1209), who wrote the *Deeds of Philip Augustus*, also announced that the end was imminent. He added the detail that the Antichrist had been born in Babylon, which fitted exactly with terminology found in Revelation regarding the source of eschatological opposition to Christianity. In Revelation, though, Babylon was almost certainly a code word for Rome.

In 1213, Pope Innocent III issued the encyclical *Quia maior* (Carefully and Effectively) which associated Islam with the mark of the beast (666). Unpackaged, this amounted to a claim that it was almost six hundred years since the appearance of Muhammad and so about sixty-six years remained until Islam would collapse. During the Fifth Crusade itself, Joachim of Fiore once again predicted that the end of Islam was imminent. These predictions regarding the demise of Islam were bound up with ideas of the second coming. This was revealed in the borrowing of apocalyptic imagery to describe it. When the Egyptian city of Damietta was captured a number of claims were made that soon Antichrist would appear. Clearly— those who claimed this believed—he would appear in defense of Islam. He would be defeated by two Christian kings.

When Emperor Frederick II reached the Holy Land in 1229, he appeared to be fulfilling the prophecy that Frederick I would return. Finally, it seemed to some at least, the "Last Emperor" had arrived in Jerusalem. He was crowned King of Jerusalem in the Church of the Holy Sepulcher. He presented himself as the hoped-for "King of the Latins and the Greeks" who would rule until the return of Christ. His allies proclaimed him to be "*stupor mundi*" (wonder of the world).[182] However, end-times speculations are complex. Although Frederick II had presenting himself as the Last Emperor, his opponents later accused him of being the Antichrist himself.

In the 1240s Franciscan monks who opposed the imperial pretensions of the emperor were applying the ideas of Joachim of Fiore against him. Far from being the Last Emperor from the west, who would march to Jerusalem in defense of Christianity, they saw him as the Antichrist in whom, to quote the Franciscan chronicler Salimbene, "all the mysteries of iniquity should be fulfilled."[183] There was much about the personal behavior, cruelty, and lack of Christian virtue of the emperor that might cause such an identification to be made.[184] At the same time, his amicable attitude towards Jewish and Islamic philosophers was met with grave suspicion by many Christian observers. They did not approve of his harem, guarded by African eunuchs, either. He was altogether too "oriental" and "other." More significantly, he had a reputation for sacrilegious and blasphemous opinions and he challenged papal power. As early as 1239, Pope Gregory IX (pope 1227–41) had made the same identification as Salimbene, when he issued *Ascendit de Mari Bestia* (The Beast Rising from the Sea), in which he declared that, in Frederick II, "The beast filled with the names of Blasphemy has risen up from the sea." It was a direct reference to Revelation 13:1. For the pope, the main reason for this accusation was the emperor's opposition to papal authority: "He who now arises to destroy the name of the Lord from the earth directs an injurious sword against us."[185] In 1240 he repeated this emphatic identification and accused Frederick of allying with Islamic forces again the Christian cause.

Frederick returned the apocalyptic accusation in 1239, in a letter that accused the pope of being the rider of the red horse of Revelation 6:4, who brings conflict to the world; and also the red dragon, with seven heads and ten horns of Revelation 12:3–4, who is defeated by Michael and his angels (Rev 12:7–9). In addition, the emperor accused the pope of being the angel from the abyss bearing bowls to pour out and harm the sea and the earth (Rev 16:1–3).[186] This latter accusation was rather confusing since the exact words of Revelation picture these angels (plural) as doing *God's* will in bringing seven judgements. One gets the impression that verses were being flung as insults by the protagonists in this conflict, with little analysis of their content or suitability as end-times accusations. Rhetoric appears to have trumped theology.

Eberhard II of Regensberg, the Prince-Archbishop of Salzburg, who was a supporter of Frederick II, identified the ten horns/kingdoms in prophecy as the Turks, Greeks, Egyptians, Africans, Spaniards, French, English, Germans, Sicilians, and Italians, who were the inheritors of the Roman Empire.[187] In 1241, at the Council of Regensburg, he accused Pope Gregory IX of being the "little horn" of Daniel 7:8. Eberhard was excommunicated for refusing to denounce the emperor and died in 1246.

The conflict continued under Pope Innocent IV (pope 1243–54). In language clearly based on Daniel 7:8, he accused Frederick of having "in his forehead the horn of power and a mouth bringing forth monstrous things." He further accused him of changing times and laws and uttering blasphemies, in direct reference to Daniel 7:25.[188] In 1245, the conflict became so heated that, at the Council of Lyons, the pope deposed the emperor. Frederick reacted by once again deploying familiar prophetic terminology in an argument that purported to show that the title "*Innocencius papa*" signified 666.[189] The accusation of being Antichrist was being flung back and forth. The supporters of the pope looked for the defeat of the Antichrist-emperor when Christ returned in 1260. However, Frederick died of dysentery in 1250; and the second coming did not occur in 1260. Franciscan writers—by now staunch opponents of the emperor—later reported rumors that the emperor was not dead but slept under the fiery volcano of Etna and would return for the last battle against Christ. That Frederick's body was escorted to its burial (actually in Palermo cathedral) by his Saracen bodyguard further encouraged the idea that this Antichrist-emperor had gone to a fiery location. Pope Innocent IV was very pleased with the outcome and declared: "Let heaven exult and the earth rejoice."[190] This rather side-stepped the fact that the Antichrist accusation had clearly been wide of the mark.

Other rulers would have the moniker "Last Emperor" applied to them, but it would not again have quite the intensity of disagreement that had occurred around its application to the crusading Holy Roman Emperors.

A new age yet to come?

The whole approach to end-times timetables and the course of history was challenged by the writings of the Italian theologian Joachim of Fiore (died 1202), whom we have already met in passing. He had a huge impact on apocalyptic thinking. For the first time since the fifth century, a major theologian rejected the outlook of Augustine of Hippo and reinstated the belief in an actual future millennium. However, it was done in a way that promoted a new approach to the millennium and stood in contrast both to the way it had been understood in the first three centuries of Christian faith and in the way it had been adapted in the concept of the Last Emperor.

Joachim argued that there were great historic ages within God's providential plan. These were, in order: the Age of the Law, the Age of the Gospel, and, finally, the Age of the Holy Spirit. His ideas provided a great deal of energy to medieval discussions about the millennium and prophecies were also later attributed to him. For Joachim and his followers, the third age was imminent and would follow the defeat of Antichrist. Then, monastic influence would lead an era of peace on earth.

While he stands out due to his writings, it is clear from the way millennial ideas had surfaced over the previous centuries that debates and popular ideas about it had long occurred under the surface of Augustinian church orthodoxy. In this sense, Joachim was lighting a fuse that had long been primed and ready to explode. Nevertheless, it has been asserted, with reason, that "Joachim revitalized every aspect of medieval millennialism."[191] And the product of this exemplified what the previous orthodoxy had kept a lid on. Apocalyptic predictions, either attributed to him or associated with his methodology, cast as end-times players monastic orders (such as the Franciscans and Dominicans) and emperors and popes (sometimes seen as rulers returning from the dead). While the *dramatis personae* and permutations of events shifted and reformed, what remained consistent was the sense of imminent cosmic change.

But when would the new age begin? Calculations fixed on 1250 or 1260. Then new calculations followed. And how should one prepare for it or hasten its coming? Among the Franciscans some opted for an inquisitorial rooting out of "ungodliness"; while some became radical millenarian preachers of an upturned social order. By 1300 the, sometimes esoteric, debates had turned violent. The so-called "Spiritual Franciscans" or *Fraticelli* (Little Brethren) condemned the established church as corrupt and worldly. Those who were part of this sinful structure would be damned. As so often, before and since, millenarianism was becoming socially revolutionary, and people were dying as a consequence. In 1296 their beliefs were declared to be heretical. But they did not go away. Throughout the fourteenth and fifteenth centuries the suppressed *Fraticelli* continued to appear in parts of Italy. Some still considered themselves the true Franciscans. Others, such as the "Apostolic Brethren," were rooted in the laity and set their faces against the Franciscan order (and monasticism generally), as being now too corrupt and worldly to be reformed. In 1300 the founder of the Apostolic Brethren, Segarelli, was executed. This set off a campaign of violent millenarian activism led by one Fra Dolcino.[192] Dolcino led something of an insurgency in north-western Italy against those maintaining Catholic orthodoxy, feudal overlords, and the wealthy. A mini-crusade was launched in response. He was captured and burned in 1307. In 1322, about thirty of Dolcino's followers were burned in Padua. Umberto Eco's novel *The Name of the Rose* (1980) is set in the aftermath of the crushing of Dolcino's movement and in the context of ongoing inquisitorial conflict with the *Fraticelli*. It is set in 1327.

Other groups among the laity, but lacking the political edge, were the *Beguines* (female) and *Beghards* (male). Living in communes, they became associated with mysticism and were regarded with suspicion. The Council of Vienne (1311) condemned the *Beghards* for holding libertine views and abandoning Christian morality (being "antinomian"), although it is difficult to decide the accuracy of the accusation. In 1310 one of the French *Beguines*, Marguerite Porete, was burned for heresy in Paris. In her book, *The Mirror of Souls*, she had claimed that the soul could achieve union with God while still on earth. It was a kind of personal apocalypse. However, by the fifteenth century they had largely achieved a measure of toleration from the authorities.

The Black Death: the end of the world?

It is not surprising that the Black Death pandemic in the 1340s and the Hundred Years War between England and France caused some people to interpret those events in apocalyptic ways. In the Franciscan community at Kilkenny, Ireland, one chronicler (who did not survive the disease) wrote: "I leave parchment to continue this work, if perchance any man survive and any of the race of Adam escape this pestilence."[193] The Swiss chronicler, John of Winterthur, writing in 1348, noted that people expected the return of Emperor Frederick II, who would massacre the clergy and break the barriers between rich and poor.[194] It was a combination of the Last Emperor belief with the urge to take revenge on the powerful, so common among the most radical millenarian movements over the centuries. In 1356, a

Franciscan, John of Roquetaillade, prophesied plagues, social unrest, and the imminent appearance of Antichrist (or antichrists). This would lead, in 1367, to a godly pope and the beginning of a millennium of peace under a French Holy Roman Emperor.[195]

Such expectations could take a violent turn in the context of the suffering of the fourteenth century and feudal oppression. In 1320, an uprising of the so-called *Pastoureaux* (Shepherds) sacked Paris as part of their demand that the king (Philip V) should go on crusade to the Holy Land. In ways reminiscent of the violence associated with the First Crusade, they launched pogroms against the Jews. They also murdered clerics and academics. An earlier *Pastoureaux* uprising had occurred in 1251. There is evidence that they thought they could hasten the second coming by their actions.[196]

In the years following the plague's arrival in Europe in the late 1340s, so-called Flagellant Movements arose in Central Europe and rapidly spread. Engaging in acts of self-mortification, they believed that their pain would avert the wrath of God as exemplified in the plague. They acted independent of the church structure and, at times, proclaimed messianic statements such as the movement lasting for thirty-three years (the age of Jesus at his crucifixion and resurrection) and only ending with the arrival of the millennium.[197]

As in the earlier years of the crusades, panic at plague mortality led to mass murders of Jews. As the living embodiment of the "alien other," they were held responsible for outbreaks of disease. Thousands were slaughtered. In Germany and in the Low Countries the Flagellant movement played an enthusiastic part in committing these atrocities.[198]

Then, in 1358, a violent lower-class revolt occurred in northern France. Termed the *Jacquerie*, it involved horrifying levels of violence, if the chroniclers, such as Jean de Venette and Jean Froissart, are to be believed. While no manifesto accompanied these uprisings, they had a millenarian character reminiscent of Fra Dolcino. This was something that would occur again, in the sixteenth century, at Münster. Certainly, at least one contemporary observer, Villehardouin, believed that the rebels had been inspired by the prophecies expressed by Roquetaillade, which had end-times themes.[199]

In 1380 the coincidence of the name of the French king, Charles VI, with that of Charlemagne caused prophecies (of the Last Emperor kind) to be expressed regarding him. These were repeated about other French kings named Charles in the later fourteenth and then in the fifteenth century.

The state of end-times beliefs by the close of the Middle Ages

As the Middle Ages drew towards a close, the radical fervor associated with belief in the allegedly impending second coming showed no signs of abating. The late-fourteenth-century English preacher John Wycliffe (died 1384) associated the pope with Antichrist. In fifteenth-century Bohemia, the most radical wing of the Hussites (something of a proto-Protestant movement, like Wycliffe's Lollard followers in England), who were called the Taborites, believed that their militant revolutionary activities would bring in the reign of Christ. They were eventually bloodily defeated in 1434, by more moderate Hussites, in alliance with Catholic forces. After 1452 they ceased to exist as a militant movement.

In the aftermath of the defeat of the Taborites—and clearly influenced by roaming bands of mercenaries who continued to reference some Taborite terminology, while actually terrorizing the Bohemian borderlands—a rogue Franciscan declared himself one called "the Anointed Savior" who would employ such mercenaries to destroy Antichrist (the pope), the clergy, and all who opposed him. In this heretical take on end-times millenarianism, his spokesmen (Janko and Livin of Wirsberg) claimed that this "Anointed Savior," not Christ, was the Son of Man of Old Testament prophecy, who would inaugurate the third and last age (the millennium kingdom). The year 1467 was proclaimed to be the year when the "Anointed Savior" would establish his rule. However, in 1466 the church authorities crushed the movement.[200]

At other times of economic and political stress others also proclaimed the imminence of the second coming, such as in 1476 when the so-called "Drummer of Niklashausen" (near Würzburg, in Franconia, Germany), Hans Böhm, announced "messages" from the Virgin Mary. These included denunciations of the clergy and the arrival of the New Jerusalem, focused on Niklashausen. This was a highly localized view of the geography of the *parousia*. Thousands of peasants flocked to hear him. To crush the movement, the authorities arrested him, and he was tortured and then burned as a heretic.[201]

What is clear from all this is that millenarian beliefs operated at *all levels* of society in the Middle Ages. Some people buttressed imperial politics using them, some looked to contemporary kings to implement God's program, others condemned the elites—including those in the church itself—for standing against the will of God, some turned to extreme violence in order to bring in the millennial kingdom as they understood it, and the accusation of Antichrist was thrown back and forth. The belief in the end-times was variously used. It could provide material for conservative proponents of the political and ecclesiastical status quo; and also for radical preachers who claimed that they were authorized to tear society down in order to bring in the millennium. It has been stated, with good reason, that these varied beliefs are "among the most profound and versatile of medieval ideologies of social change."[202] The most populist lower-class medieval movements exhibited a striking hostility towards Jews, the better-off, church authorities, and the intelligentsia. "They also displayed the anger, paranoia, and violence that would dominate one strain of anti-modern Christian millennialism found in the pogroms of the Crusaders to the genocidal persecutions of the Nazis."[203]

In the century that followed 1500, the range of such apocalyptic beliefs would expand and would, at times, involve quite extraordinary violence.

9

The Impact of the Reformation
on End-Times Beliefs

THE WAY THAT HISTORIANS divide up the past into categories, such as
"medieval" and "Early Modern," provides us with useful tools for mental
compartmentalization. However, they have the drawback of leaving us
with categorizing past experiences in ways that, while conveniently book-
ending them, does so in a way that fails to accurately describe the flow and
complexity of real events and movements.

The Reformation and the Early Modern period of history (the latter
describing events c.1500–1800) are cases in point. The former, describing
changes and upheavals in the Western Church following Luther's publication of his *Ninety-five Theses* of 1517, unfolded differently in various
geographical and cultural settings and as experienced by different classes
of people. And it, of course, was not solely started by Luther; nor was
its course dictated by him alone, far from it. What later emerged in the
reformed Geneva of Calvin was related to, but strikingly different from,
what eventually settled down as the Lutheran mainstream in large parts of
Germany and elsewhere. And the way these changes were understood and
acted on had radically different characteristics if one is comparing a German peasant protesting at social inequalities with a Swiss reformer seeking
to establish a semi-theocracy, or a Protestant monarch seeking to benefit
from the dynamism of the new movement in national state-building. The
way each viewed the world had gained a new "Protestant focus"—similar
to the way that an optometrist might drop a new lens into a pair of testing
spectacles—but the underling conditions of each had an immense effect on
how they "saw" the world. And, anyway, the lens dropped before their eyes
differed from place to place. It was not the same "Protestant focus lens" in

Geneva as it was in the Netherlands, or in the royal court of London. Consequently, we should not expect uniformity among those breaking away from the historic Catholic Church. This applied to the way they interpreted these turbulent experiences as end-times events. There were certainly common features; but a whole lot of differences too.

Similarly, the fifteenth-century changes—encapsulated in the concept of the "Renaissance" and the dissemination of new ideas via the movable type of Johannes Gutenberg's printing presses from the 1450s—meant that changes often associated with the sixteenth century had their roots in the late Middle Ages.[204]

The same can be said of the end-times beliefs that characterized the Middle Ages and that stretched back into the Roman period. These changed in emphasis and interpretation as Western Christendom fragmented in the sixteenth century, but many common features remained. Continuity, as well as novelty and invention, characterized the way that these well-rooted beliefs were deployed in the Reformation period

However, there was one significant and wide-ranging change in officially sanctioned ideology. Following the Reformation and a galvanized re-engagement with the detail of Scripture as the definitive statement of belief, Protestants again read the prophecies as historical and predictive in a newly energized way. Futurism was back on the agenda. As we have seen, this was not new, and biblical prophecies had become increasingly approached in this manner during the Middle Ages (regardless of official Augustinian orthodoxy). Indeed, there had been a determined push-back against this Augustinian approach to prophecy. However, following the Reformation, this push-back became the norm across many of the groups who broke away from Roman Catholicism. This change in emphasis influenced events across Europe, from mainstream theological statements to revolutionary Anabaptist uprisings. If not a novel approach, its increasingly widespread nature was striking. It was a shift in emphasis that was encouraged by the extreme turbulence of the times. Old conflicts between pope and emperor seemed to pale in comparison with the schism that rent the Western Church in the sixteenth century. Then conflicts, such as the Thirty Years War (1618–48) and political crises in Britain in the 1640s and 1650s, only added to this sense of being in the middle of apocalyptic events. The radicalization started early. In fact, it was there from the start.

Apocalyptic radicalization and the Reformation

In 1521, Martin Luther had made his decisive break from the authority of the pope, following the Diet of Worms before the leaders of the Holy Roman Empire. Luther himself had wanted no such break but rather had been hoping to reform the Catholic Church. It was not to be. And whatever Luther had once wanted, others of his contemporaries were in favor of a more radical break with the past and were committed to challenging society as well as church. Things were about to get very radical indeed.

While they were not strictly part of this process of church reformation, the peasants who rose in revolt across Germany in 1524 and 1525 took their cue from a sense of radical change being possible. This, in principle, was due to the theological conflict that was brewing. Huge numbers died in the course of the so-called German Peasants' War and its defeat; and the violence sparked wildly differing reactions among early Protestant reformers. Martin Luther, for one, condemned the uprising. It is possible to get a flavor of his attitude towards the peasant revolutionaries from the title of a pamphlet that he wrote: *Against the Murdering Plundering Hordes of Peasants*. In it he advised lords to crush the revolt. In contrast, some other Christian leaders, of a more revolutionary disposition, applauded it and later sought to emulate its attack on the wealth and power of the world. This soon morphed into a sense of enacting God's judgement on a sinful society, while offering the promise of an imminent New Jerusalem as part of a millennial new world order.

As a result, among many south German peasants there would be calls for a much more radical definition of "Reformation," in defiance of Luther and the established order. This only served to up the ante. Later radical revolutionaries, such as those at Münster in Westphalia, in 1534–35, would see themselves as the heirs of the revolutionary tradition of bloody violence of the German Peasants' War. For them, social upheaval was interwoven into apocalyptic beliefs. These were the "Anabaptists," whose exploits would later thrill or horrify different Protestant groups, including the seventeenth-century British "godly," depending on their predilection. It soon became clear that the Reformation was to have both a socially conservative and a revolutionary track. But apocalyptic beliefs were integral to both, even if expressed in different forms. A distinct Protestant apocalyptic identity was emerging.

From the year 1529 the term "Protestant" entered the vocabulary as a number of German princes backed Luther's calls for reform. Just as the Holy Roman emperor in the Middle Ages had done, they also were keen to restrict the power of the pope. However, this time the Holy Roman emperor backed Catholic orthodoxy and these German princes were keen to reduce his power too. By 1541, any hope of reconciliation between Catholics and Protestants broke down following the Diet of Regensburg. Years of indecisive warfare then followed between the Catholic emperor and German Protestant princes. This finally led to the Treaty of Passau, in 1552, which recognized the continued existence of the Protestant German states. Finally, the Peace of Augsburg (1555) ended this period of fighting. But it was far from being the end of religious warfare.

In these years of fragmenting faith communities, the charge of being the agent of Antichrist, indeed of being Antichrist himself, was once more thrown about as those engaged in these conflicts framed the opposition as the cause of this crisis within Christendom. Unlike the conflict between Emperor Frederick and the pope—when everyone considered themselves members of the one true church, regardless of the insults being exchanged on a personal level—this sixteenth-century conflict was centered on which community represented the true church, and which the apostate church of Antichrist. It was such a severe crisis that many believed that it presaged the imminent time of tribulation and the second coming.

Millenarian beliefs became prevalent among sixteenth- and seventeenth-century Protestants and they tended to identify the pope as the Antichrist. Various attempts were made to identify the "mark of the beast" (666) in Revelation 13:18 as applicable to other contemporary rulers and events too. Imaginative Protestant writers contrived numerical systems which made it represent the pope's name. Luther, for example, accused the pope of being the Antichrist in the 1530 edition of the German Bible and continued to do so in later editions.[205] For Luther, it was the proclamation of the true gospel (as he and his supporters presented it) that would defeat the false prophet Antichrist.[206] He was certain that the last days were at hand and that what had been prophesied in Revelation was being fulfilled in his conflict with the papacy and the supporters of the Roman Catholic Church.

In 1545, the engraver Melchior Lorch produced a shocking illustration, *The Pope as Wildman*, in which the pontiff is shown having the tail and animal attributes traditionally associated with the devil. Frogs spew from his mouth in direct reference to Revelation 16:13 where impure spirits in the form of frogs issue from the mouths of the dragon, the beast and the false prophet. The figure also resembles the so-called "Wild Man" of medieval demonology (a figure associated with destructive and erotic forces). In keeping with this association, the papal cross carried by the pope/beast is in the form of a tree trunk. The way in which Reformation outlook drew on pre-existing medieval motifs is clear from this illustration. Lorch dedicated the illustration to Luther.

In Switzerland, John Calvin in his 1559 edition of the *Institutes of the Christian Religion*, also identified Antichrist as being the pope. The same connection was made in the commentary accompanying the Geneva Bible, translated in 1560 by English Protestant exiles living in Geneva.[207] For the Reformed believers in Switzerland, as the Lutherans of Germany, the link was clear and beyond debate. It was one that would influence the outlook of many Protestants for centuries and remains a potent association among some in the twenty-first century.

When the King James' Authorized Version of the Bible was published, in 1611, its dedication thanked the king for identifying the pope as the man of sin, or lawlessness, referred to in 2 Thessalonians 2:3. It was an identification that the king (then king of Scots) had made as far back as 1588. By 1611, the identification had become mainstream. In Edmund Spenser's *Faeri Queen*, of 1596, the character representing Catholicism is described as "a dreadful Beast with sevenfold head." Everyone listening would have got the point. Mistress Quickly in Shakespeare's *Henry V* (written in 1599) wistfully recalls how Falstaff frequently referred to "the whore of Babylon." The sexualization of this eschatological term was clearly designed to tease and amuse Elizabethan audiences in the playhouses. Again, everyone would have got it.[208]

In addition, Luther—mindful of the expansion of Ottoman power at the time—identified this Islamic power as being the fulfilment of the prophecy regarding Gog of the land of Magog in Ezekiel 38.[209] Some Catholic writers also adopted a similarly eschatological interpretation of the Ottoman Turks.[210] This was despite the continuing Catholic Augustinian orthodoxy, which eschewed such literal interpretations of prophecy. Similarly, some Catholic defenders of the pope threw back at Luther the accusation of being Antichrist. This futurist approach can be seen in the commentary on Revelation written by the Spanish Jesuit Franciscus Ribeira, published in 1591.[211] However, many others held the line and continued to argue that the fulfilment of scriptural prophecy lay beyond history and could not be read in the details of contemporary events and persons. This continued the allegorical reading of prophecies that was rooted in the thinking of the Late Roman church.

When it came to the implementation of these eschatological events, Luther and his supporters looked to God to bring in the millennium. Once the pope had been defeated, the situation would be ready for the return of Christ; judgement on those who had opposed the godly movement of Luther and his allies; and the heavenly kingdom would be established. Armed millenarian revolts were certainly not envisaged. Calvin, though inclined towards a theocratic form of government and the rule of the saints in Geneva, was also opposed to major changes in the economic status quo. The godly should take power, but there would not be an upending of the economic hierarchy. For Luther (and also for Calvin) this was for a number of reasons. Firstly, only God could bring in such a millennial kingdom. Secondly, such revolts disturbed the social order and got in the way of spreading the new Protestant message. Thirdly, such political and social upheavals would discredit the Reformation.[212] This was the emergence of a generally premillennialist position; although other millennial timeframes would be mooted by other reformers after him (including postmillennial ones). But the officially promulgated concept was one shorn of eschatological activism on the part of believers.

However, in sharp contrast to Luther and Calvin, there were others who adopted an altogether more muscular and proactive approach towards bringing in the millennial kingdom. It is to these radicals that we will now turn.

Anabaptists: the end-time "Reds" of the Reformation

The most radical, among those who believed that they lived in the last days, tended to gravitate towards the "Anabaptist" wing of the Protestant Reformation. The term itself simply described those whose theological position rejected the validity of infant baptism in favor of adult believers' baptism. Many of these groups were the forerunners of Baptist churches, which emerged in the seventeenth century; although many of these later fellowships came directly out of infant-baptizing churches and did not have roots in the earlier Anabaptist movement. In the sixteenth century people died for this belief in believers' baptism.

The Anabaptist movement was amorphous and included both violently militant groups and pacifist fellowships. The one thing they had in common was a belief in the need for adult believers to make their own declaration of faith (leading to salvation) that was independent of the power and sacraments of Catholic priests on one hand, and Lutheran and Reformed pastors on the other. As a consequence, some died at the hands of fellow Protestants, such as Michael Sattler who was burned at Zurich; while others were killed by Catholic authorities, such as Balthasar Hubmaier, who was burned at Vienna. The latter's wife was executed by drowning, which was clearly chosen to mirror the Anabaptist practice of adult full-immersion baptism. All these died in the 1520s. They died because their core belief was personally empowering and challenged established ecclesiastical structures. It was a short step from this to challenging secular structures too. Luther publicly denounced them in 1535.[213] They were regarded as highly dangerous, and they suffered as a consequence. In such a situation of radicalized groups suffering widespread lethal persecution, it is no surprise that many began to adopt millenarian beliefs in the judgement of God that would vindicate the suffering poor and bring down the mighty. Some of these radical groups promoted a redistribution of wealth and the holding of goods in common. They claimed scriptural validity for this from the practice of the very early church, as revealed in Acts 2:44–45; another group whose socio-economic radicalism was developed in the context of belief in the impending *parousia*.

This apocalyptic preaching that the poor would tear down the rich was promoted in Germany by Thomas Müntzer and Niklas Storch, at the time of the German Peasants' War. They attracted a following among unemployed silver miners at Zwickau; and then among peasants and copper miners in Thuringia. Müntzer went on to ally himself with Heinrich Pfeiffer, who was leading agitation against the wealthy oligarchs in the town of Mühlhausen. From there, Müntzer issued a manifesto which called for uprisings and quoted eschatological passages from Ezekiel 34, Daniel 7, Matthew 24, and Revelation 6. For Müntzer, the end-times showdown was at hand. He eventually relocated to a nearby camp of peasants who were in revolt against the German aristocracy. In May 1525, this uprising was bloodily suppressed by an army loyal to the German princes. Müntzer was captured and tortured; and then beheaded (along with Pfeiffer) in the camp of the German princes. Storch died while on the run.

Luther supported the violent suppression of Müntzer and his "League of the Elect."[214] Luther and Müntzer represented two very different approaches regarding how to establish the kingdom of God on earth and how to live in the light of their faith in the second coming of Christ. Müntzer explicitly attacked Luther and his social conservatism in a pamphlet entitled *The Most Amply Called-for Defense and Answer to the Unspiritual Soft-living Flesh at Wittenberg*. What the pamphlet lacked in a snappy title, it more than made up for in the severity of its criticism of Luther. Müntzer declared that Luther was the beast, and the whore of Babylon, both depicted in Revelation. In contrast to Luther, Müntzer called for social revolution. Luther, in 1524, had dedicated his tract (*A Letter to the Princes of Saxony concerning the Rebellious Spirit*), setting out his opposition to Müntzer, to "Lord Friedrich, Electoral Prince, and Johann, Duke of Saxony, Landgrave of Thuringia and Margrave of Meissen."[215] In pointed contrast, Müntzer dedicated his riposte to "Christ, King of kings and Duke of all believers."[216] It was clear that Müntzer considered that Luther had sold-out to worldly authorities, whereas he was true to the spiritual calling of one anointed as a prophet of Christ. In the end, it was Luther who won; and Müntzer who was destroyed. So perished a self-proclaimed prophet who was, arguably, "obsessed by eschatological phantasies which he attempted to translate into reality by exploiting social discontent."[217]

Müntzer never actually described himself as an Anabaptist, although he was later venerated by the Anabaptist movement in the aftermath of the crushing of the German Peasants' War.[218] However, Anabaptists and radical violent politics were firmly and irrevocably (if incorrectly) connected by many contemporaries. It is not surprising that, later in the seventeenth century, the term Anabaptist became "just a loose term of abuse like, 'Red.'"[219] As late as 1662, the English *Book of Common Prayer* found it necessary to assert that, "The Riches and Goods of Christians are not common, as touching the right, title, and possession of the same, as certain Anabaptists do falsely boast."[220] The Anabaptists (the most extreme ones anyway) had clearly made an impact on the consciousness of those in power. And it was a radical agenda that often had end-times dimensions, as was vividly demonstrated at Münster in Westphalia, Germany.

In the year 1534, John Mathias or Matthys of Haarlem (in the Netherlands) and John Buckhold or Bockelson of Leiden (also in the Netherlands) led a group of extreme Anabaptists who seized control of the German city of Münster. What occurred after this went far beyond theological experiment and social change. The entire social order of the city was violently upended and a reign of terror was implemented. Old patterns of behavior were abandoned or violently suppressed. There had been precedents for this in the so-called *Bundschuh* (peasants' clog) uprisings that had eventually escalated into the earlier German Peasants' War. Both the *Bundschuh* and the seizure of Münster represented lower-class revolt.[221] They proclaimed nothing less than a God-sanctioned overturning of the entire social order. It was active millenarianism being enforced in earthly communities. The New Jerusalem was being built by the hands of the most radical Protestants.

The violence began to spiral out of control. Both Lutherans and Catholics were expelled from the city. The Anabaptists there hated one group as much as the other. Then the city itself was besieged by the Catholic Bishop of Münster, who had found himself locked out of his own town. It was then that the millennial kingdom really took off in the minds of the most extreme revolutionaries. Mathias claimed to be a prophet and he and his supporters began a reign of terror against all critics and perceived enemies. The kind of social experiment that had terrified better-off citizens in the German and Czech lands (and which had led to the execution of Anabaptists there) was now finally being implemented. The radicals seized all gold and silver and held it communally. All books were destroyed, because they offered alternative sources of knowledge. This was a "Year 0" moment. In March 1534, Mathias was so certain of his prophetic status, and so convinced that he had been ordered by God to take a small force out of the city to break the siege, that he did so. He was killed. Following his death, he was replaced by John Buckhold, who was later remembered in some radical circles as "Jan of Leiden." Now the apocalyptic gloves were off. Buckhold adopted the title "King of Justice, King of the New Jerusalem."[222] The end-times certainty was clear for all to see. Whether this should be seen as a version of the Last Emperor motif or a heretical messianic self-promotion was not immediately clear. That matter would soon be clarified.

Buckhold, as "King of the New Jerusalem," proclaimed a policy of polygamy and then took fifteen wives. The policy was used to justify the sexual excesses of others in the leadership too. As so often in religious cults—and frequently so in those possessing a distorted and militaristic apocalyptic ideology—the sexual appetite of the leader was ruthlessly promoted. As the harbinger of a new world order, and as one elevated above the norms that applied to lesser beings, the radical leader was embodying both authority and liberation from restraints. It was a long way from any kind of apocalyptic vision found in Revelation; or in any other part of Scripture for that matter. And it was ruthlessly enforced. Any woman who refused to marry one of Buckhold's supporters was executed. Women who argued with their husbands were also executed.[223] All sexual norms had soon broken down in the city. A nightmare descended on the citizens of Münster, who were now at the mercy of the most extreme (male) members of the community.

Then things escalated even further. Given the way that things had developed so far and the increasing megalomania of Buckhold, what occurred next was almost predictable. In August 1534, Buckhold declared that he, not Christ, was "Messiah of the last days." This new messiah would rule the world as a descendant of the Old Testament's King David. Buckhold's coinage proclaimed that "The Word has become Flesh and dwells in us." It was clear that this referred to King John Buckhold.[224] While the rest of the city starved, he lived in luxury, but proclaimed that, since he was dead to the world, there was no sin in this. Again, it was a trope of the self-styled "apocalyptic dictator," which would not be confined to Buckhold. He also claimed that the cobblestones of the town would turn into loaves of bread in order to feed the starving people who were trapped there.[225] According to a near-contemporary engraving, made by Heinrich Aldegrever, King John's motto was "*Gottes macht ist myn cracht*" (God's power is my strength).

Finally, in 1535, the chaos ended as those besieging the place finally gained entry to the town. Following this, they slaughtered the Anabaptists and captured King John. In 1536, he was tortured to death with red-hot irons as an example to all such would-be messiahs. Apparently, he died without making a sound.[226]

Despite the bloody crushing of the revolt, others still took inspiration from the example of Münster. Indeed, it was remarkable what an after-life it would have, since millenarian groups continued to extol its virtues into the middle of the seventeenth century. They claimed that the bad things said about it were invented by the enemies of those who had seized control of the town. In 1567, a cobbler named Jan Willemsen set up yet another "New Jerusalem," and this one was also in Westphalia. In a manner comparable to Buckhold, he too declared that he was the end-times messiah. In time, he and his supporters were captured and executed, like their predecessors in Münster. Willemsen himself was burned at Cleves in 1580.[227]

Dating the second coming

Despite the clear scriptural instructions not to attempt to date the second coming, some Christians continued to do so, as they had in the past. In 1597 the English writer, Thomas Lupton, in a publication entitled *Babylon is Fallen*, named the year 1666 as the date. Then, in 1610, he followed this with a second work entitled *A Prophesie That Hath Lyen Hid, Above These 2000 Years*. This reiterated the claim concerning the date. It seems clear that he was drawn to it because of the number of the beast in Revelation, although that had no dating associated with it whatsoever. In 1593, another writer, John Napier, calculated that the key date would be 1688. This claim appeared in his book entitled *A Plaine Discovery of the Whole Revelation*. It hinged on calculations based on computations of numerical references (many of them complex and/or mysterious) that he culled from various scriptural passages; but particularly from Revelation. He was not the first to do this. He would not be the last either.

A post-Reformation foundation of end-times calculations and specula-tions was being laid down. This reminds us that it was not simply the pre-serve of extreme groups such as the Anabaptists. End-times reflections were mainstream in Protestant Europe and nowhere more so than in England. These would be built on by Puritan co-religionists in the 1640s and 1650s as order broke down in Britain during the Civil Wars. Some of those who were influenced by these ideas would have extreme beliefs comparable to some of those held by the revolutionaries at Münster. Others, who were influenced by these end-times beliefs, were leading parliamentary figures.

In England, the late-sixteenth-century writings of Cambridge-educat-ed Thomas Brightman (died 1607) and Joseph Mede (died 1638)—along-side the German theologian Johannes Heinrich Alsted (died 1638)—greatly influenced the later Fifth Monarchy Men, as we shall see in the next chapter. Brightman wrote a commentary on Revelation in which he identified the Church of England as the Laodicean church of Revelation 3:14–19 (neither hot nor cold); the Philadelphian church of Revelation 3:7–13 (loved by God) he identified as the church of Geneva and the kirk of Scotland. In his commentary on Daniel (as well as in his commentary on Revelation), he identified the pope as Antichrist, whose reign is limited to 1,290 years and who will then be destroyed by God. In his publication *Shall They Return to Jerusalem Again?* published in 1615, he advocated the return of the Jews to their ancestral home in the Middle East. As such, he was one of the first Christians to do so. Joseph Mede's commentary on Revelation, *Key of the Revelation Searched and Demonstrated out of the Naturall and Proper Charecters of the Visions*, gave two possible dates for the second coming based on his numerical calculations: 1654 or 1716. He also predicted the conversion of the Jews prior to the second coming.

Johannes Heinrich Alsted, like the other two writers, was an example of a mainstream churchman who held strong millennialist beliefs without becoming a social revolutionary or a heretic. He was particularly influential in promoting premillennialism (that Christ will return in order to establish his thousand-year-reign on earth). This was most clearly expressed in his publication *Diatribe de mille annis Apocalypticis* (Discussion about a Thousand Year Apocalypse), which was published in 1627. Prior to this, he had expressed ideas in line with the orthodoxy of Augustine of Hippo, which did not envisage a future literal millennium (amillennialism). This appears in his 1614 work entitled, *Methodus Sacrosanctae Theologiae* (Method of Sacred Theology).[228] There is evidence that this shift in his theological position was caused by his experiences of the devastation caused by the Thirty Years War in Europe, which he interpreted as being signs of the approaching last days.[229]

The legacy of the Reformation for end-times thinking

The Reformation, through its removal of papal authority, gave rise to an explosion of radical millenarian ideas. It also shattered what remained of the old Augustinian amillennialist orthodoxy. That had already taken a battering as a result of the medieval re-examination of the application of prophecy, such as that associated with Joachim of Fiore; not to mention the popular (and populist) outbreaks of millenarian enthusiasm and violence associated with the crusades and the Black Death.

At the same time, the sixteenth-century rupture of Western Christendom caused such intense infighting within the church that each side accused the other of being the Antichrist. In such turbulent times it seemed as if the known world *was* indeed coming to an end. This sense of the impending end accelerated in the wars of religion, which were occasioned by the fragmentation that occurred within the Christian community. The terrible, ideologically driven slaughters seemed reminiscent of the days of the tribulation described in Revelation. The end of days really did seem very close.

In addition, the Protestant reformers' emphasis on a personal relationship with God was accompanied by expanding access to Scripture in the vernacular among ordinary people. This made it increasingly difficult to police orthodoxy and almost impossible to keep the lid on extreme radical beliefs, even of heresies as judged by any historic standard. Inevitably, this led to the emergence of some very varied and controversial interpretations among some who were now deeply convinced of their own personal spiritual insight and personal authority. This proved to be especially the case when disturbances to the social order allowed determined (even fanatical) groups to project their views onto their wider society. We have seen how the bloody events of the Anabaptist seizure of Münster, in 1534, soon took on a millenarian character. And it was no isolated incident. Apocalyptic fears and hopes, and extreme millenarianism, flourished (then as now) in times of uncertainty and upheaval. After the suppression of Münster, other millenarian prophets proclaimed the imminent arrival of the New Jerusalem in the 1560s. Such views continued to circulate among the more extreme Anabaptist groups. Then, conflicts such as the Thirty Years War and the British Civil Wars added to this sense of being in the middle of apocalyptic events. As a result of this, millenarian beliefs were very much in the Protestant (and, in Britain, the Puritan "godly") mainstream as events unfolded in the seventeenth century. Millenarian beliefs were certainly not just the preserve of fringe groups. As political order broke down in the British Isles in the 1630s and 1640s, homegrown interpretations of the prophetic texts mingled with those that had originated in Germany and that had entered Britain via the conduit of the Protestant Netherlands. A heady cocktail of end-times ideas was being mixed that would intoxicate huge numbers of people on the parliamentary side as the country spiraled down to civil war.

10

When Order Breaks Down

The British Civil Wars

In the 1640s and 1650s the British Isles were convulsed by civil wars. These wars are often called the "English Civil War," but, as the conflict affected England, Ireland, Scotland, and Wales in a number of conflicts, they should really be called the "British Civil Wars." During this time of upheaval, millenarian preaching accelerated. This accompanied turbulence that was as much religious and social as it was political and military. In this respect, the trend mirrored similar occurrences in Germany during the dramatic changes of the Reformation in the previous century.

In the British Isles, as on the continental mainland, apocalyptic politics was energized by the reemphasis of the literal reading of prophecy, which was encouraged by the Reformation changes. Overall, large numbers of people were becoming radicalized, and this radicalization revealed itself in millenarian beliefs alongside political demands. In England, in 1653, there was even a (failed) attempt to establish a theocratic parliament as a response to these beliefs. This was, indeed, a dramatic episode in the developing history of end-times beliefs and their application.

Who truly is king in the end times?

The regicidal events in London, in January 1649, prompted profound questions relating to ultimate authority. While this gripped all who were trying to establish a new republican constitutional settlement, it also had profound religious implications. This was especially so in a nation where the king had previously headed-up the national church (a legacy of Henry VIII's break with Rome in the previous century) and where recent monarchs had developed a highly exalted concept of the divine origins of their power. However, there was a growing minority who had come to a very different conclusion as to how monarchical power should function in the nation.

In 1649, following the beheading of King Charles I in January of that year, the radical Welsh preacher Vavasor Powell published a poem summing up his assessment of the political and religious turmoil of that momentous year. It contained these striking lines:

> Of all kings I am for Christ alone,
> For he is King to us though Charles be gone.[230]

Shortly before he wrote these words, an anonymous Scottish pamphlet-writer had urged the English parliament to overthrow King Charles because, in his view, there was a stark choice that lay before the people of the British Isles: "The quarrel is whether Jesus shal be King or no"? This went to the heart of the debate over the source of governmental power and raised questions over how it should be exercised in a period when increasingly large numbers of people thought that the second coming was imminent. As if that earlier question was not enough to shock readers out of any support for earthly monarchy, the Scottish pamphleteer hammered the message home. "O that England may never seek the death of crowned King Jesus! May never comply with dying Antichrist . . . ."[231] The choice, according to the Scottish pamphleteer, was stark: King Jesus or Antichrist (Charles I and earthly monarchs generally)? People must choose: either embrace God as King or subject themselves to the agent of the devil. The choice could not have been put more clearly and its millenarian tone was apparent to all.

Such millenarian preaching, often conducted by increasingly radicalized Presbyterian preachers, accelerated in the 1640s during the civil wars.[232] These preachers looked forward, with some enthusiasm, to the imminent suffering to be imposed on those who had once persecuted God's "saints." In this coming violence they saw the avenging sword of God about to fall on "this Babylonish company." This phrase was found in a pamphlet written by William Bridges, in 1641, and tellingly titled *Babylon's Downfall*.[233] The terminology drew on Revelation and on the Old Testament denunciations of Babylon. But now "Babylon" consisted of the royalist cause and all who lacked sufficient enthusiasm for the side of parliament and the Puritan-inspired purging of the nation in preparation for the return of Christ. This was no fringe radicalism; it was a view preached before Parliament and within the New Model Army, which was fighting the king and his eventual successor (Charles II). Such apocalyptic politics had become mainstream.

The prophecies revisited

The radical preaching was accompanied by a detailed search of prophetic texts in order to corroborate the political demands of those who had taken up arms against the king and the established church. A number of numerical calculations occurred in consideration of prophecy and its interpretation. These built on earlier interpretative traditions and applied them to contemporary events. Many involved speculation relating to Antichrist and similar figures.

The amount of time that the beast/false prophet/Antichrist would have power over the earth was taken to be "a time, and times, and half a time" (Rev 12:14). In Revelation, this period comes from a vision in which a symbolic woman (the church?) is pursued by a red dragon/serpent (the devil) who eventually gave power to the beast from the sea with ten horns and seven heads bearing blasphemous names (Rev 13:1–2). Some interpreted this as three-and-a-half years. Or as 1,260 days, since Revelation 12:6 used this number to describe the duration of the woman's time in the wilderness (protected from the dragon). However, there were widely differing views on this. Some read "days" as "years." This was based on the correlation of days with years in Numbers 14:34, in the Old Testament, where forty years in the wilderness matched forty days investigating the promised land. On this basis, and by starting the calculation in the fourth century AD with the supposed rise to power of the papacy (c. 390), it was expected that the downfall of Antichrist would occur in the 1650s. Some claimed corroboration for this interpretation in the number of 1,260 days also appearing as a time when "two witnesses" of God would declare his message (Rev 11:3); before being killed by the beast from the bottomless pit, and lying dead for three-and-a-half days (Rev 11:7–9). These repeated time-periods clearly echoed similar time-periods found in the book of Daniel; and their study led to varied interpretations.

Daniel 12:11 referred to when the daily sacrifice shall be taken away, and "the abomination that desolates is set up, there shall be one thousand two hundred and ninety days." Some took this period (1,290 days or three years and 195 days) as indicating the reign of Antichrist, since "the abomination that desolates" indicates blasphemous activities; and the time-period seemed similar to (though not the same as) the one in Revelation 12:14. This left the identity of Antichrist open to question, along with exactly when his reign would occur. As we shall see, there was competing speculation regarding this identification.

However, the *Geneva Bible* commentary (popular with many Puritans) considered it the period of time between Christ's death and his second coming. It also suggested that the timeframe simply meant "the time shall be long of Christ's second coming, and yet the children of God ought not to be discouraged" (since a literal length would have culminated in c. 1323).[234] This is a reminder that there was no settled consensus regarding how these numerical verses should be interpreted. Not even among committed Puritan writers.

Daniel 12:12 then added, "Happy are those who persevere and attain the thousand three hundred and thirty-five days." The addition of forty-five days was interpreted by the *Geneva Bible* commentators as simply meaning nobody could calculate Christ's second coming—and so be patient. However, to many others the end-times clock could be set running at the rise to power of anyone that they labelled Antichrist. Once done, the second coming would be expected about three-and-a-half years later. Such a precise timetable and end date was in direct contradiction of specific New Testament prohibitions concerning such a calculation. This did not stop the many who continued to engage in such speculations.

The radicalized end-times groups of the British Civil Wars

While millenarian ideas and end-times speculations were mainstream by the middle of the seventeenth century for many Protestants, there were those who took these beliefs to extremes. For some, this meant that their apocalyptic outlook was expressed through support for the godly cause of parliament and the New Model Army in the conflict with the royalists. However, others took the ideas in an even more radical direction. These envisaged an overturning of the social order, which soon brought them into conflict with more powerful (and they would have said, vested) interests within the Puritan cause. It was where the legacy of Münster conflicted with that of Geneva.

The Diggers

The group known as the Diggers called for nothing less than the total re-ordering of the system of land ownership in the country. In any period of history this would have been revolutionary, but when about 83 percent of the English population lived in the countryside in 1650, and wealth was still measured primarily in terms of land and agricultural products, the idea of the communalization of agriculture was truly shocking.

It is not, therefore, surprising that some modern writers have catego-rized the Diggers as seventeenth-century anarcho-communists. But their outlook went deeper than this. The first critic of the Digger community, which established itself at St George's Hill in Surrey, England, described one of its leaders, William Everard, as being, "once of the army but was cashiered, who termeth himself a prophet . . . ."[235] This is a telling descrip-tion and reminds us that, although the Diggers have become the historic "poster community" of the modern Left, they were people of their time and their politics had a theological underpinning. In January 1649, in the pamphlet entitled *The New Law of Righteousnes*, the Digger leader, Gerard Winstanley, promised that the economic order would change soon, since Christ would rise in his people and lead them to a more righteous rela-tionship with each other.

While a little vague, there is more than a hint of contemporary mil-lenarianism about this claim. This is clear from his terminology, where he explains "it is the fullness of time" and the "restorer of the earth" will soon "make the earth a common treasury" again.[236] Analysis of Old Testament prophecy and also the incarnational and eschatological language of the New Testament will pick up echoes of it in these words of Winstanley, as he looked forward to the transformation of the world order. For example, the reference to Christ's second coming, in Ephesians 1:10 refers to God's "plan for the *fullness of time* [italics added], to gather up all things in him, things in heaven and things on earth." Winstanley was prophesying the restora-tion of the earth and of fallen sinful society through the implementation of a communal ownership of the land. This was as eschatological as it was socio-political. It was realized eschatology.

The Digger manifesto—*The True Levellers Standard Advanced* or more formally titled *A Declaration to the Powers of England*—claimed that all the well-known Old Testament prophecies about the "restoration of Israel" (referring to justice and freedom from want) involved what these radicals called "digging" (communal agricultural work). The Diggers believed that the process they were starting on St George's Hill would be part of (perhaps even trigger) the restoration of the whole of fallen creation. How else should we interpret words of Everard such as "True religion and undefiled is to let everyone quietly have earth to manure"?[237] It is just too concrete an interpretation to conclude, as the historian Christopher Hill appeared to do, that this was primarily about the means to feed cattle over the winter; to have sufficient fertilizer for the land. While Hill claimed that, "'Manuring' is the crucial word in Winstanley's programme,"[238] it is more persuasive that the crucial operative words really were, "True religion and undefiled." The Digger program was not just about a reorganization of crop routines and improved cattle management. But it was eschatology that was less dramatic and supernatural than usually envisaged. For Winstanley, the second coming of Christ was not to be looked for in a dramatic event such as Christ coming in the clouds, as traditionally taught. Instead, he emphasized Christ "rising up" within the saints. This would restore humanity from its fallen state and would liberate society from its enslavement to private ownership. His 1648 pamphlet, entitled *The Saints Paradice*—which predated his Digger activities—reveals this. It is almost as if the act of digging would trigger supernatural agency. One can see this in statements such as, "The curse shall be lifted from the creation, fire, water, earth and air, . . . there shall be no barrenness in the earth or cattle, for they shall bring forth abundantly. Unseasonable storms of weather shall cease."[239]

Similarly, and earlier in 1648, he wrote a tract entitled *The Mystery of God*. In it he advanced a dispensationalist belief that he was living in the last-but-one dispensation and was awaiting the imminent restoration of creation by the action of God. This was clear evidence of his millenarian hopes. It was rooted in the idea that the Bible account and history generally are divided into discernible periods (dispensations) marked at beginning and end by events of great religious importance and, together, driving history forward to a point predetermined by God.

The prophetic nature of Winstanley's outlook is further emphasized by the way in which he described how the command "work together, eat bread together" was seen in a visionary experience. This was "receiving a word from the Lord," and was the kind of "prophesying" that irritated more mainstream seventeenth-century Protestants when they viewed the saints of the Independent churches and the gathered congregations. Despite this, the Diggers, in their time, had considerable reach. Many early Quaker communities in the English Midlands probably had Digger-connections to start with. However, this was suppressed by later Quakers who wanted to remove traces of the influence of the earlier movement from their own spiritual DNA.[240]

Winstanley's eschatological outlook survived as late as 1649. In that year he published *The True Levellers Standard Advanced*, in which he pondered on Revelation 12:14—where the rule of the dragon would last (as we examined earlier) for, "a time, and times, and half a time." In 1649, Winstanley was convinced that the time referred to was almost over and that momentous end-time events were imminent. But his confidence and faith in the impending transformation of all things did not last; and this later change in his outlook has masked his earlier eschatological beliefs.

In 1651 he was faced with the failure of his revolutionary venture. Local and national elites had swung into action. Toughs and soldiers had broken up the peaceful little Digger community. The power of property was asserted against the end-times hopes of the realized eschatology of the Diggers. It was then that Winstanley wrote a tract entitled *The Law of Freedom*, in which he proposed state action to bring in the necessary rural reforms. The radical hope was morphing into economic and social policy. He even dedicated it to Oliver Cromwell in the hope that he might look favorably on the concept. The plea was ignored. Winstanley's millenarian hopes seemed a distant memory, although only separated from his disillusionment by a couple of (traumatic) years as far as the Digger movement was concerned.

Soon he had abandoned all traditional forms of religion. This included: giving up prayer to an external God (since he now believed that God was within the individual); abandoning traditional concepts of heaven and hell; soon he even gave up using the term "God" and replaced it with the term "Reason." His drift from unconventional millenarian to Quaker (a sect which emphasized searching for God within) was apparent from this. In 1676 he was buried as a Quaker. By his death, God's kingship, for Winstanley, had become an inward matter and no longer implied the outward reordering of society. He no longer believed in the end times.

The Fifth Monarchy Men

There was no such ambiguity with regard to the Fifth Monarchy Men. This group was particularly active in the 1650s, during the Commonwealth and Protectorate periods, when Britain was a republic. Their distinctive name was derived from the content of Daniel 7:1–28, with its vision of four kingdoms (or monarchies) that would be succeeded by the rule of "one like a son of man" who would appear with the clouds of heaven and would be established as ruler of an eternal kingdom by the Ancient of Days. This constituted the Fifth Monarchy and was interpreted as referring to the millennial kingdom of Christ whose second coming was predicted in this vision of one like a son of man. Christ would reign on earth with his saints for one thousand years (the millennium we have already discussed), before the final judgement and the creation of a new heaven and a new earth.

The Fifth Monarchy Men were convinced that the prophesied time of the Fifth Monarchy was about to begin. Those, who believed this, would be instrumental in creating the context within which this Fifth Monarchy would be established. The story of this group reveals the direct application of belief in the rule of the saints, in which a form of government and society would see God established as the sole King on earth. As the "prophetess" Anna Trapnell put it, in 1654, in a pamphlet entitled *The Cry of a Stone*:

> Oh King Jesus thou art longed for,
> Oh take thy power and raign . . . .[241]

These members of the godly were determined to implement a theocracy of the saints ruling for, and then alongside, Christ himself.

As a consequence, they rather mixed premillennial and postmillennial beliefs since they both saw themselves as reigning as a revolutionary theocracy who were preparing the ground for Christ's return (a semi-postmillennial position) but also then ruling alongside Christ as the millennium unfolded (basically a premillennial stance).

Fifth Monarchists could be found among both Baptists and infant-baptizing Independents (derived from Church of England congregations); among Calvinists and believers in free will. As a consequence, they formed something of an umbrella organization that was united by its end-times focus. Meetings in Fifth Monarchist fellowships were characterized by prophesying and sharing of dreams and visions from God ("revelations"). Their most famous visionary was Anna Trapnell. In late 1653, she spent eleven days semi-conscious and uttering prophecies.

However, the Fifth Monarchists differed from many of their contemporaries among the godly in their very literal application of prophecies to contemporary events (especially the execution of the king); in their confident calculations of dates for the destruction of Antichrist; and in their extreme self-confidence and belief that they were the saints chosen by God to rule under Christ. They combined this with the belief that they were called to active insurrection. This muscular activism aimed to overthrow all worldly government, which they believed would be part of the process by which Christ's literal kingdom would be established on earth. Many were committed to violent acts in order to achieve this. Their declaration of 1656, for example, resolutely declared: "God's people must be a bloody people."[242] And they meant it. The Fifth Monarchist Mary Cary wrote a book tellingly entitled *The Little Horn's Doom and Downfall* (1651)—a title prompted by the prophecy of Daniel—in which she expressed her hatred for the rich and her willingness to fight them. In this, she clearly thought she was looking at life from the perspective of God as judge of the world. In sharp contrast, some other Fifth Monarchists were active but non-violent.

The question was: who was whom, in the realization of prophetic imagery? Mary Cary identified Charles as the little horn. In 1649, John Canne also claimed that Charles' execution, in January of that year, was the fulfilment of God's judgement on the fourth monarchy's little horn, fore-told in Daniel 7:21–22. Later, Fifth-Monarchist-inclined members of the parliamentary army made a similar assertion, in the 1650 *Declaration of Musselburgh*. They went on to state that they had "proclaimed Jesus Christ, the King of Saints, to be our King."[243]

Much of this rested on confidence that the final days had arrived or were imminent. Such dating was influenced by a calculation that 1,656 years elapsed between the creation of the world and the judgement of the flood and, so, 1656 was identified as a key year. This fairly arbitrary date suited those determined to see end-times events unfolding around them. In addition to this, the 1,260 days of the witnesses, in Revelation 11:3, were interpreted as years, starting in 396—when it was claimed that the pope had assumed political authority—and also culminating in 1656. This would not be the first time that arbitrary numerical interpretations would be made from prophetic verses; and then combined as if to provide ac-cumulating and corroborative evidence.

When this date passed, the year 1657 was chosen as it was three-and-a-half *literal years* since the start of the Protectorate (linked to the 1,260 days of Revelation and a similar number in Daniel). This identification labelled Cromwell as the beast or the little horn, since clearly this could no longer be applied to the defeated (and executed) Charles I. Such a switch-ing between *literal* and *symbolic* time-periods was somewhat arbitrary and not unique to this group.

The Fifth Monarchy Men took planning for the impending theocratic government seriously. After all, they believed that they would play a key part in it. Thinking they would initially rule on behalf of Christ, they were far from egalitarian. Some of them argued for an assembly elected by the "gathered churches" (the fellowships of which they approved). On the other hand, John Rogers wanted Cromwell to personally select godly co-rulers to make a modern Sanhedrin (the ancient Jewish ruling council). Clearly, he had not yet adopted the Cromwell-is-Antichrist view. John Spittlehouse wanted representatives chosen by the officers of the godly parliamentary army. Later he changed this to a call for Cromwell, as a second Moses, to select men. After the failure of the Barebone's Parliament (see below), many Fifth Monarchists came to the opinion that only they were loyal to Christ and so should rule for him. By the end of 1653 they were of one mind that Cromwell's protectorate was not the rule endorsed by God and referred to in the prophecies. Any last lingering support for Cromwell had evaporated.

When it came to the kind of society that such a theocracy should aim to establish, there were mixed outlooks. Some, like Mary Cary, identified the rich as the prime target of the godly. Others argued for the implementation of the Old Testament law of Moses. Others advocated the abolition of all existing titles; refused hat-honor (removing hats) to social "superiors"; and used the non-deferential terms "thee" and "thou" to these elites, as the Quakers did. Predictably this infuriated the judges, MPs, and army officers so addressed. Looking forward, it was envisaged that the elect (i.e., they themselves) would rule like kings.

Some Fifth Monarchists took a radical socio-economic line and wanted redistribution of land, accompanied by work schemes to assist the poor. Most, in contrast, believed in private property. None of them preached common ownership. In this they can be contrasted with the Diggers. They looked forward to God's transformation of health, weather, crop fertility, personal wealth, and social harmony in the new millennium.

The Quakers

Today, we would not think of the Society of Friends (Quakers) as a radical millenarian group. That is because a lot has changed since its seventeenth-century origins. For early Quakers, though, the struggle that a believer went through in the process of gaining spiritual enlightenment became known as the "Lamb's War." This echoed imagery from the book of

Revelation. For most Quakers, this inward experience of Christ replaced the expectation of the second coming in outward form that was held by almost all of the godly and was the driving belief of the Fifth Monarchy Men. However, this Quaker belief could still become quite radical in its application. For, if Christ was to be so fully known internally, then this could lead to perfect sanctification in this life. The Quaker leader Edward Burroughs put it this way: "the saints of God may be perfectly freed from sin in this life so as no more to commit it."[244]

This Quaker view of egalitarianism (at least for those considered enlightened) could, at times, be expressed in words that looked towards an attendant radical change to the social order. As Isaac Pennington expressed it in 1658,

> That which is high, that which is wise, that which is strong,
> that which is rich, that which is full, that which is fat:
> the Lord will lay low.[245]

However, unlike the Fifth Monarchists, the early Quakers did not devise a program of political action in order to trigger such a change. Rather, they looked to God to implement it. Such divine intervention would be brought about by the inner transformation of men and women, which then changed society, because Quaker millenarianism did not usually look to an outward second coming.

Despite this, the Quaker belief in enlightened perfectionism could still have some dramatic consequences for some individuals who felt that they had achieved a deep inner unity with Christ. In one famous case, at least, this re-envisaged a form of the second coming through realized eschatology. This occurred in 1656 in Bristol and involved a Quaker named James Nayler. One of his followers wrote of him: "Thy name shall no longer be James but Jesus" and another described him as "Thou lamb of God."[246] This was a combination of Quaker perfectionism and millenarian zeal. And it was heresy to any mainstream Christian, including most other Quakers. On Palm Sunday, 1656, Nayler entered Bristol in an imitation of Christ's Palm Sunday entry into Jerusalem. His followers laid branches before him and called out "holy, holy, holy" as he came into the city. This was the apocalypse lived out on the streets of an English town.

His contemporaries were horrified at these actions, and he was imprisoned and branded on the forehead with "B" for Blasphemy, his tongue was bored through, he was whipped through London and Bristol, placed in the pillory, and then subjected to indefinite confinement. The Quaker leadership, notably George Fox, disowned Nayler. This was clearly where eschatology met heresy. It was not a unique occurrence, as events at Münster had already shown.

Cromwell and an end-times theocracy

In 1651 Oliver Cromwell wrote a letter to John Cotton, the minister of the Puritan church in Boston, New England, expressing the excitement that many others around him also felt, "Surely, Sir, the Lord is greatly to be feared, as to be praised!" And he raised the question and its apparent answer: "What is the Lord a-doing? What prophecies are now fulfilling?"[247] That he believed that prophecies were being fulfilled seems clear from the letter. In the absence of anything more specific in this letter, and when compared with the equally non-specific language he used to the so-called Barebone's Parliament in 1653, it is fair to assume that he meant it in the most general terms: God was about to do (unspecified) wonders.

Cromwell was not a Fifth Monarchist and, unlike them, he did not make detailed claims about specific fulfilled prophecies. Nevertheless, he was confident that he stood on the cusp of a monumental movement of God that was of end-times significance. And, as part of this, he was convinced that a theocratic form of government should be established in order to facilitate the further fulfilment of prophecy.

Major-General Harrison—a Fifth Monarchist and a senior army officer—suggested to Cromwell that a ruling body should be established that was based on the Old Testament Sanhedrin of seventy members. The members of the new body should be carefully selected from among the saints. Being a Fifth Monarchist, Harrison firmly believed that such an assembly—which he thought was based on scriptural precedent—would pursue a godly agenda and would be the prelude to the establishment of the reign of Christ.

In the end, a modified version of Harrison's idea was accepted by Cromwell and the Army Council. As a result, in May 1653, letters from Cromwell and the Army Council were sent to Independent churches across England to nominate those they thought suitable for invitation to the new assembly. This caused great excitement among the most committed millenarians. Many Fifth Monarchists, at that point, declared that God had raised up Cromwell as a new Moses and that, as a result, he would lead the nation to a point where the reign of Christ on earth would be revealed.

When the nomination process was complete, a total of 140 men were selected for membership (129 from England, five from Scotland, and six from Ireland). A minority of them were from congregations with strong Fifth Monarchist sympathies. This parliament—which finally sat for just over five months—is now remembered as the "Barebone's Parliament," the "Nominated Parliament," or the "Parliament of Saints." The unusual first name is taken from the striking surname of one of its members: Praise-God Barebone. He represented the City of London.

Cromwell declared to the assembled members, "You are as like the forming of God as ever people were. . . . You are at the edge of promises and prophecies."[248] Millenarian excitement ran high. Addressing the opening of the Parliament, in July 1653, he further declared: "Truly God hath called you to this Work by, I think, as wonderful providences as ever passed upon the sons of men in so short a time." Reflecting on the convoluted path that had led to this point he revealingly concluded, "It's come, therefore, to you by the way of necessity; by the way of the wise Providence of God—through weak hands."[249] He was convinced that, though the road to this point had been twisting and difficult, a godly assembly had finally been formed. The future seemed to promise more wonders. But it was not to be.

The Barebone's Parliament met from July to December 1653. Never before had the Fifth Monarchists been so influential in national politics. While under 9 percent of the assembly were Fifth Monarchists,[250] they could find allies among other radicals on key issues. However, their influence would not last.

To begin with, these Fifth Monarchists members pursued a radical reform of the legal system and the total separation of church and state. With regard to the Anglo-Dutch War (1652–54) that was being fought, they hoped that it would spread across Europe until Rome fell and the pope was overthrown. But the Fifth Monarchists had reached the high watermark of their influence and now the political tide was turning. They lost the votes that aimed to abolish tithes and restrictions on public preaching. Despite this failure, the aims of these millenarian radicals alarmed those of a more conservative disposition. Within six months, the conservatives organized a vote for the dissolution of the assembly in December 1653. This critical vote occurred while the millenarians were absent at a prayer meeting. Soldiers then denied the radicals access to parliament. The rule of the saints was eventually replaced by the Army Council's Instrument of Government, which led to Cromwell becoming Lord Protector.

The Fifth Monarchists were shocked. One of them asserted that, by making himself Lord Protector, Cromwell "tooke the Crowne off from the heade of Christ, and put it upon his owne."[251] Another, Vavasor Powell, asked rhetorically: "Lord, wilt thou have Oliver Cromwell or Jesus Christ to reign over us?"[252]

Earlier, in May 1653, preachers at Blackfriars in London had declared that they had been told "by revelation" of the urgent "necessity of Monarchy in this Nation but bestowed it . . . on a new Line [King Jesus]."[253] This miraculous establishment of Christ's kingdom would be triggered by the rule of the saints. Some believed that Christ would appear and reign; others that he would appear and then leave the rule to the saints; others that the saints would rule until Christ appeared after one thousand years; yet others thought the saints would rule until perfection had been achieved and only then would Christ appear. But now the assembly embodying these hopes was no more.

Cromwell countered with, "A notion I hope we all honour, and wait and hope for: that Jesus Christ will have a time to set up his reign *in our hearts* [italics added]."[254] That was not how the Fifth Monarchists envisaged it. They now began plotting Cromwell's downfall, and his replacement by King Jesus (whose reign would initially be revealed by themselves taking political power). Accompanying this was a reworking of prophetic identifications. The Fifth Monarchist prophetess, Anna Trapnell, declared that those who did the bidding of the protectorate were "of the Beast."[255] This was comparable to a Fifth Monarchist resolution of 1656, which identified Cromwell as the "little horn" of Daniel's prophecy (earlier identified as Charles I).[256] Cromwell struck back. Leading millenarians were imprisoned or removed from military commands. Two millenarian plots against Cromwell failed: in 1657 and then in 1659. The ringleader of the 1657 one, Thomas Venner, was imprisoned (he was only released when the protectorate ended in 1659).

For those who had looked to see the reign of Christ established on earth in the 1650s, the decade had ended with deep disappointment. And worse was to come.

11

Years of Disappointment and Re-Thinking

1660 to 1918

THE STUART RESTORATION OF 1660 led to a collapse of widespread radical millenarian activities in Britain. But this was, by no means, an end to it. In 1661 and 1685 there were millenarian uprisings in England. However, a high watermark had been reached in the 1650s and what came after was a retreat from such millenarian confidence.

The same apocalyptic mood permeated the Puritan settlements of New England in the 1640s and 1650s, but here it did not suffer the same degree of decline as the century wore on. Then, in North America, the "Great Awakening" (c. 1720–40s) and the "Second Great Awakening" (c. 1795–1835) both included end-times enthusiasm. In fact, the nineteenth century laid the foundation for many beliefs about the end times, and approaches to both prophecy and politics, that remain highly influential—especially in the USA and UK—in the twenty-first century. From there, these ideas have spread globally. Consequently, the period saw a shift from disappointment to re-thinking that was foundational for modern ideas.

In addition, this American millenarianism eventually led to a number of new religious movements, such as the Seventh-day Adventists, the Mormons, and the Jehovah's Witnesses. In each one of these movements, a strong emphasis on the end-times was a defining feature and remains so.

The shock of the Restoration in Britain

If the protectorate of Oliver Cromwell was deeply disappointing to millenarian radicals, then the restoration of Charles II in 1660 was devastating. Fifth

Monarchists who were guilty of regicide were hanged, drawn, and quartered in October 1660. Others of the group were imprisoned as the sect was driven further underground by vengeful royalists. On his way to his execution, a bystander shouted at ex-Major-General, and Fifth Monarchist, Thomas Harrison: "Where is your Good Old Cause now?" Harrison replied, "Here in my bosom, and I shall seal it with my blood."[257] Other accounts indicate he claimed that he would soon return with Christ, to judge those who had so recently judged and condemned him. It was not to be.

The catastrophe of 1660 was the latest blow to eschatologically driven millenarianism; for while the restoration of Charles II was regarded by them as the ultimate failure of godly rule, it came about precisely because nobody among the godly had definitively established what form godly rule should take. The most radical of the millenarians had been certain that the death of Charles I would usher in an era when God would rule. This had influenced Cromwell's outlook too. However, all had failed to implement a coherent or consistent plan of what this meant in practice. The most radicalized, like the Fifth Monarchists, had aspirations, but few consistent programs.

Ultimately, this was because their reading of prophecy was so wide of the mark. In order to occur, these hoped-for events required God himself to directly intervene to establish his rule. Even the more postmillennialist among the radicals assumed a supernatural intervention that would eventually confirm and complete the cause they were implementing. Few actually assumed that they would need to wait one thousand years to see this (they were only semi-post-millennialist in practice). But whether this meant the visible and actual second coming of Christ, the transformative theocracy of the Puritan saints, or the revelation of God's will through providential signs and dramatic social change was never established. The second and third possibilities were open to much debate as to whether they were actually happening. Only the first was unequivocal and, even there, there was fierce disagreement over how to interpret its imminence or otherwise. Consequently, internal conflict was inadvertently hardwired into the whole eschatological system of the millenarian godly.

Then the Restoration proved that all the eschatological speculation had been in error. Or had it? As so often in the recent and more distant past, the collapse of specific claims did not lead to a questioning of the whole project of calculation, identification, and speculation. While some were disillusioned and drifted away, others doubled down on new calculations and identifications. This remains a recognizable feature of such enterprises throughout history.

The last millenarian uprisings in England

In January 1661, a couple of leading Fifth Monarchists, Thomas Venner and Vavasor Powell, led an abortive uprising in London against Charles II. Over the course of four days the revolt, led by Venner, caused panic. The evocative battle cry of the uprising was: "King Jesus and the heads upon the gates."[258] The revolt was finally put down with the deaths of some twenty-two of the rebels. Later, another twenty were executed. These including Venner himself, who was hanged, drawn, and quartered. In the face of such resolute government action and the failure of their prophetic hopes to materialize (the significant year of 1666 did not prove to be of end-times significance) the Fifth Monarchy movement rapidly faded away. Many of its members drifted into Baptist churches or into Nonconformist Congregational churches.

It was over, but it was not over. Not quite. There are, in fact, reports of some Fifth Monarchist activity continuing as late as the 1680s. A Fifth Monarchist was among those who stole the Crown Jewels from the Tower of London in 1671. Then a small group of Fifth Monarchists, which including the son of Thomas Venner, took part in Monmouth's Rebellion, of 1685, against King James. The Duke of Monmouth—the illegitimate son of Charles II—landed at Lyme Regis in Dorset with only three small ships and eighty-two men. The poorly prepared invasion lacked money, weapons, and other supplies, and it ended badly. But before it did so, millenarian beliefs were noted among his West Country followers,[259] with a Fifth Monarchist tasked with raising London for the cause.[260] It looked as if the army of saints was again on the march, as in the 1640s. However, this one lacked the equipment and the leadership necessary for victory and it all ended in disaster at the Battle of Sedgemoor in July 1685. The army was scattered. Then, in the so-called "Bloody Assize" that followed the defeat, hundreds were hanged, drawn, and quartered (including some of my own ancestors). Monmouth, as a noble, was beheaded. Political millenarianism would be taken off the agenda in Britain. However, across the Atlantic the story was only just beginning.

The millenarian contribution to the cultural DNA of the USA

Despite the fame of the Mayflower Pilgrims of 1620, most of the godly who emigrated to North America travelled there in the decade 1630–40 (triggered by the personal rule of Charles I and mounting pressure on Puritans). It was a movement that has become known as "the Great Migration." In this movement of godly colonists, perhaps the most important occurred in 1630 when John Winthrop led the so-called "Winthrop Fleet," which contained seven hundred colonists on eleven ships, to settle at what became Boston.

While the Pilgrims were "separating Puritans," who wished to break away from the established English church, most who came after them were "non-separating Puritans," who wanted semi-independence while still being part of an overarching ecclesiastical body. What all had in common was a clear sense of being called to North America by God. As Winthrop explained to his companions on the sea voyage to the New World, their colony should be a "City upon a hill" (Matt 5:14) in the words of the Geneva Bible that he and others of the godly used. The kind of theocracy, which would later be explored by members of the 1653 Barebone's Parliament, looked like it really might be constructed in New England. In their view, "they were a new Chosen People of God destined to found a New Jerusalem—a New City of God in the midst of the wilderness."[261] The idea was redolent with end-times implications. However, this involved a complex mixture of biblical themes.

On one hand, they imagined themselves as a New Israel crossing the Jordan River (in this construct, the Atlantic Ocean). So, Increase Mather, in 1676, wrote of, "the Heathen People amongst whom we live, and whose Land the Lord God of our Fathers has given to us for a rightful possession."[262] They had embarked on a seventeenth-century exodus, leaving sinful "Egypt" (or "Babylon" in other re-workings of biblical terminology) behind them. They spoke of a "New England Canaan," as part of their reimagining of themselves in the role of God's chosen people, embarking on the conquest of a new promised land.[263] In this construct, the indigenous peoples were presented at idolaters, slated for extermination. This could fit a historicist perspective on prophecy as it was being fulfilled across the broad sweep of history.

However, there was also a futurist and eschatological aspect to this, for they believed that North America had become a new sacred space within God's plan for history.[264] In this sense, it was an "American Israel," playing a key role in the events leading to the second coming of Christ.[265] Increase Mather, in 1676, saw America as a forerunner of the New Jerusalem. Fellow Bostonian, Samuel Sewall, in 1697, thought that "the seat of the Divine Metropolis" might be in North America not the Middle East.[266] This had echoes of the "supersessionism" and "replacement theology" that we have seen had developed over the first four centuries of the Christian era. It became a vital ingredient in the development of US nativism and "American exceptionalism."

However, some Puritan preachers did not subscribe fully to the "American Israel" construct and looked instead for the conversion of the original Israel—the Jews—and their return to the Middle East as a key component of the end times.[267] Then, as now, navigating the complex landscape of providential history could be complex.

Key features of the ideology of the twenty-first-century evangelical right in the USA—influencing its national, as well as eschatological, outlook—can be traced back to these formative years of the mid-seventeenth century.[268]

Later, in the nineteenth century, the Mormon movement (The Church of Jesus Christ of Latter-day Saints) would take this relocation of Israel to North America in a very different direction and to another level. This was by claiming (as found in *The Book of Mormon*) that a migration of Jewish tribes to North America had occurred in the distant past. In this, "it shifts the center of the Judeo-Christian world away from the Near East and places it in North America." The eschatological implications of this are such that "Israel and America are conflated . . . to an unprecedented extent" and through the second coming—and reinstatement of a paradise-earth—"this paradise will have its origin point and center in the United States."[269] The role played by *The Book of Mormon*, and other documents only accepted as canonical within Mormonism, means that Mormon eschatology and its details lie beyond the boundaries of this study of the end-times as viewed from a biblical basis. However, it should be added that the Mormon view has much in common with the wider tradition and references the biblical prophecies (expanded by particular Mormon literature). "The end," in Mormon theology, is essentially premillennial and involves: great signs announcing its imminence; translation of the righteous; the visible second coming of Christ; staged resurrections; judgement and the cleansing of the earth; recognition of Jesus as God's true Messiah by the Jews; the theocratic rule by Christ during the millennium; final release of the devil, followed by his destruction by the archangel Michael and the saints; final judgement and restoration of the earth, as it is "celestialized" to be the dwelling place of God and Christ with the righteous. When tied to the claimed eschatological significance of Mormon experiences during the nineteenth century, the overall nature of the second coming takes on the nature of a process (eventually leading to Christ's revelation in glory and then the unfolding judgements and transformations of the earth) and not one single event.[270] Many of the futuristic details are outlined in the Mormon *Doctrine and Covenants*; but Mormonism does not calculate or speculate with regard to the date of this, very Americanized, second coming.

To return to the Puritan legacy within mainstream Christianity: in the eighteenth century the original Puritan stream was much diluted in the emerging colonies of North America, but its influence never went away. The 1730s and 1740s witnessed the beginning of a number of religious revivals. The first became known as the "Great Awakening." This meant that the Puritan legacy gained a new buoyancy and influence. The attendant apocalyptic expectation lasted until after the American Revolution.[271] The Massachusetts preacher Jonathan Edwards (died 1758) believed the millennium was approaching, but he took a postmillennialist stance, believing that Christ would return *after* an age of grace, "that glorious work of God" which would "renew the world of mankind."[272] This would probably begin in America and would culminate in the second coming of Christ.

The Great Awakening had a number of cultural effects. The first was the continued influence of the Puritan sermon's denunciation of current sin and its focus on future transformation (sometimes termed a "jeremiad," after the Old Testament prophet, Jeremiah). The second was a continued influence of the Puritan emphasis on personal sin and salvation, and an individual calling that was married to a sense of national destiny. This was certainly not simple theological or ecclesiastical continuity, since huge changes occurred in American churches and culture in the eighteenth century. It was more the continued influence of an outlook, an idea, which survived through this period of change and has had remarkable longevity.

The movement that came out of the Great Awakening flowed across the boundaries of individual church communities and created something of a common evangelical identity that would have a lasting effect on large areas of the church in the eventual USA (as in the UK). It contributed significant aspects to that emerging cultural DNA. This "could encompass both the pursuit of supernatural signs and spiritual manifestations and the systematic study of the Bible and the natural order and the logical thought which accompanied it."[273]

The continuity of imagery and outlooks could be viewed in surprising areas. When the British Parliament passed the Boston Port Act in 1774 (a response to the Boston Tea Party)—to force the town to compensate the royal treasury and East India Company for losses incurred—several local ministers announced a fast day and preached against the British crown as a tool of "Satan," who had unleashed King George, "the great Whore of Babylon," to ride her "great red dragon" upon America.[274] "The language was taken from the verbal toolbox of millenarianism which had been used by earlier saints to condemn their enemies in prophetic terms drawn from the Bible."[275] Now it was being deployed against King George III.

Eschatology went hand-in-hand with American patriotism; and among its more extreme exponents looked forward to "a star-spangled Millennium."[276] In 1776, Timothy Dwight (grandson of Jonathan Edwards) hailed the new state in the words of Isaiah: "Arise, shine, for thy light is come." He looked forward to two centuries of US progress, which would climax in the year 2000.[277]

In the nineteenth century, the westward advance of the frontier, which became known as "Manifest Destiny," owed much to both the individualistic personal self-confidence, and the sense of providentially approved community purpose, that was inherited from the earlier national myth. "It satisfyingly justified the precocious confidence of a newly minted and assertive state."[278]

This was greatly enhanced by the "Second Great Awakening," which influenced large areas of US society between 1800 and the 1830s. It made evangelical outreach and enthusiasm a major part of what it meant to be an American Christian. By the late 1850s, the idea of the revivalist camp meeting had become engrained across America and was also well known on the expanding frontier.[279] Within this, eschatological expectation played a significant part. This was because, in North America as in Britain, the years of disappointment had given way to a radical re-thinking with regard to prophecy and the course of world and salvation history.

The triumph of dispensationalism

During the nineteenth century, ideas were developed that continue to shape eschatological thinking across wide areas of the church in the twenty-first century. Today, most of those for whom the study of prophecy is a major part of their teaching and preaching hold to a doctrine known as the "pre-tribulation rapture." In fact, as we will see in a later chapter, this is taken as a given in most modern end-times teaching and in constructing timelines of events leading to the second coming of Christ. The belief forms part of a wider set of ideas that constitute a literalist eschatological belief known as "premillennial dispensationalism," which is now the norm among most students of prophecy. It may come as a surprise to many of these teachers, preachers, and writers that this very precise belief (as it is now held) is a comparatively new addition to end-times thinking and dates from the nineteenth century in its current form. In fact, it would have puzzled many—if not most—earlier believers in the second coming. This is because it was a doctrine that was largely unknown for the bulk of Christian history, until the nineteenth century. And when it was touched on in earlier periods, it was not the centerpiece of the end-times timeframe that it now is. Suggestions that evidence for it can be found in some aspects of the writings of Irenaeus (second century), Victorinus (fourth century), Joseph Mede (seventeenth century), and Increase Mather (seventeenth to eighteenth century) do not challenge the general conclusion that it did not form a central part of church eschatology.[280] Even the most committed modern exponents of rapture theology struggle to add many theologians to this very limited list, despite two thousand years of church history and thought.[281] The nineteenth century changed that.[282]

We will look at it in more detail later but, put simply, dispensationalism holds that God has two covenant relationships with two different groups of people: the Jews and the Christian church. These two relationships form part of two dispensations in salvation history. The idea of the pre-tribulation rapture is that the church (meaning those who are "true believers") will be instantly and supernaturally removed from the earth prior to the culmination of a time of unprecedented terrible judgement and suffering (the tribulation), which will immediately precede the second coming of Christ. With the church no longer on the earth, God's covenant relationship with the Jews (which has never been abandoned) will, in effect, be revived and will come center-stage in salvation history. Jews will accept Jesus as the Messiah; other people too (not previously part of the church) will also do so. Then Christ will return. The belief is closely related to the view that the establishment of the State of Israel is a key point in the last days and in God's end-times relationship with the Jewish people. It is also closely associated with condemnation of the visible church as being largely apostate (and so constituting part of "Babylon"); fallen from purity in its doctrines and practices; and soon to be shaken and divided by the removal of "true believers" from its ranks as a result of the rapture. This has been summed up as offering: "reward for a faithful Church, a future for the Jews, and wrath for the apostate and ungodly." As such, it has been posited that the doctrine performs the function of "neatly tying together a number of eschatological loose ends."[283] The scriptural base that is claimed for this and its impact on modern outlooks will be examined in another chapter. At this stage, we will simply examine how it first emerged as a developed doctrine.

Arguably, the first formulation of the idea (as we would now recognize it) occurred in the writing and preaching of Edward Irving and the Albury Prophecy Conferences; and was drawn to the attention of a wider readership through their publication, The Morning Watch.[284] Between 1823 and 1831 Irving was a well-known London preacher and led one of the largest congregations in the city: the Church of Scotland Caledonian Church at Hatton Garden. The idea in question was sometimes referred to as a "secret [original italics] rapture of the Church at a secret coming [of Christ],"[285] since it was thereby differentiated from the open events of Christ's final appearance, which would be witnessed by all people. This idea was promulgated in publications, such as in Irving's introduction to The Coming of the Messiah in Glory and Majesty (1826). The word "rapture" was first used to describe the translation (rather than death) of Christians, as the way by which they will meet the Lord, in the June 1830 edition of The Morning Watch.

Irving, along with a number of his contemporaries, felt that something significant had occurred in terms of end-times events during the period 1789–93[286] (at the time of the upheavals of the French Revolution) and its aftermath. Irving believed that the 1,260-year rule of "Babylon" (Rev 11:3; 12:6)—the Catholic Church—had ended in 1792.[287] This rule had also represented the "little horn" of Daniel 7. He believed he lived in a period of trial that would last for seventy-five years. This time would see the Jews restored to the promised land and would culminate in the second coming in 1867.[288] Given the turmoil of the revolutionary and then Napoleonic wars, and the economic, political, and social turbulence that continued to affect

Europe in the decade after the final defeat of Napoleon, it is perhaps not surprising that some students of prophecy sought to identify these events in Scripture. They also projected on events their own prejudices, such as when they saw campaigns for the political emancipation of Catholics in the UK as evidence of collaboration with "Babylon."[289] Irving preached that the bowl of wrath poured by the seventh angel (Rev 16:17) would soon occur.[290] This would then be the prelude to the rapture and then the tribulation, which came immediately prior to the second coming.

Although the belief is now a given among modern students of prophecy, it was strongly criticized by some at the time and in the century afterwards. This criticism could go as far as claiming that the belief was held by "no one in all Christian History from the Apostles to Edward Irving,"[291] and "is not taught in the Bible."[292] The intensity of this opposition is exemplified in the further accusations (underpinning both these attacks on the belief) that the new theology originated in the statements of women prophets among Irving's company and that this was due to spiritual influence that was not of God. How much of this attack was due to opposition to the belief itself, and how much to the idea of woman prophets, their speaking in tongues, and the eventual accusation of heresy levelled against Irving's Christology (he was excommunicated from the Church of Scotland and removed from his post in 1830–31) is difficult to disentangle. But it is clear that the belief generated considerable heat from some who opposed it. This is why the impact of John Nelson Darby (see below) is so important, because his work lifted the doctrine out of the tangled and controversial context of Irving and his associates. Nevertheless, it has been argued that Irving played a major part in shifting the interpretation of prophecy in Britain from postmillennialism (Christ will appear *after* the prophesied millennium) to premillennialism (Christ will first appear and *then* instigate the millennium).[293] That Irving and the Albury Conferences had a big influence on early Brethren gatherings is clear.[294] And these early Brethren conferences were attended by Darby, who would prove highly influential in later prophetic analysis.[295]

While it seems correct to argue that the roots of this doctrine in its current form stretch back to Irving, it was Darby whose work hugely extended the reach of the belief and popularized it in North America; and whose work then proved highly influential in the twentieth century and beyond. Other proponents of the belief were keen to separate Darby from earlier work by Irving since rejection of Irving's orthodoxy by the Church of Scotland threatened to taint the concept. As a result, the idea is now almost always assumed to have originated with Darby and to have had no connection to the writings and statements of Irving and his associates. Darby was later to state that he himself had held these beliefs since 1827; but there is persuasive evidence pointing to his being somewhat undecided as late as 1843. Nevertheless, he had clearly been reflecting on the matter since the 1830s and the roots of the concept (for him at least) can be dated from there.[296]

Darby had a huge influence on dispensationalism in the UK and in the USA, such that by the 1870s it had become popular across many church groups. In the early years of the twentieth century, it would contribute to the development of fundamentalism in the USA and then to Christian Zionism. After belief in premillennialism had received a severe shock in the 1840s (see below), this later surge in dispensationalism would put the belief once more centerstage in eschatological studies.[297] And it has remained so.

Darby (died 1882) renounced his ordination in the Church of England and became a founder member of the Plymouth Brethren. With a focus on biblical literalism and premillennialism, he went on to found a more exclusive group within the Brethren and travelled widely in the USA. This brought the idea of the pre-tribulation rapture and belief in the related but different dispensations of the Jews and the church to a wide audience and readership. The spread of this message was accelerated by the publication of the *Scofield Reference Bible* in 1909, in which Cyrus Ingersoll Scofield incorporated many of Darby's ideas in his annotations. In the same way that the commentary found in the *Geneva Bible* had influenced the outlook and interpretation of prophecy among seventeenth-century Puritans, the *Scofield Reference Bible* influenced (and continues to influence) biblical literalists across the globe (but especially in the USA). By 1943 it had sold two million copies and remains in print and highly popular. In fact, in 2011 it seems that it had become the best-selling book in the five-hundred-year history of the Oxford University Press and the best-selling reference Bible in US history with over ten million sales, although strict verification is difficult to achieve.[298] But the point is clear: it has sold a huge number of copies and influenced a vast number of people. Today, dispensationalism is a global religious phenomenon and dominates prophetic belief, with tens of millions of adherents. And the *Scofield Reference Bible* played a major part in that process.

It is difficult to overstress the significance of such reference Bibles since they inculcate particular interpretations of Scripture so firmly in the minds of regular users that the interpretation can become as familiar as the scriptural text itself. This process also means that texts are often assumed to have one clear significance and way to be interpreted (i.e., that espoused in the references), which informs (both consciously and unconsciously) the scriptural worldview of the reader. In this way, we can hear echoes of *Scofield* in the work of later writers of popular religious books, such as Hal Lindsey, Edgar C. Whisenant, and Tim LaHaye; and in the preaching of Billy Graham, and later US evangelical preachers to the present day. Those who read and accept the *Scofield* references engage with a confident quantification and classification in which an almost scientific methodology has been applied to literalist and fundamentalist interpretations of the Bible in general and prophecy in particular. The effects of this are profound.

"The Great Disappointment"

A striking example of both the impact of end-times beliefs in the USA and the way that communities espousing them are capable of overcoming apparently catastrophic errors in predicting the second coming can be found in the early history of the group that became the Seventh-Day Adventists.

In the 1830s, the followers of Baptist minister William Miller proclaimed that the second coming would occur in 1843 or 1844. Under Miller's influence they had developed an approach towards the letters to the seven churches, found in Revelation chapters 2 and 3, which identified them as referring to different stages in the history of the church. This approach could be traced back to the writings of the Puritan Thomas Brightman (died 1607). According to this historicist construction, the Millerites thought they were living in the Age of the Church of Laodicea (a lukewarm church that, famously, was neither hot nor cold). This final age was to last from 1798 to 1843–44.[299] Like the Brethren, the Millerites were premillennialists and, in the USA, this was a shift from the postmillennialist position that had been common in North America since the influential preaching of Jonathan Edwards. In this earlier view there was a tendency to see history closing with more and more people converting and then the prophesied millennium finally *culminating* in the return of Christ.[300] However, in the nineteenth century the tectonic plates of prophetic study moved.

The influence of the Millerites was huge and vast numbers of people expected the coming end. The timeframe was eventually narrowed down further and the date set at 22 October 1844. This was based on Daniel 8:14, which referred to 2,300 "days" occurring before the sanctuary is cleansed. This, Miller believed (one might add without any direct scriptural evidence), referred to the second coming of Christ. This was then converted from days into years—an arbitrary decision, it might be argued, given that Daniel specifically refers to "evenings and mornings," but one often adopted in such calculations. Miller dated this from Artaxerxes' decree to rebuild the Jerusalem temple. Miller believed this was in 457 BC and so the date 1844 emerged. The precise date of 22 October was chosen as it was the Day of Atonement (*Yom Kippur*) in 1844 and Christ, as High Priest of the new covenant (as in the letter to the Hebrews), would appear (it was claimed) on this day.[301] There is no scriptural basis for this dating of the second coming to be associated with the Jewish Day of Atonement, but it soon gained considerable traction. However, even this precise date had hidden complications, since the Millerites took it from the minority-Jewish Karaite calendar, not the rabbinic Jewish calendar.[302] The latter would have given a different date of 23 September; with *Yom Kippur* beginning on the evening of 23 September in the Jewish reckoning of the duration of days.[303]

The second coming did not occur and the event became known as "The Great Disappointment." Many drifted out of the movement as a result of this, but others remained and, in 1863, became the Seventh-Day Adventist Church. Miller had been expelled from the Baptist Church and died in 1849.

These early Seventh-Day Adventists advanced a re-worked view of Miller's interpretation of prophecy that, in its revised form, stated that something significant had occurred in 1844—*but in the invisible, heavenly realm*. A trigger-event had indeed happened (Christ had come to cleanse the sanctuary of heaven); and so the second coming was still imminent.[304] This heavenly transition point was impossible to objectively prove (unlike the event that had actually been expected in 1844 but had not occurred), but it became a way of moving on from "The Great Disappointment" while still remaining a community defined by its emphasis on eschatology, although no longer setting a date. Rather than admitting a terrible mistake had occurred, they refocused their efforts based on the revised understanding of what had (they now claimed) occurred in 1844. Some, in a splinter-group called the Second Adventists, even named a new date for the second coming: 1873/4.[305]

Similarly, the debacle of 1844 did not diminish their confidence that they represented the true church, as defined by their keeping of the Jewish Sabbath (on Saturday), rather than Sunday, as the rest of the global Christian community. Indeed, their official position was that the keeping of Sunday was a defining feature of the apostate church (which was, as a consequence, "Babylon"). Keeping Sunday was seen as the mark of the beast and the Catholic Church (surprisingly in alliance with mainline Protestant churches) had adopted this "mark."[306] Eventually these organizations, it was claimed, will compel the world to mark Sunday as a sacred day. This will occur at the behest of Antichrist. This will be the deciding characteristic of who is in the true church (keeping Sabbath/Saturday) and who is not (keeping Sunday).[307] Those who refuse to obey this law will be persecuted, culminating in the second coming and the *start* of the millennium. The preceding time of tribulation is sometimes known as the "time of Jacob's trouble." This was a novel interpretation of what was meant by the mark of the beast.

At the second coming, the living righteous will be translated and the righteous dead will be resurrected. This constitutes the "first resurrection" (Rev 20:5). Both groups of the righteous will be taken to heaven to reign with Christ for one thousand years. This is a very unusual version of the millennium belief. During this time, the punishment of the wicked will be determined. The rest of mankind (that is, the unrighteous) will die but not be judged at the time of the second coming. During the millennium (while the righteous are with Christ in heaven), the devil and his angels will occupy the earth. This is how the binding of the devil is understood. At the end of the thousand years, Christ will return with the righteous; the wicked will then rise from death (the "second resurrection") to surround Jerusalem in the company of the devil. There they will face judgement and annihilation through fire coming down from heaven (Rev 20:9) and in the lake of fire (Rev 20:15). The devil and his angels will be destroyed in the lake of sulfur and fire (Rev 20:10). It is then that the New Jerusalem will be established, having come down from heaven (Rev 21:10) and the earth will be remade. There the righteous will live forever in a world without sin.[308] With variations, these beliefs have informed the eschatology of the Seventh-Day Adventists since the mid-nineteenth century. (Seventh-Day

Adventists, it should be noted, do not accept the traditional doctrine of hell as a place of conscious eternal punishment.)

At about the same start-point, and in the same aftermath of "The Great Disappointment," another group was started that, like the Seventh-Day Adventists, responded to the failure of specific end-times predictions by doing more of the same. This was the beginning of a movement that eventually became the Jehovah's Witnesses. In 1879 the early group first began to publish a magazine entitled *Zion's Watch Tower and Herald of Christ's Presence*. The movement also began to believe that it was the true church, although their non-Trinitarian Christology separated them from mainstream Christianity as it had defined itself since the Late Roman Empire. Like the earlier Millerites, they also named a date: 1914. Prior to this, the Jews would return to Palestine (this had started as a result of nineteenth-century Zionism); then in 1914 God would begin to directly rule the earth. These ideas were expounded in a series of books entitled *The Millennial Dawn*, between 1889 and 1904.[309]

The date of 1914 was clearly hugely significant in world history, but it did not see the second coming. However, the tumultuous events suggested to followers that the prediction was not entirely invalid. The outbreak of the war was interpreted as the *start* of God's decisive end-times actions, with the final date identified as 1918. But that date saw the end of the war, not the beginning of Christ's reign on earth. However, the year 1914 was then reinterpreted as the start of the *"invisible* rule" of Christ.[310] As with the Seventh-Day Adventists, what had once been clearly predicted in concrete terms was reworked as an *invisible* event, rather than judged a predictive error. As in so much in the history of erroneous eschatological calculations, *plus ça change.*

As well as having a Christology that set them apart from the mainstream of Christian creedal orthodoxy, the Jehovah's Witnesses developed a version of the premillennial belief that mixed traditional views with new interpretations: first, the Battle of Armageddon and the victorious return of Christ; a millennial period of time on earth, but one in which the devil will test the veracity of the faith of the saved; a final judgement and the destruction of the devil and those who have failed during the millennium; then everlasting life for the fully saved on a transformed earth; while an elite 144,000 will rule with God in heaven (an interpretation based on Revelation 7:4 and 14:1–3).[311] This interpretation of the meaning of the 144,000 is particularly associated with the Jehovah's Witnesses.

This brings us into the twentieth century; a century that saw new developments in radical eschatological thinking and the global communication of these ideas. The legacy of that is very influential in the contemporary world, with significant political ramifications in a number of areas. So, to developments in the twentieth century we now turn.

12

From the Second World War to the "End of History"

1945 to 1991

IT IS CLEAR THAT, over two thousand years, many who applied end-times prophecies to their contemporary situation felt strongly that these ancient texts resonated with current events. The ability to do this, regardless of the failure of such applications in the past, is one of the striking characteristics of communities focused on applied eschatology.

However, it can plausibly be argued that the situation since 1945 has been significantly different to the previous two millennia. For the first time in history, humans have the ability to obliterate life using weapons that were undreamed of in the past. Fire raining from the sky, great clouds of smoke, vast destruction, unimaginably large numbers of casualties, appalling sickness, are the hallmarks of nuclear warfare. It is not surprising that the threat of this has been seen as the fulfilment of prophecies that, in the past, were considered to only be possible due to direct divine intervention. Now, it seems, the judgement that falls on the world could be the direct result of human action.

A number of commentators have suggested that nuclear warfare is referred to in 2 Peter 3:10: "But the day of the Lord will come like a thief, and then the heavens will pass away with a loud noise, and the elements will be dissolved with fire, and the earth and everything that is done on it will be disclosed." Wilbur M. Smith's booklet *This Atomic Age and the Word of God* (November 1945) was based on this interpretation and reached a wider audience via a condensed version published in the *Reader's Digest* in January 1946. An expanded book, with the same title, was published in

1948.[312] More recently, climate change has the potential to radically affect all life on the planet. Suddenly, the apocalyptic scenarios have become very imaginable in the here and now.

In the generation that followed 1914 the interpretation of prophecy shifted dramatically in favor of premillennialism.[313] Postmillennial optimism was difficult to sustain in the face of the capacity for destruction that was demonstrated in the first half of the twentieth century. As Scofield commented in 1918: "The prophetic Word . . . [gives] not the least warrant for the expectation that the nations . . . will or can make a permanent peace."[314]

This trend towards a premillennialist outlook has increased since the end of the Second World War. It has encouraged the belief that we do, indeed, now live in the last days. The premillennial perspective has been further energized by globalization. Then there are the interconnections brought by the expansion of information technology, the worldwide web, and social media. In addition, complex financial arrangements and instruments involve millions in networks of economic interactions and dependency. The idea that global institutions could malignly control the lives of the human population is easier to envisage. In addition, supranational bodies such as the United Nations and the European Union have drawn nations closer together but have also excited opposition from those who see in them the potential platforms of international power from which Antichrist will operate. That the latter occupies an area including territories that once formed part of the Roman Empire has only added to this interpretation.

None of this means that the second coming must be imminent. However, these factors help explain the fresh explosion of interest in the topic. And, without doubt, many of these developments are unprecedented and thought-provoking. Furthermore, the development of widespread literacy across the globe, and the rise of mass media, has meant that these ideas have spread to an extraordinary degree. What Caxton's printing press did for the later dissemination of Reformation ideas (including eschatological ones), modern technology and social media have done for modern communications, including eschatological speculation.

In this chapter we will examine how the impact of these changes between 1945 and 1991 (the collapse of the USSR) resonated with eschatological ideas. Then we shall see how the interaction of global complexity with eschatology has developed from then until the present.

First, though, we need to consider the one single development that, in many ways, is the most significant in the modern explosion of end-times thinking. Over the centuries many events have been considered as candidates for starting, what one might call, the "end time clock." In the twentieth century, the event that has a greater claim to be a trigger event than most of those (erroneously) identified in the past is the establishment of the State of Israel in 1948. This was, and is, an event of enormous significance. The question for many students of prophecy is: "Has it started the end-time clock running?" Most premillennialists would answer with a resounding "Yes."

Israel returned to "the land"

For many Christians, the establishment of the State of Israel in 1948 is interpreted as the direct fulfilment of Old Testament prophecy.[315] This outlook is not confined to Christians, since many religious Jews would also view the event in eschatological terms. Indeed, some subscribe to "catastrophic messianism," whereby the secular Israeli state is the precursor to the recreation of the fully restored ideal nation of Israel due to the actions of the Messiah.[316] However, the secular nature of much traditional Zionism, and the difference in numbers between the two religions, has meant that it is among Christian Zionists (especially those with a dispensationalist outlook) that the belief has gained most attention. The belief has impacted on modern politics in a number of ways. Most obvious is the support of the US evangelical right for Israel.

Almost all Old Testament prophecy assumes the presence of a Jewish community in the Middle East. What we might call "Israel in the land" is a given. Old Testament prophecies refer to the scattering of the people of God (e.g., Deut 28:64) and of them eventually being returned to the land (e.g., Jer 23:3; Isa 11:12). Academic experts might suggest this referred (preteristically) to the historic Babylonian exile. However, the sense of ultimate restoration is clear in these passages, which gives them an end-times character and possibly two applications.

While New Testament prophecy is less geographically specific, parts of it can be read in the same way. There is a widespread belief that Jesus will return in person to the Mount of Olives. This being a direct interpretation of the words spoken by angels to the disciples at his ascension from that location outside Jerusalem: "This Jesus, who has been taken up from you into heaven, will come in the same way as you saw him go into heaven" (Acts 1:11).

Between 70 and 1948 this was difficult to read literally. Those that did so—and had not subscribed to supersessionism—often assumed that there must be a return of the Jews to their ancestral lands. We find this idea explicitly stated from the seventeenth century onwards. Then, in 1948, this occurred. It is little wonder that it is a major component in all modern end-times thinking. The establishment of the State of Israel is, for many, the event that has started the end-times clock running. As early as 1917, the entry into Jerusalem by the British General Allenby (having defeated the Ottomans to gain control of the city) prompted Scofield to comment that, "Now for the first time we have a real prophetic sign."[317] Jesus' image of a fig tree's leaves signaling the coming of summer, being like the signs indicating the imminent last days (Matt 24:32–33), is often taken as a reference to the restoration of Israel. It should be noted that Jesus does not actually make this connection and the gathering-in that he has just referred to is one accomplished by angels, not human agency. And it occurs *after* the return of the Son of Man (Matt 24:30–31). His reference to "this generation" not passing away until all is accomplished (Matt 24:34) was once taken by modern prophecy enthusiasts as a generation starting in 1948. That interpretation is now rarely referred to, as a biblical generation would have ended in the mid-1990s.

The Israeli capture of the whole of Jerusalem in the 1967 Six Day War was regarded as a direct fulfilment of prophecy, since now Israel was both in "the land" and in control of the ancient capital city, which features so prominently in prophecy.[318]

Leading evangelicals, post 1945, from preachers and church leaders—such as Billy Graham (died 2018), Jerry Falwell (died 2007), Pat Robertson, Robert Jeffress, and John Hagee—to popularizers of end-times beliefs—such as Hal Lindsey and Tim LaHaye—have strongly argued for Israel playing a major part in God's plans in the time immediately preceding the second coming.[319] From 1970 onwards, huge numbers of evangelical Christians have visited Israel and volunteered on kibbutzim and on archaeological digs as part of their solidarity with a nation they regard as the key end-times state.[320] In recent years (see chapter 13) this has developed into political influence within the USA that is unprecedented.

As time has gone on, this evangelical support has expressed itself in many ways, as we shall see in the next chapter, but one of the most controversial is in support for the rebuilding of a Jewish temple on the Temple Mount in Jerusalem. Since this would require the demolition of the Islamic *al-Aqsa* Mosque, the Dome of the Rock and the Dome of the Chain, as well as four minarets, the conflagration this would cause is difficult to exaggerate.[321] In the 1980s the hopes for the rebuilding brought together conservative evangelicals in the USA and radical Jewish groups such as the "Jewish Temple Builders."[322] In the mid-1980s, the Israeli security services caught a number of Jewish and Jewish-Christian groups who were planning to blow up the Islamic sites on the Temple Mount.[323]

The "northern enemy": the USSR and the Warsaw Pact nations

The existence of the atheistic communist USSR and its support for the Arab opponents of Israel made it a strong candidate for "the northern army" referred to in Joel 2:20, which would be destroyed by God because it had come against Israel. The vivid descriptions of destruction in Joel were frequently interpreted as nuclear war: "fire has devoured the pastures of the wilderness" and "flames have burned all the trees of the field" (1:19); "The sun and the moon are darkened, and the stars withdraw their shining" (2:10); from the destroyed northern army, "stench and foul smell will rise up." (2:20) When added to descriptions in Zechariah of the flesh, eyes, and tongues consumed away of "all the peoples that wage war against Jerusalem" (Zech 14:12), the idea that this referred to the effects of nuclear radiation was rapidly adopted by many interpreters.[324] That Zechariah called this a "plague" from the Lord was seen as the use of contemporary language to describe the future event.

Before the collapse of the USSR in 1991 a great deal of end-times speculation centered on identifications of Old Testament tribes as the countries of the Warsaw Pact, as a Christian companion to Cold War politics. These tribes, who are "latter years" enemies of Israel, are named in Ezekiel as "Gog, of the land of Magog, the chief prince of Meshech and Tubal" (Ezek 38:2). They lead a confederation of Persia, Ethiopia, Put, Gomer, and Beth-togarmah (Ezek 38:5–6). Some of these ancient tribes are easy to identify. Persia was basically what we now call Iran; Ethiopia or Cush referred to African lands south of Egypt;[325] Put can be read as Libya.[326] The others are more complex. Gog of Magog appears to refer to Scythian and/or Tartar tribes north and north-east of the Black Sea.[327] Meshech and Tubal seem to have been tribes of the Caucasus region and north-east of the Black Sea.[328] Gomer was understood to be tribes further west in Central and Western Europe.[329] Beth-togarmah (House of Togarmah) refers to horse-breeding peoples of Armenia or Scythia.[330] The phrase "chief prince" has also been translated as a proper-name: "Rosh." In which case it might refer to Slavic peoples and some later commentators linked it to Russia.[331] It is not surprising that what Ezekiel regarded as tribes of the far north should be viewed during the Cold War as the USSR and the nations of the Warsaw Pact.[332]

In 1983 it was to a group of Christian broadcasters that President Ronald Reagan delivered his "Evil Empire" speech, which condemned the USSR. We can only speculate whether Reagan meant this in an eschatological sense. But we can be certain that many of those who heard the speech did.

The same occurred with regard to communist China and some scriptural verses referring to an end-times army from the east (notably, Dan 11:44; Rev 16:12) were considered to point to this nation intervening in the politics of the Middle East. Overall, though, China's role in prophetic interpretation drew much less attention than that accorded to Russia.

Even when tensions eased, there was still a reluctance to move away from describing the USSR as the northern enemy. Mikhail Gorbachev might have been working hard to reform his country and avoid nuclear catastrophe, but this did not stop him from being described in some quarters as the potential Antichrist. By adding the initial of his patronymic ("S" for Sergeyevich) it was concluded that the letters of his name totaled 1,332 or 666 doubled. But this was not all. His commitment to peace rendered him suspect, because Antichrist would be a bringer of false peace.[333] This claim was based on Jeremiah 6:14, which referred to people proclaiming "Peace, peace, when there is no peace." Earlier, the prophet had warned that "evil looms out of the north." (Jer 6:1). It should be noted here that, in Jeremiah's day, Israel's enemy was Babylon, to the north-east.

The peace-characteristic had caused suggestions in the 1970s that Henry Kissinger might be the Antichrist. It was as if students of applied eschatology were opponents of peace. This despite the clear message of Matthew 5:9: "Blessed are the peacemakers, for they will be called children of God." Evangelist Paul Olson was preaching that the Soviet Union would lead an attack on Israel—quoting Ezekiel and Jeremiah—in November 1989, even as the Iron Curtain was coming down.[334] It is still stated that a form of this alliance will constitute an end-times invasion of Israel.[335]

Eschatology in the bookshops

The focus on the millennium and the rapture has gained increasing traction among millions of Christians since the 1970s. In this, a number of aspects reoccur: the key role of the State of Israel; the threat posed by global super-powers (other than the USA); belief in clandestine religious movements, with alleged occult involvement; the perceived threat posed by transna-tional organizations such as the UN and the EU.

One of the most popular manifestations of this was the publication of *The Late, Great Planet Earth* in 1970, written by Hal Lindsey, co-written with Carole C. Carlson. It was bought in huge numbers and was sold in mainstream bookshops as well as in supermarkets. It took a particular dis-pensationalist interpretation of prophecy to the mass market. It even led to a movie narrated by Orson Welles and featuring monologues by Lindsey.[336] Its pacey and accessible style outlines beliefs that are now virtually *de ri-gueur* among most students of prophecy. These include the significance of the establishment of Israel, the impact of the rapture, the escalating seven years of the tribulation with its attendant rise of Antichrist, and the mark of the beast. This accompanies condemnation of secular humanism, and warnings about the threat of one-world government, secret organizations forming what would now be called an international "deep state," a one-world religion, and the malign use of technology as a means of control and of the destruction of enemies.[337] It also included identification of the EEC/EU (in 1970 made up of only six states) as the revived Roman Empire in fulfilment of prophecies in Daniel and Revelation regarding numbered empires, and beasts with numbered features. Its application of biblical prophecy to twentieth-century military weaponry "turned the Bible into a manual of atomic-age combat."[338] This drew on verses such as those from Zechariah referred to earlier. Critics noted a lack of empathy in Lindsey's work, even suggesting that he seemed to find the violent events exciting and attractive.[339] Other suggested he was confusing modern weaponry for divine supernatural judgements.[340]

When it came to timetabling the end (as found in Lindsey's writings), common approaches linked many commentators (with some variations). Most subscribed to something similar to the timeline of events that under-pins the *Left Behind* novels, which we will now explore.

The *Left Behind* series was produced by the writing team of Tim La-Haye and Jerry B. Jenkins. The phenomenon of the "prophecy novel" dated, in the USA, from the 1930s and early writing in this genre set the scene for the later *Left Behind* series by including dramatic coverage of the imagined impact of the rapture on society.[341] However, none of the earlier writing enjoyed the huge success of the *Left Behind* series. Set in Chicago suburbia (not the stereotypical southern "Bible Belt"), it follows the story of characters not taken in the rapture. Consequently, they face the seven years of the tribulation. While the novels are works of fiction, they conform to a timetable of events, drawn from a number of combined prophetic passages, to form a program that is now accepted by huge numbers of Christians.

In the books, while the rapture is of huge significance, another key event is a seven-year peace treaty between the Antichrist and Israel which follows it and begins with the rebuilding of the Jerusalem temple. This future rebuilding is accepted by most modern eschatological commentators.[342] It ushers in a period of worldwide peace, but this peace is a deception.

The Antichrist of the series is a fictional man of Italian origins, named Nicolae Carpathia.[343] Unlike many earlier versions of Antichrist, he is not presented as a Jew (as in the second-century opinion of Irenaeus) or as the pope.[344] The character is highly mutable. His being Italian maintains the focus on Europe as the origins of Antichrist that is found in *The Late, Great Planet Earth*, even as he is given a base in Baghdad or "New Babylon." This means that the "Babylon" that is condemned in the Bible is given its literal geographical location; the ancient site of Babylon being fifty-three miles (eighty-five kilometers) south of Baghdad. Most academic commentators consider the original use of "Babylon" in Revelation to be a coded reference to the Roman Empire.[345] Not so in the literal rendering of the prophecies in the *Left Behind* series.

At the mid-point of the seven-year-long tribulation, the two witnesses of Revelation 11:1–12, who have condemned Antichrist, are martyred; then brought back to life and are taken into heaven. It is at this mid-point that the suffering of the tribulation accelerates, as the judgements of Revelation increase in intensity. These are the ones described in Revelation chapters 9 and 11 (the "trumpet judgements"). At this point, Antichrist himself suffers a fatal head wound and is revived. This is a literal reading of Revelation 13:12, which refers to the beast "whose mortal wound had been healed." This begins the three-and-a-half year period of the "great tribulation." As Antichrist (the beast) increases his grip on global power, he is supported by one described as the false prophet, who works miracles on his behalf to deceive the people of the world. It is then that the number 666 is used to control people. Biblically, the false prophet is also described as "another beast that rose out of the earth; it had two horns like a lamb and it spoke like a dragon" (Rev 13:11); and as "the false prophet" later in the account (Rev 19:20). Revelation 13:2–4 indicates that it is "the dragon" (the devil) who empowers Antichrist. In the *Left Behind* series, it is clear that Nicolae Carpathia (Antichrist) is empowered by the devil and is the personification of evil and deception.[346] It should be noted that at no point does the book of Revelation actually use the title "antichrist." The one who is represented as this person in the series—as generally in modern eschatological literature—is actually described in Revelation as "a beast rising out of the sea" (Rev 13:1) or simply "the beast."

The Jerusalem temple is rebuilt. The Dome of the Rock and the *al-Aqsa* Mosque are transported to New Babylon.[347] At first, this garners Jewish support for Carpathia. But eventually he, as the Antichrist, declares himself God in the Jerusalem temple, with all sacrifices being reserved for him. This is how the predicted "abomination that desolates" (Dan 9:27), referred to by Jesus as "the desolating sacrilege standing in the holy place" (Matt 24:15), is interpreted. Most modern eschatologists would probably subscribe to this interpretation. It should be stated that neither of these prophecies, as found in the Bible, refer explicitly to the Antichrist. Nevertheless, one can see why the connection has been made, given the opposition to God that is integral to the rebel who is described in these various passages.

In the series, this is all conveyed in a dramatic and accessible manner, with references to modern political systems and technology, but interwoven with spiritual events. Two examples from *Desecration: Antichrist Takes the Throne* will suffice to make the point. The mark of the beast is applied at loyalty-mark application centers, open twenty-four hours a day. But the announcement of punishment for those lacking the mark is interrupted by an angelic declaration that breaks in on the broadcast and cannot be stopped by the broadcasting network. Those receiving the mark are covered with sores sent as punishment by God. Water turns to blood. Another example would be the "flood from the serpent's mouth" (Rev 12:15). This becomes a modern motorized army set on destroying the enemies of Carpathia. But then divine intervention rips open the ground around Petra and the armored columns plunge into it, to their doom. What is described as supernatural intervention and what is described in physical terms is at the discretion of the writers. This bears comparison with the way other commentators have moved between literal and symbolic interpretation of various numbers appearing in prophecy while at all times claiming to be following scripture literally.[348] The writers use the book of Revelation to construct their timetable.

As the book progresses, those who come to faith in Christ (including Messianic Jews) become embroiled in a guerrilla war with the vicious forces of Antichrist. Those who oppose him are called the "Tribulation Force." This resonates with modern experience of insurgency, while placing it in an end-times context. One can see why the books have been so popular. They have influenced the outlook of millions of believers, in a way comparable with the influence of the *Scofield Reference Bible* almost a century earlier.

It should be added that most of those who have taken on board this way of reading the end-times are within the evangelical community, both in the USA and worldwide. Within other Protestant churches the influence is harder to measure, but from what data and evidence is available, it is far less. In contrast, Catholics are members of a church that has repeatedly condemned millenarianism and continues to do so.[349] However, some millenarian beliefs have appeared among fringe Catholic groups.[350] Despite this suspicion over millenarianism, it should be noted that belief in the second coming is an integral part of official Catholic doctrine.[351] However, end-times speculation is frowned on.

Some thoughts on the rapture

As noted in an earlier chapter, the phenomenon known as the rapture is a major component in most modern end-times thinking and proposed time-tables. Indeed, the pre-tribulation rapture is the foundation for much of the way the last seven years of human history, prior to the second coming, are now envisaged in prophetic analysis.

Given the significance of this belief, the scriptural basis for it is questionable. Zephaniah 2:3 enjoins believers to seek the Lord and "perhaps you may be hidden on the day of the LORD's wrath." In the New Testament, 1 Thessalonians 4:17 states: "Then we who are alive, who are left [after the Christian dead are raised on Christ's return], will be caught up in the clouds together with them to meet the Lord in the air." The key word is the Greek *harpazo* meaning "to snatch or catch away."[352] It is this word that is now well known in its Latin form, *raptus* (rapture). Then, 1 Corinthians 15:51 states: "Listen, I will tell you a mystery! We will not all die, but we will all be changed." The belief, it is claimed, is also revealed in "the blessed hope and the manifestation of the glory of our great God and Savior, Jesus Christ"

(Titus 2:13). It is a hope because believers will not face the coming tribu-lation.[353] Within this verse it is said that two stages are implied: firstly, the "blessed hope" (the rapture) and secondly, the "manifestation of the glory [of Christ]" (the actual second coming).[354]

These verses, it is often stated, describe "the sudden mass disap-pearance of millions upon millions of people from the face of the earth." Those left behind (as in the famous book series) will have witnessed "a miraculous event of astonishing proportions."[355] This will cause, as one might imagine, chaos on earth in every area of society, economy, and government. Then will occur the rise of Antichrist and the seven years of the tribulation.[356] During this time there will be many who turn to Christ despite fierce persecution.[357]

The rapture is sometimes claimed to be what Jesus referred to in John 14:1–3, when he talked about taking believers to be with him in his Father's house. Some commentators draw a parallel with words of Jesus, in Matthew 24:39–41, regarding two in a field, one taken the other left; and two women grinding flour, one taken and one left. Further corroboration is said to be the absence of the Greek word for "church" during the description of the tribulation in Revelation. This, it is suggested, is because the church will not be on earth at that time.

While this belief has become foundational in modern end-times thinking, it can be argued that (in its current form) it brings together com-plex and mysterious concepts, interprets them in a preconceived way, and then makes of them a precise timetable as if they had been written of a piece but scattered across Scripture. Then it corroborates them with verses that do not refer to this concept at all and will not bear the weight of the artificial construction placed on them.

However, the verses in question can be read very differently. 1 Thes-salonians 4:17 simply assures living believers that they will be reunited with the Christian dead on Christ's return. There is nothing about it to suggest it significantly precedes his second coming. Furthermore, it seems clear that the image of meeting the Lord in the air is drawn from the custom that, when a dignitary visited a city, representatives would go out to greet them and lead them back into the city. Consequently, here, the Lord comes to the earth and its Christian citizens go out (which in this instance is upwards due to where the Lord is coming from) to greet him and welcome him. There is no reason to read this as implying being taken away while life carries on back on the earth. 1 Corinthians refers to the same concept of those believers alive when Christ returns entering glory without experiencing death. The "two stages" interpretation of Titus is not convincing. The concept imposes an artificial construct on the verse; it is clearly describing one event: union with Christ at his second coming. There is nothing whatsoever in John 14 to support the idea of the pre-tribulation rapture, as this reassures believers of a home in heaven, and not the timetable of how it will be achieved. This leaves Matthew 24:39–41. The comparison in that passage, when read in context, is with the judgment of Noah's day when those who were not saved in the Ark "knew nothing until the flood came and swept them all away." The key point is that those who are "taken" at "the coming of the Son of Man" are those swept away by the Final Judgment. Those who are "left" are those who survive the judgment, like Noah and those with him. The text is very clear about that. This is the exact opposite of the rapture interpretation. In conclusion, the overall "rapture-concept" can be argued to be a questionable product of attempts to both timetable the end times and gain assurance that believers are exempt from the suffering preceding the return of Jesus. But it is now mainstream and hugely influential.

End-times thinking at "the end of history"

After 1945, the combination of the establishment of Israel, a succession of wars in the Middle East, the Cold War, the threat of nuclear annihilation, increased globalization and economic connectivity, and unity in Western Europe leading to the formation of the EEC (now EU), led to great confidence that the second coming was imminent. The common interpretation of Jesus' words in Matthew 24:34, "this generation will not pass away until all these things have taken place," caused many to expect the *parousia* by about 1990, since that was the end of a generation since the establishment of Israel in 1948. The setting of precise dates was discouraged among most prominent commentators, but the implications seemed clear.

By the time that the Cold War effectively ended in 1989, and the USSR imploded in 1991, there had already been a sea change in eschatological outlooks. Between 1945 and the 1980s, the earlier optimistic post-millennialist legacy of Jonathan Edwards and those in the Social Gospel movement had given way before dispensationalism and what has been described as the "social pessimism of end time rapturists."[358] There was no positive aspect to the arc of human history, except that its inevitably disastrous denouement would usher in the millennium. The stage indeed seemed set for dramatic and catastrophic events and there were times when a Soviet-led invasion of the Middle East, though hard to envisage, did perhaps seem possible. That this occurred at the same time as the enlargement of the EEC (later called the European Union [EU] after 1993) only added to the combination of factors that could be presented as indicative of the approaching fulfilment of prophecy.

As a consequence, the period after the collapse of communism in the USSR was a disappointment to many end-times commentators. The most likely scenario for an invasion of Israel by Gog, Magog, Meshech, and Tubal was now hard to construct. The road to Armageddon seemed to have been diverted. China, on the other hand, still seemed to pose a threat in the wake of its brutal suppression of protest in Tiananmen Square in 1989. No *Glasnost* was happening there. But then, China had never played such a key role in the eschatological timetables as the USSR had done, despite the dramatic interpretation sometimes connected to Revelation 16:12 and the "kings from the east" crossing a dried-up River Euphrates.

Despite this, disappointment was a stimulus to rework the analysis. The existence of the State of Israel remained a strong argument for the times being unlike any that had come before. And in the Middle East there was more than enough potential for future conflict. Syria, Iraq, and Iran might yet prove to be major players in widespread conflagrations centered on Israel and, like Russia, were to the north. Nuclear proliferation had not been fully curtailed by changes in the relationship between the USA and what had once been the USSR. Europe remained the focus of much eschatological attention.

However, time was passing and 1948 was already forty-three years (a generation) in the past when the USSR ceased to be a major player. In some ways this sharpened the need to identify key indicative events to replace previous ones. The search for "signs of the times" intensified, in line with the idea that the "prophetic stopwatch" was, as it were, suspended during the "Great Parenthesis" of the Church Age but restarted towards its end.[359] Now, that stop watch was thought to be ticking and had been doing so for over forty years.

In 1992, the American political scientist Francis Fukuyama wrote the provocatively titled *The End of History and the Last Man*. It was not, of course, an eschatological text, despite the dramatic first part of its title. Instead, it celebrated the alleged ideological triumph of Western liberal democracy and the free market in the wake of the collapse of Soviet communism.

While its content has been much debated and misunderstood, to many observers it seemed to point the way towards a positive (indeed triumphant) future for these institutions. In the decade that followed this, such confidence in the West arguably led to the peak of influence in the USA of so-called "neocons" during the presidency of George W. Bush (2001–9). Associated with both the defense, as they saw it, of Israeli national interests and also with promoting and planning the invasion of Iraq in 2003,[360] they set the scene for much of the turbulence that has characterized the Middle East in the following two decades after that invasion. It was in these ensuing twenty years that US evangelical eschatology and a right-wing international agenda became intimately intertwined.

These two decades witnessed an extraordinary surge in evangelical influence in US right-wing politics, culminating in the election of Donald Trump in 2016. As that political influence has increased, end-times beliefs have become highly significant in US Middle Eastern policy. The period that Fukuyama described as marking *The End of History*, has been seen by millions of Americans as literally signaling the imminent end of history and the world itself. It is to this that we now turn.

13

The "End Times" Are "Now Times"

1991 to Today

The end-times after the "end of history"

THE CONTINUED INFLUENCE OF dispensational and pre-tribulation rapture beliefs alongside the rising influence of US neo-conservatives in the 1990s and early twenty-first century has been described as "two kinds of fatalism."[361] This evaluation is contentious, but the premise is that, together, they have underpinned US "imperial power" abroad, providing both its ideological and its economic drive. In a world where things are expected to get much worse before they get better, extreme measures may not only be justifiable; they may actually be desirable. This was (and arguably has continued to be) a potent mix. It may even be seen as necessary to bring on the apocalypse in a final showdown.

This is not simply speculation. In 2008 a review of attitudes found that 25 percent of Americans believed that the second coming would take place in their lifetimes. In effect, before 2050. Almost 66 percent (including President George W. Bush) believed in the literal accuracy of biblical prophecies as relating to the end times.[362] From what we have seen, we can assume that this includes belief in the removal of believers via the rapture, the crisis of the tribulation, and the rise to power of the Antichrist culminating in the Battle of Armageddon,[363] followed by the second coming of Christ. The potential impact of this on US attitudes towards both domestic and foreign policy is intriguing.

This is the legacy of a growing attitude towards the threats of global annihilation which see such destruction as pre-ordained and part of God's plan. The almost subliminal effect of this outlook can be "passive acquiescence."[364] At one time this occurred in the face of Cold War annihilation, but latterly in the face of nuclear war triggered by other forms of conflict (such as over Iran) or even climatic catastrophe. Although, it should be noted, many who adopt what some could call a providential fatalism do not accept the reality of climate change caused by human activity. But if they do, any response to it is often marginalized by belief that either the second coming will occur long before it fully takes effect, or it is part of a preordained plan. And the rapture will have removed believers from the earth before the worst of the tribulation occurs anyway.

Conservative evangelical belief in eschatology does not inevitably mean fatalism, as was exemplified by Billy Graham, as far back as 1984, in *Approaching Hoof Beats: The Four Horsemen of the Apocalypse*, when he commented that: "Every person who is a follower of Christ is responsible to do something for the hungry and sick in the world. We must do what we can, even though we know that God's ultimate plan is the making of a new earth and a new heaven."[365]

Despite this, there is plenty of evidence to show that, for many, such eschatologies can encourage political and social passivity in the face of global threats to human existence. Those who work to reduce such threats might even be presented as, inadvertently, working against the grain of providence. Or worse, they might actually be preparing the way for the Antichrist's claim that he brings (illusionary) peace as part of his one-world government. One can see how this can easily shade from mainstream belief into the extreme positions of, for example, US militia and survivalist groups who are preparing to either resist these malign (left and liberal) internationalist forces, or are preparing to sit-out the tribulation (at least until the rapture). In this way, "God and guns" can become eschatologically combined in a way conducive to encourage extreme right-wing positions. Life in an uncertain and threatening world can accelerate such tendencies and their popularity.

Within a decade of the attacks on the Twin Towers, the FBI estimated that somewhere in the region of 1,500 apocalyptic cults existed in the USA.[366] As far back as 1993, the bloody siege of the Branch Davidians, led by David Koresh, at Waco, Texas, illustrated the deep commitment of some to apocalyptic visions of the world. That this movement was freely entered into is often missed by simply dismissing the group as "a cult."[367] And it is often forgotten how closely related to the mainstream the Branch Davidians were, having come out of the Seventh-Day Adventists.[368] Belief in the impending end-times and an eschatological timetable (as outlined above) is held within most US evangelical churches. By 2011 it had been estimated that somewhere in the region of forty million Americans subscribed to dispensational beliefs of the kind we have explored earlier.[369] Assuming that these are adults, this amounted to almost 17 percent of the US adult population. Globally, many more tens of millions of Christians are influenced by US conservative evangelical media outlets expressing these beliefs.

We have seen how the *Left Behind* series of novels provides something of a barometer regarding these opinions. They are "indicative of the reenergized political and cultural power of a Christian Right that in the late 1990s had seemed to be in retreat."[370] *Desecration* was released about six weeks after 9/11. It became the best-selling hardback book of the year, pushing John Grisham out of the number-one spot that he had held every year since 1994; and it achieved this just three months after publication.[371] The sixteenth and last in the series (*Kingdom Come: The Final Victory*) was published in 2007. When Tim LaHaye died in 2016, the series had sold somewhere in the region of eighty million copies, according to the publisher, Tyndale House.[372]

What is striking is the way that end-times reflections have increasingly become associated with the outlook of the evangelical right in the USA; and this has influenced the political flavor of such views when adopted by those globally, who are influenced by US evangelical culture. This rightward political shift is highly significant and in direct contrast with the way that eschatological beliefs in periods of the past have been associated with political radicalism. The contrast with the sixteenth and seventeenth centuries is notable. In short, contemporary enthusiastic eschatological commentary and speculation has become increasingly intertwined with conservative politics and with Christian nationalism.

In the USA this can be dated from the 1930s, when many prophecy writers expressed politically conservative criticisms of Roosevelt's New Deal.[373] State intervention (especially if associated with the concept of reform bringing peace and prosperity) were, and are, often roundly condemned as indicative of trends that will culminate in the actions of the Antichrist. One US commentator, in the 1930s, even went so far as to suggest that the blue eagle badge of the NRA (National Recovery Administration) was reminiscent of the mark of the beast.[374] Arguably, such politically orientated interpretations express pre-existing conservative ideology and outlook, and view events and alleged prophetic fulfilment through this political lens. Fulfilment is looked for in line with established political views, and is then "found" in events that offend this outlook or are in line with it. This is no different in principle to Anabaptist condemnations of wealthy landowners, or Puritan views of royalist activities. What is striking, though, is its current *conservative* nature. The effect of this is that it can now be difficult to disentangle end-times interpretations of events—that would find acceptance across faith communities regardless of political outlooks—from those that are deeply politically partisan and are indicative of right-wing nationalist views.

This rightward shift in eschatological interpretation is a twentieth-century trend, which has accelerated in the twenty-first century. In 2001, in the aftermath of 9/11, President Bush laid out his response in a speech to religious broadcasters in Nashville, Tennessee. His explicit outlining of US intentions to confront enemies abroad, and defend allies, would be successful he opined because it is "the angel of God who directs the storm."[375] The message was clear that "the storm" was moving in the direction being followed by US foreign policy.

It should be noted that, while the rightward trend is undeniable, the dispensationalist outlook that accompanies it means that antisemitism (so often associated with the nationalist right) is not a feature in the eschatological mainstream. In the 1940s this had led to suggestions that Hitler might be the Antichrist. It was suggested that if A was given the value 100 (a rather arbitrary decision one might suggest), B the value 101, and C the value 102, etc., then the letters of HITLER added up to 666. Since the 1920s, though, Mussolini—an Italian who had signed a concordat with the pope—had been regarded as a more likely candidate.[376] This condemnation of antisemitic politicians is due to a positive attitude towards Israel and the hope that end-times conversion of the Jews is imminent. As a result, current conservative eschatological politics usually also includes a strong commitment to Christian Zionism. This differentiates it from the pattern of beliefs usually associated with highly conservative and nationalist politics.

What is clear is that there are a number of features of contemporary eschatological interpretation that continue trends that have been developing since the 1960s and 1970s and were prevalent in the 1980s up to the collapse of the USSR in 1991. These usually include determined support for Israel and opposition to critics of that state's policies; support for nationalist Israeli politicians and the settler movement; a highly negative attitude towards international bodies and obligations; a deep suspicion of state intervention in society and the economy; antipathy to concerns such as climate change, which suggest too much human agency in world problems and their possible solutions; a conservative stance in the so-called "culture wars" that have divided Western societies since the 1960s and continue to do so; and a noteworthy tendency to accept and communicate conspiracy theories.

"Babylon in Europe"? The European Union in the firing line

A striking example of an organization that has attracted high-profile criticism, couched in end-times terminology, is the European Union.

Attempts to unify Europe have often been interpreted as fulfilments of prophecy: from the medieval papacy to Napoleon and, since the Second World War, most clearly in attitudes towards the EEC/EU. In this process, Christian millenarians have attempted to draw parallels between EEC/EU-related events, and prophecies found in the Old and New Testaments. The UK's 2016 EU Referendum saw the re-emergence of end-times ideas concerning the EU gaining a higher profile than at any time since the 1970s. This affected a significant amount of the conversation within evangelical communities, and online, prior to the referendum. Nothing of this surfaced in official "Leave" arguments. But, informally and online, it contributed a great deal to the negative mood-music regarding the EU among a section of the UK's evangelical community.

Much of this was encouraged by recent literature and commentary. However, as far back as the third-century theologian Hippolytus (died c.235), it had been suggested that a ten-nation revived Roman Empire would be an end-times fulfilment of Daniel 2:42 (a fourth kingdom with toes mixed of iron and clay), Daniel 7:7 (a fourth beast with ten horns), and Revelation 13:1 (a beast from the sea, with ten crowned horns and seven heads). The 1957 Treaty of Rome (which laid the foundation for a Common Market) was presented as a bringing together of a revived Roman Empire. This became a given among many eschatological commentators in the USA and UK by the 1970s, as seen in the pronouncements of David Wilkerson and Tim LaHaye.[377] This influenced the global community in fellowship with these evangelical and Pentecostal churches. By the 1980s the EEC/EU had replaced the USSR as the future seat of Antichrist.[378]

By 1994 the EU had twelve member states, but this in no way defused the identification of it as the revived ten-nation Roman Empire because, in Daniel 7:8, a "little horn" is described coming up among the ten horns and destroying three of them to make room for itself. This was interpreted as the ten-nation confederacy increasing to thirteen and then the "little horn" (Antichrist) destroying three nations, so that the membership would drop back to ten.[379] However one interprets Daniel 7:8, this is simply *not what the text says*. It plainly states that three of the pre-existing ten horns are removed. This ability to read Scripture differently to what is plainly there, in order to advance a pre-conceived position, is striking. It is even more so when one reflects on the fact that it is done by biblical commentators who would claim that they read the Bible literally and who would be critical of less fundamentalist commentators. In 1995, the EU added three more member states; in 2004, ten more countries joined; in 2007 two more joined; then in 2013 yet another. When the UK had its EU Referendum in 2016 the number of states in the EU stood at twenty-eight. This was massively in excess of the ten states featuring in prophecy and stretched from the North Sea to the eastern Baltic and the borders of Russia. It incorporated huge swathes of territories in Central and Eastern Europe that had never, at any point, been part of the Roman Empire. And yet the same charges were (and are) repeated that it is a fulfilment of the prophecies found in Daniel and Revelation, with inventive suggestions regarding why it now far exceeds "ten nations."[380]

In the UK, a number of prophecy commentators claimed there were explicit and negative associations between the EU and biblical prophecy. David Hathaway was prominent among these and chose a memorable title for his influential book: *Babylon in Europe* (2006). He claimed that the European Parliament building in Strasbourg is deliberately designed in the shape of the Tower of Babel, as depicted in the oil paintings of Bruegel the Elder.[381] Hathaway tellingly merged this painting with the parliament building on the cover of the book. The impression is clear that the EU is an ungodly organization. In fact, the parliament building is based on structures and shapes drawn from Classicism and the Baroque; from Roman and Greek theatres to the ideas of Galileo and Kepler. It is meant to depict the evolution of the institutions, evolving from central power to a democratic organization.[382] It is unfinished as, at the time of its construction, Europe was "unfinished" as no country from the former Soviet bloc had yet joined the EU. However, urban myth has overshadowed architectural reality.

As with many of those who oppose the EU on alleged grounds of prophetic fulfilment, the arguments of Hathaway and others largely repeat those found in the 1970s in *The Late, Great Planet Earth* and similar publications. These critics of the EU charge it with being the last world empire; claim that current European political structures provide the geopolitical base from which Antichrist will operate; and assert that from these events will occur the seven-year tribulation of wars, plagues, and earthquakes, which will culminate in the Battle of Armageddon and then the second coming of Christ.[383]

In 2016, one UK church website even claimed that the seat 666 is kept free in the European Parliament, for dark purposes. In fact, in Brussels this seat was then occupied by a Croatian member of the Greens/European Free Alliance and in Strasbourg by a Slovak member of the Group of the European People's Party (Christian Democrats).[384] This fact was very easily checked,[385] but clearly nobody in this particular church bothered to do a search that could be done in five minutes.

In 2016 the UK voted to leave the EU; the infamous "Brexit" that divided the nation then and since. When the UK finally left the EU in January 2020 the remaining states numbered twenty-seven. How the prophetic opponents of the EU will continue to insist that this represents a ten-nation revived Roman Empire is anyone's guess. But, based on previous experience, a way will be found round this. What seems clear is that the end-times-Brexit position reveals as much about Christian nationalism in the twenty-first century as it does about the attempted application of biblical prophecy. That the prophecy-based attacks on the EU, in the UK, occurred at the same time as a surge of nationalism and anti-immigrant sentiments is a combination of events that is undeniable. This is not to suggest that the proponents of the former are complicit in the latter. However, that all form part of a recognizable cultural phenomenon seems impossible to deny.

The attacks on the European Union are often associated with related beliefs about what is termed "Mystery Babylon," an anti-Christian world religion of the last days. In Revelation chapters 17 and 18, there is dramatic denunciation of "Babylon the great, mother of whores and of earth's abominations" (Rev 17:5). While most biblical experts believe this was a preterist coded reference to Rome, or Jerusalem, or to any religious system that opposes God—there is a popular current belief that it refers to a one-world religion promulgated by Antichrist. And many subscribe to the belief that this will be based, literally, in a re-built Babylon in Iraq.[386]

However, assertions that Roman Catholicism represents part of the one-world end-times phenomenon continue to circulate in prophetic circles.[387] This revives a longstanding Protestant antagonism towards Rome and Europe that pre-dates the current EU.[388] The alleged influence of the Catholic Church on the evolving EEC/EU is often claimed;[389] despite the large numbers of Protestants and those of other faiths who are citizens. Only now it is sometimes accused of being part of a secret occult empire or linked to the *Illuminati*, who feature in many conspiracy theories. This is where Protestant prejudices can shade into the extreme theories of QAnon and belief in a liberal "deep state" that is governed by an international organization of devil-worshipping pedophiles. This outlook extends into other areas of conspiracy theory involving liberal secularists, the UN, and (in the USA) federal government and gun control.

Regarding "Mystery Babylon" or "Babylon the great," other interpretations can also be found. These range from asserting that it represents apostate Jerusalem (and Judaism) in the time of the great tribulation[390] as it embraces the false messiah;[391] to the USA;[392] to Islam.[393] The matter is interpreted variously, but the idea of a new one-world religion based in Iraq is one that has gained a great deal of traction due to the influence of the *Left Behind* series and associated publications.

The end-times in the USA of Donald Trump

The election of Donald Trump as US president in 2016 was achieved with the support of about 81 percent of white US evangelicals. There is a great deal of evidence that shows that support for a conservative political agenda was in line with US evangelical end-times values and expectations. This shows itself in antagonism towards international obligations and support for repudiation of action to combat climate change. However, its most obvious focus was on Israel.

Christians United for Israel (CUFI) is the most influential Christian Zionist organization in the USA today. CUFI was founded in 2006 by evangelical pastor John Hagee. By 2019 it had over six million members.[394] Membership figures of over ten million are also quoted.[395] Its mission is to support Israel, as it believes that Israel is the fulfilment of prophecy. In support of Israel, CUFI is highly active in US politics. The Israeli Prime Minister, Benjamin Netanyahu, stated that: "I consider CUFI a vital part of Israel's national security."[396]

The widespread US evangelical support for Israel is hugely significant and it "can largely be explained in terms of their literalist rather than allegorical readings of scripture: the land is viewed as God's covenantal gift to his chosen people and, for the 'dispensationalists' among them, the in-gathering of the Jewish people is associated with prophecies concerning the second coming of Christ."[397]

This constitutes "a huge voting bloc of evangelicals who are taught not to question Israel's divine right to the land."[398] This has become in-creasingly controversial as it has developed into something approaching unquestioning support for an Israeli administration that some others feel has become increasingly hardline and nationalistic. Support for Israel need not be the same as total support for all policies pursued; but it can seem as if that is expected. This has led some to suggest that there is a "cri-sis of contemporary Christian Zionism" and its cause is "not bad theology, but bad praxis."[399] Unquestioning support for the actions of any state, in an imperfect world, runs the risk of muting legitimate Christian views on some governmental behavior. The Old Testament prophets, who are often quoted to justify unquestioning support for Israel, teach that "violations of God's eternal moral law could never be justified by the necessity for prophetic fulfilment."[400] This kind of unquestioning support, though, can have a direct impact on government policy.

Decisions, such as the movement of the US embassy to Jerusalem (announced in 2018) and support for Israeli sovereignty over the Golan Heights (announced in 2019), have been explicitly praised within US evangelical circles as end-times fulfilments. As John Hagee prayed, at the consecration of the ground for the new embassy, in May 2018: "Jerusalem is and always shall be the eternal capital of the Jewish people."[401] Robert P. Jones, CEO of the Public Religion Research Institute (PRRI), was quoted in an article in NBC News in April 2019, explaining that "The end goal isn't what's good for the Jewish community, the end goal is what's good for the second coming of Christ."[402] One might say that this is where "policy and apocalypse meet."[403]

Emphasizing the connection between Old Testament prophecy and recent US policy decisions, Israeli Prime Minister Netanyahu spoke by video link to the CUFI Conference in July 2019. He worded his message to Washington, DC, "from 'Jerusalem, DC'—Jerusalem, David's capital." He went on to thank Hagee for the support of "millions and millions of devout Christians." And he remarked: "You remember the Cyrus Declaration—the proclamation that said to the exiles in Babylon 'you can come back to Jerusalem'?—well, I think that this [the USA embassy move to Jerusalem as Israel's capital] is a [comparable] historic proclamation."[404] Netanyahu's reference was to Isaiah 45:13. Many evangelicals had declared Trump to be a modern Cyrus, the agent of God.[405]

In January 2020, Trump hosted Netanyahu, in Washington, DC, to declare US recognition of Israeli sovereignty over all Jewish settlements in the area known to the Israeli government as "Judea and Samaria" and to Palestinians as the "Israeli-occupied West Bank." It was a truly historic moment, coming as it did on top of the movement of the US embassy to Jerusalem. Many leading US evangelicals were at this momentous meeting.

Commenting outside was Barak Ravid, former diplomatic correspondent for *Haaretz* newspaper and, in January 2020, a diplomatic correspondent for Israel's Channel 13 News. Reflecting on the events of the day, he posed two challenging questions: "What's the endgame? How is this all going to end?"[406]

How indeed?

14

"Let Lights be Brought . . ."

IT IS MID-FEBRUARY 2021 and I am listening to a recording of Scott Lively, on the US radio program "Swamp Rangers" Sunday show (broadcast on 31 January 2021), explain that Vice President Kamala Harris might be the Whore of Babylon and Barack Obama might be the Antichrist. Regarding Harris, he remarks that "all of the biblical references to the Whore of Babylon and the Jezebel that plays such a huge, huge role in the last days prophecy, all sort of rise to the surface." In the case of Obama, we are told that "he more than anyone else that I've ever seen does fit the model."[407]

It could be the thirteenth century, with Pope Gregory IX and the Franciscan chronicler, Salimbene, accusing Emperor Frederick II; or the emperor throwing back the accusation of Antichrist against Pope Innocent IV. Perhaps the accusation is reminiscent of the sixteenth-century attack on the papacy by Luther. There again it could be the seventeenth century, as the Fifth Monarchy Men accuse, first Charles I, and then Cromwell, of being the Antichrist, or the little horn. Or perhaps it is the eighteenth century and Boston patriots accusing George III of being "the great Whore of Babylon," riding the "great red dragon" upon America. However, it is 2021 and, in the bitterly divided context of US politics, many within the evangelical right once more select from the apocalyptic toolbox in order to express themselves against those they consider their enemies.

What this reminds us of is that, for many within the Christian community, there remains a ready enthusiasm to deploy end-times terms and imagery in their political conflicts. Indeed, the use (and, arguably, misuse) of the biblical prophecies has had a resurgence in the polarized world of the twenty-first century. And the confidence of those utilizing them is as high as it was among Frankish chroniclers surveying the tenth-century

Magyar threat; Cold-War-era writers framing the USSR as Gog of the land of Magog; and later Christian nationalists accusing the European Union of preparing a throne for Antichrist, with its empty seat numbered 666. Caution has not usually been a hallmark of apocalyptic identification and calculation, in two millennia of speculation, despite New Testament warnings to the contrary. *Plus ça change.*

However, there are aspects of the current focus on eschatology that stand out. It is now largely dominated by the political right. This is certainly not a forgone conclusion. Nor is it an intrinsic characteristic of end-times thought; far from it. For the early church, the confident hope in the second coming of Christ was part of the radical agenda of a persecuted minority whose founder had been executed as a political prisoner and whose membership and message controversially transcended ethnicity, gender, and class. They were at odds with the world order; powerless except in their trust that the power of God would eventually decide history in their favor. Then, God would overthrow worldly corruption and finally establish a new heaven and a new earth. Whatever else the writer of Revelation felt should be understood from the dramatic words of that unique New Testament apocalyptic text, it seems clear that a future transformation of the world and the cosmic order was very much in mind. But it was the hope of the powerless. It was to resonate with powerless men and women over two millennia. If we are to connect with the core meaning of end-times thought, in its original form, then this seems unescapable.

This makes its current place within right-wing ideology all the more remarkable. From the US nationalism that has characterized the evangelical right in alliance with Donald Trump, to the UK Christian Brexitnationalists denouncing the EU, eschatology has become the preserve of many who wish to promote nationalism and conservatism, oppose international commitments and supranational organizations, and resist aspects of modernity as varied as credit cards, vaccination, gun control legislation, and action on climate change. It has become, for many, a component part of a besieged outlook that pits them against disconcerting aspects of the modern world and expects justification in the form of future catastrophe—from which they will be rescued, while those left behind will suffer tribulation. In the past, this outlook underpinned political *radicalism*, but now, more often than not, *conservatism*. In many ways, this is rooted in aspects of the Cold War, which caused a rightward turn in eschatology, in opposition to Soviet atheistic communism.

This legacy remains potent and accumulative. As a result, a relationship has developed between the US right and the Israeli right in which unconditional support for nationalist perspectives becomes the litmus test of "true support" for Israel and, thus, for the biblical prophetic heritage. It is, however, noteworthy that many of the Old Testament prophets, who looked towards future transformation, were also highly critical of the policies and injustices present in their contemporary society. They were far from being conservative defenders of the national status quo or power-politics.

The current complexity also shows itself strikingly in antipathy towards action regarding climate change. Fossil-fuel conservatism in the coal, oil, and gas communities—in conjunction with opposition to governmental and international controls and targets—takes encouragement from an outlook that considers environmental catastrophe largely irrelevant in the context of imminent Armageddon. And across the global field of eschatological reflection and speculation it is the dominance of the USA and of US evangelicals that has decided much of the present discourse. In many places today, where end-times thoughts are expressed, they are spoken (in effect) with an American accent. And with a politically conservative tone.

Much of modern eschatological discussion seems to favor disengagement (even passivity) and denial regarding the pressing issues of society. It can seem unengaged with the social and environmental crises around us. As such, it has become fused with both political conservatism and right-wing populism. However, this is not inevitable. Belief in the second coming can be a core tenet of faith without giving rise to a retreat from the world and its problems.

There is a story told—which may be apocryphal—that, in the seventeenth century, a very dark day caused the members of a New England assembly to think that the end of the world was upon them. Their debating chamber was deep in premature shadows. A motion was presented, that they should disperse to their homes and await events with prayer. At last, the speaker made his ruling. It allegedly went as follows: "Either this is the end of the world or it is not. If it is not, then we have business to attend to. If it is, then I would have it that Christ finds us attending to our duties. I rule, let lights be brought."

That is a challenging thought: to believe in the second coming but to still be fully engaged with the responsibilities of life. And engagement with such responsibilities does not have a prescribed political flavor or agenda. Eschatology is not the preserve of one political wing, however it might now seem. The early church was a powerless radical community that engaged in transformative behavior, even as it awaited the return of Jesus.

We would do well to heed the advice of that legendary New England speaker. Facing the assumption that the second coming was imminent, he decided on engagement with the tasks of the day, rather than on speculation regarding the coming *parousia*.

"Let lights be brought."

Endnotes

1. Daniel 7:1–8, and 17–26.
2. Revelation 13:1.
3. Whittock, "I Believe in Prophecy."
4. 1 Thessalonians 5:2–3, *NRSV*. All Bible quotes are from this version, unless otherwise stated.
5. Belgium, France, Italy, Luxembourg, the Netherlands, West Germany since 1957, and enlarged to Denmark, Ireland, and the UK in 1973.
6. Whittock, "The Sword Drawne."
7. Matthew 24:36; 25:13; Acts 1:7.
8. "America's Changing Religious Landscape," line 29.
9. "America's Changing Religious Landscape," Table 1.
10. Roberts and Whittock, *Trump and the Puritans*, 18.
11. Olsen, "Opinion," line 13; PRRI "The 2020 Census of American Religion," lines 6–7.
12. Schonhorn, *Defoe's Politics*, 18.
13. Whittock and Whittock, *Christ: The First 2000 Years*.
14. Whittock, *When God Was King*.
15. Roberts and Whittock, *Trump and the Puritans*.
16. Bump, "Half of Evangelicals Support Israel."
17. Bump, "Half of Evangelicals Support Israel."
18. Flannagan, "Covid World."
19. Stefon, *Judaism*, 31.
20. Baker, *Joel, Obadiah, Malachi*, 205.
21. Baker, *Joel, Obadiah, Malachi*, 146.
22. Ellis, "Prophecy," 538.
23. Unger and White, *Nelson's Expository Dictionary*, 190.
24. Travis, "Eschatology," 228.

25. For an interesting exploration of approaches to Daniel, see Howe, *Daniel in the Preterists' Den*. With regard to considerations of the date of the text, see Collins, "Current Issues," 1–15.

26. The literal meaning of the Hebrew term *mashiach*, from which our modern term *messiah* is derived, and which is represented in Greek as Christ.

27. Chilton, "Kingdom of God," 408.

28. Theissen and Merz, *The Historical Jesus*, 459.

29. Rowland, *Christian Origins*, 177.

30. For an examination of this apocalyptic view of Jesus' outlook, see Ehrman, *Jesus: Apocalyptic Prophet*.

31. Doudna, "The Sect of the Qumran Texts," 95–107.

32. Vine, *An Expository Dictionary*, 532.

33. Vine, *An Expository Dictionary*, 532.

34. "Bauckham, "Apocalyptic," 34.

35. Travis, "Eschatology," 228.

36. Tabor, "Jewish and Christian Millennialism," 257.

37. Sanders, *Jesus and Judaism*, 61–76.

38. See Ehrman, *Jesus: Apocalyptic Prophet*.

39. Fenton, *Saint Matthew*, 391.

40. Tabor, "Jewish and Christian Millennialism," 261.

41. Schweizer, *Good News According to Matthew*, 458.

42. Leaney, *Gospel According to St Luke*, 263.

43. Morris, Leon. *The Gospel According to Matthew*, 612.

44. Morris, Leon. *The Gospel According to Matthew*, 612–13.

45. Wright, *Jesus and the Victory of God*, 317.

46. Porter, "Millenarian Thought," 70.

47. Porter, "Millenarian Thought," 69–70.

48. Porter, "Millenarian Thought," 64.

49. Schweitzer, *Mysticism of Paul*, 92.

50. Court, *Approaching the Apocalypse*, 35.

51. Percy, "Whose Time is it Anyway?" 30.

52. Porter, "Millenarian Thought," 76.

53. See Swete, *The Apocalypse*, 261–62; Court, *Myth and History*, 2–3.

54. 1 John 2:18 (both singular and plural form used) and 1 John 2:22, 1 John 4:2–3, 2 John 1:7 (all singular). Jesus also warned against "false christs" (plural) in Matthew 24:24 and Mark 13:22.

55. Court, *Approaching the Apocalypse*, 48.

56. Cohn, *The Pursuit of the Millennium*, 23.

57. Cohn, *The Pursuit of the Millennium*, 23.

58. The text known as *Sanhedrin* 29c.

59. Kelly, *The Birth of Jesus*, 16–17.

60. Ice and Demy, *The Return*, 115.

61. Ice and Demy, *The Return*, 115.

62. Ice and Demy, *The Return*, 115.

63. Bryce Ervin, *One Thousand Years with Jesus*, 118.

64. Clifford, *A Brief History of End Time*, 126.

65. Roberts et al., *Ante-Nicene Fathers Volume I*, 146–47. Barnabas, *The Epistle of Barnabas*, chapter XV.

66. Tabor, "Jewish and Christian Millennialism," 259.

67. Mounce, *The Book of Revelation*, 22.

68. Cohn, *The Pursuit of the Millennium*, 26.

69. Court, *Approaching the Apocalypse*, 58.

70. Mounce, *The Book of Revelation*, 11.

71. Mounce, *The Book of Revelation*, 22.

72. Mounce, *The Book of Revelation*, 22.

73. Cohn, *The Pursuit of the Millennium*, 25.

74. Court, *Approaching the Apocalypse*, 52.

75. Court, *Approaching the Apocalypse*, 53.

76. Cohn, *The Pursuit of the Millennium*, 25.

77. Cohn, *The Pursuit of the Millennium*, 26.

78. Court, *Approaching the Apocalypse*, 46.

79. Porter, "Millenarian Thought," 64.

80. Mounce, *The Book of Revelation*, 11.

81. Tabor, "Jewish and Christian Millennialism," 259.

82. Mounce, *The Book of Revelation*, 23–24.

83. Court, *Approaching the Apocalypse*, 56.

84. Tabor, "Jewish and Christian Millennialism," 258.

85. Cohn, *The Pursuit of the Millennium*, 28.

86. Cohn, *The Pursuit of the Millennium*, 28–29.

87. Court, *Approaching the Apocalypse*, 52.

88. Cohn, *The Pursuit of the Millennium*, 26.

89. Mounce, *The Book of Revelation*, 25.

90. Tixeront, *Handbook of Patrology*, 135.

91. Moreschini and Norelli, *Early Christian Greek and Latin Literature*, 397.

92. Quasten, *Patrology*, 413.

93. Mounce, *The Book of Revelation*, 25.

94. Bryce Ervin, *One Thousand Years with Jesus*, 142–43.

95. "Eschatological Attitude," lines 47–51.

96. Poole, "The Western Apocalypse," 108.

97. Poole, "The Western Apocalypse," 108.

98. Fredriksen, "Apocalypse and Redemption," 151; Mounce, *The Book of Revelation*, 25.

99. Mounce, *The Book of Revelation*, 25.

100. Andrew of Caesarea, *Commentary on the Apocalypse*, 26–28.

101. Andrew of Caesarea, *Commentary on the Apocalypse*, 28.

102. Andrew of Caesarea, *Commentary on the Apocalypse*, 38.

103. Allen, *Manuscripts of the book of Revelation*, 109

104. Andrew of Caesarea, *Commentary on the Apocalypse*, 5.

105. Johnson, *A History of Christianity*, 76.

106. Dockery, *Christian Scripture*, 103.

107. Stanton, *Kept from the Hour*, 148.

108. Clouse, *The Meaning of the Millennium*, 9.

109. Palmer, *The Apocalypse*, 32.

110. Clifford, *A Brief History of End Time*, 126–27

111. Clifford, *A Brief History of End Time*, 126.

112. Landes, "The views of Augustine," lines 65–74.

113. Landes, "The views of Augustine," lines 121–30.

114. Cohn, *The Pursuit of the Millennium*, 32.

115. Reinink, "Political Power and Right Religion," 155.

116. Berkey, *The Formation of Islam*, 98.

117. Savory, "Christendom vs. Islam," 127.

118. Whitelock, *English Historical Documents*, 842.

119. Whitelock, *English Historical Documents*, 843.

120. Whittock and Whittock, *The Viking Blitzkrieg*, 20.

121. Whittock, "Vikings: When the Hammer Met the Cross," lines 36–39.

122. Whittock and Whittock, *The Viking Blitzkrieg*, 42.

123. Whittock and Whittock, *The Viking Blitzkrieg*, 42.

124. Hadley, *The Vikings in England*, 208.

125. Roach, *Æthelred the Unready*, 279–83.

126. Whittock and Whittock, *The Vikings: From Odin to Christ*, 191.

127. Roach, *Æthelred the Unready*, 241–42.

128. Roach, *Æthelred the Unready*, 243.

129. Roach, *Æthelred the Unready*, 204–5.

130. Roach, *Æthelred the Unready*, 205.

131. Roach, *Æthelred the Unready*, 244.

132. Keynes, "Apocalypse Then," 260.

133. Roach, *Æthelred the Unready*, 246.

134. Westrem, "Against Gog and Magog," 56.

135. Westrem, "Against Gog and Magog," 57.

136. Grumeza, *The Roots of Balkanization*, 108.

137. Roach, *Æthelred the Unready*, 248.

138. Landes, "The Views of Augustine," lines 65–74.

139. Shoemaker, *The Apocalypse of Empire*, 39.

140. Mounce, *The Book of Revelation*, 23–24.

141. Shoemaker, *The Apocalypse of Empire*, 39.

142. Shoemaker, *The Apocalypse of Empire*, 39–41.

143. By which is meant the period following the end of overall Roman imperial power in the fifth century and covers the emergence of successor states in the West and the survival of imperial power in the East. The early part of this transition period is sometimes also now called "Late Antiquity" (c. 284–700); although this term also includes the final period of the Roman Empire.

144. Sivertsev, *Judaism and Imperial Ideology*, 12.

145. Magdalino, "The History of the Future," 11.

146. Shoemaker, *The Apocalypse of Empire*, 42.

147. See: Northcott, *An Angel Directs the Storm*.

148. Shoemaker, *The Apocalypse of Empire*, 42–46.

149. Landes, "The Views of Augustine," lines 141–46.

150. Clifford, *A Brief History of End Time*, 128.

151. Landes, "Lest the Millennium Be Fulfilled," 197, notes 228 and 229.

152. Landes, "Lest the Millennium Be Fulfilled," 196.

153. Landes, "Lest the Millennium Be Fulfilled," 198, note 235.

154. McGinn, "Forms of Catholic Millenarianism," 1.

155. Palmer, *The Apocalypse in the Early Middle Ages*, 6–7.

156. As examples of this approach see: Brown, *The Rise of Western Christendom* and Wickham, *Framing the Early Middle Ages*.

157. MacLean, "Apocalypse and Revolution," 100–105.

158. MacLean, "Apocalypse and Revolution," 105.

159. Landes, "Lest the Millennium Be Fulfilled," 197.

160. Landes, "Lest the Millennium Be Fulfilled," 199.

161. Landes, "Patristic and Medieval Millennialism," lines 62–65.

162. Clifford, *A Brief History of End Time*, 126.

163. Paxton, "History, Historians, and the Peace of God," 28.

164. Landes, "Medieval and Reformation Millennialism," lines 100–103.

165. Ekkehard, *Hierosolymita*, 10–11; Rubenstein, *Armies of God*, 45.

166. Rubenstein, *Armies of God*, xii.

167. Rubenstein, *Armies of God*, 9, 324.

168. Walker-Meikle, "The Goose That Went on Crusade," lines 14–17.

169. Rubenstein, *Armies of God*, 47.

170. Walker-Meikle, "The Goose That Went on Crusade," lines 22–26.

171. Rubenstein, *Armies of God*, 49.

172. Walker-Meikle, "The Goose That Went on Crusade," lines 20–1.

173. Slack, *The A to Z of the Crusades*, 87.

174. Dass, *The Deeds of the Franks*, 123, note 41.

175. Landes, "Medieval and Reformation Millennialism," lines 124–27.

176. Raedts, "The Children's Crusade," 279–323.

177. Rubenstein, *Armies of God*, 341.

178. McGinn, "Forms of Catholic Millenarianism," 1–2.

179. Rubenstein, *Nebuchadnezzar's Dream*, 47–48.

180. Slack, *The A to Z of the Crusades*, 87.

181. Almond, *The Antichrist*, 165.

182. Cavendish, "Death of Emperor Frederick II," lines 52–53.

183. Coulton, *From St Francis to Dante*, 79.

184. Almond, *The Antichrist*, 169–70.

185. Mcginn, *Visions of the End*, 173–74.

186. Mcginn, *Visions of the End*, 174–75.

187. Whittock, *When God Was King*, 128–29.

188. Mcginn, *Visions of the End*, 169–70.

189. Mcginn, *Visions of the End*, 176.

190. Cavendish, "Death of Emperor Frederick II," lines 10–11.

191. Landes, "Patristic and Medieval Millennialism," lines 145–61

192. Landes, "Patristic and Medieval Millennialism," lines 145–61

193. Ziegler, *The Black Death*, 202.

194. Ziegler, *The Black Death*, 94.

195. Landes, "Patristic and Medieval Millennialism," lines 164–94.

196. Landes, "Patristic and Medieval Millennialism," lines 164–94.

197. Ziegler, *The Black Death*, 93–94.

198. Tuchman, *A Distant Mirror*, 115–16.

199. Landes, "Patristic and Medieval Millennialism," lines 164–94.

200. Cohn, *The Pursuit of the Millennium*, 223–25.

201. Whittock, *When God Was King*, 124–25, 129.

202. Landes, "Medieval and Reformation Millennialism," lines 183–85

203. Landes, "Patristic and Medieval Millennialism," lines 110–13.

204. "When Was the Early Modern Period?" lines 1–31.

205. Boyer, *When Time Shall Be No More*, 61.

206. Cohn, *The Pursuit of the Millennium*, 243.

207. Boyer, *When Time Shall Be No More*, 61.

208. Boyer, *When Time Shall Be No More*, 63.

209. Boyer, *When Time Shall Be No More*, 62.

210. Boyer, *When Time Shall Be No More*, 62.

211. Boyer, *When Time Shall Be No More*, 62.

212. Cohn, *The Pursuit of the Millennium*, 243.

213. Whittock, *The Reformation*, 32–33.

214. Whittock, *The Reformation*, 33.

215. Drummond, "A Letter to the Princes of Saxony," lines 1–3.

216. Cohn, *The Pursuit of the Millennium*, 243.

217. Cohn, *The Pursuit of the Millennium*, 251.

218. Cohn, *The Pursuit of the Millennium*, 250–51.

219. Hill and Dell, *The Good Old Cause*, 160.

220. *The Oxford Dictionary of Quotations*, 400.

221. Whittock, *When God Was King*, 15.

222. Whittock, *When God Was King*, 15.

223. Whittock, *The Reformation*, 35.

224. Whittock, *When God Was King*, 16.

225. Whittock, *The Reformation*, 35.

226. Whittock, *The Reformation*, 35.

227. Whittock, *When God Was King*, 16.

228. Clouse, "Millennialism in the Seventeenth Century," 5.

229. Clouse, "Millennialism in the Seventeenth Century," 5.

230. Capp, *The Fifth Monarchy Men*, 51.

231. Capp, *The Fifth Monarchy Men*, 52.

232. Capp, *The Fifth Monarchy Men*, 38–39.

233. Capp, *The Fifth Monarchy Men*, 39.

234. Whittock, *When God Was King*, 130.

235. Bradstock, *Radical Religion*, 52.

236. Bradstock, *Radical Religion*, 53.

237. Hill, *The World Turned Upside Down*, 130.

238. Hill, *The World Turned Upside Down*, 130.

239. Bradstock, *Radical Religion*, 63.

240. Hill, *The World Turned Upside Down*, 128.

241. Whittock, "The Sword Drawne," 43.

242. Whittock, "The Sword Drawne," 18.

243. Capp, *The Fifth Monarchy Men*, 54.

244. Bradstock, *Radical Religion*, 96.

245. Whittock, "The Sword Drawne," 37.

246. Whittock, "The Sword Drawne," 37.

247. Abbott, *Writings and Speeches of Oliver Cromwell*, Vol. II, 473.

248. Fraser, *Cromwell: Our Chief of Men*, 424.

249. Carlyle, *The Letters and Speeches of Oliver Cromwell*, Vol. III, 58.

250. Bradstock, *Radical Religion*, 122.

251. Woolrych, "Political Theory and Political Practice," 56.

252. Firth, *Cromwell's Army*, 338.

253. Capp, *The Fifth Monarchy Men*, 65.

254. Firth, *Cromwell's Army*, 338.

255. Capp, *The Fifth Monarchy Men*, 133.

256. Fritze and Robison, *Historical Dictionary of Stuart England*, 193.

257. Forsyth, *John Milton*, 148.

258. Greaves, *Glimpses of Glory*, 138.

259. Schonhorn, *Defoe's Politics*, 18.

260. Fritze and Robison, *Historical Dictionary of Stuart England*, 193.

261. Cody, "Puritanism in New England," lines 15–16.

262. "Native Americans and Massachusetts Bay Colony," lines 16–19.

263. See Bercovitch, *The American Jeremiad* and Bercovitch, *The Puritan Origins of the American Self*. Also, Kaplan, *Our American Israel*, 5.

264. Miller, *Errand into the Wilderness*, chapter 1; Zakai, *Exile and Kingdom*, 65–67, 120–23.

265. Whittock, "The 1620 Mayflower voyage," 14.

266. Boyer, *When Time Shall Be No More*, 69.

267. Smolinski, "Israel Redividus," 357–95; Coffey, "Exile & Return," 289–313.

268. See Roberts and Whittock, *Trump and the Puritans*.

269. Smith, *A Dream of the Judgment Day*, 219.

270. Blythe, *Terrible Revolution*, 31.

271. Boyer, *When Time Shall Be No More*, 69.

272. Boyer, *When Time Shall Be No More*, 71.

273. Roberts and Whittock, *Trump and the Puritans*, 50.

274. Elliott, "The Legacy of Puritanism," lines 246–47.

275. Roberts and Whittock, *Trump and the Puritans*, 52.

276. Boyer, *When Time Shall Be No More*, 73.

277. Boyer, *When Time Shall Be No More*, 73.

278. Roberts and Whittock, *Trump and the Puritans*, 76.

279. Roberts and Whittock, *Trump and the Puritans*, 75.

280. Patterson and Walker, "Our Unspeakable Comfort," 109 note 39.

281. Ice and Stitzinger, "Rapture," 316–19.

282. Patterson and Walker, "Our Unspeakable Comfort," 109.

283. Patterson and Walker, "Our Unspeakable Comfort," 100.

284. Patterson and Walker, "Our Unspeakable Comfort," 99.

285. Tregelles, *The Hope of Christ's Second Coming*, 26.

286. Patterson and Walker, "Our Unspeakable Comfort," 108.

287. It should be noted that Revelation calls these "days" not years.

288. Gilley, "Edward Irving," 106.

289. Gilley, "Edward Irving," 106.

290. Court, *Approaching the Apocalypse*, 112.

291. Gaebelein, "The Attempted Revival," 19.

292. Rose, *Tribulation until Translation*, 245.

293. Murray, *The Puritan Hope*, 194–95.

294. Murray, *The Puritan Hope*, 286, note 32.

295. Patterson and Walker, "Our Unspeakable Comfort," 114.

296. Patterson and Walker, "Our Unspeakable Comfort," 101.

297. Court, *Approaching the Apocalypse*, 123.

298. Pietsch, *Dispensational Modernism*, 249–50 note 31.

299. Court, *Approaching the Apocalypse*, 120.

300. Court, *Approaching the Apocalypse*, 122.

301. Newport, "The Heavenly Millennium," 134.

302. Newport, "The Heavenly Millennium," 134, note 16.

303. Landman, et al., *Universal Jewish Encyclopedia*, September (Tishri).

304. Newport, "The Heavenly Millennium," 135.

305. Newcombe, *Coming Again*, 303.

306. Newport, "The Heavenly Millennium," 137–38.

307. Newport, "The Heavenly Millennium," 142.

308. See Hunt, *Religious Bodies*, 22.

309. Court, *Approaching the Apocalypse*, 126–27.

310. Court, *Approaching the Apocalypse*, 127.

311. Court, *Approaching the Apocalypse*, 128.

312. Smith, *This Atomic Age and the Word of God*.

313. Boyer, *When Time Shall Be No More*, 100.

314. Scofield, *What Do the Prophets Say?* 18.

315. For example, Fruchtenbaum, "Israel in Prophecy," 155.

316. Court, *Approaching the Apocalypse*, 193.

317. Trumbull, *Prophecy's Light on Today*, 67, on the comment made to him by Scofield on 11 December 1917.

318. Fruchtenbaum, "Israel in Prophecy," 157.

319. Ariel, "Radical Millennial Movements," 679.

320. Ariel, "Radical Millennial Movements," 679.

321. Ariel, "Radical Millennial Movements," 679.

322. Ariel, "Radical Millennial Movements," 679–80.

323. Ariel, "Radical Millennial Movements," 682–83.

324. Boyer, *When Time Shall Be No More*, 123–24.

325. Jones, *Jones' Dictionary*, 90.

326. Jones, *Jones' Dictionary*, 303.

327. Jones, *Jones' Dictionary*, 232.

328. Jones, *Jones' Dictionary*, 248, 360.

329. Jones, *Jones' Dictionary*, 132.

330. Jones, *Jones' Dictionary*, 360.

331. Jones, *Jones' Dictionary*, 311.

332. For a contemporary table of identifications (including a number of those outlined here), see Hitchcock, "Gog and Magog," 119–20.

333. For an example, see Faid, *Gorbachev!*

334. Boyer, *When Time Shall Be No More*, 178–79.

335. Hitchcock, "Gog and Magog," 121.

336. Shuck, "Christian Dispensationalism," 521.

337. Shuck, "Christian Dispensationalism," 522.

338. Boyer, *When Time Shall Be No More*, 127.

339. Boyer, *When Time Shall Be No More*, 128.

340. Boyer, *When Time Shall Be No More*, 131.

341. Boyer, *When Time Shall Be No More*, 106.

342. Price, "Temple," 372–73.

343. Shuck, "Christian Dispensationalism," 523.

344. Ariel, "Radical Millennial Movements," 681.

345. For example: Murphy, *Fallen Is Babylon*, 331, 354.

346. Shuck, "Christian Dispensationalism," 523–24.

347. Ariel, "Radical Millennial Movements," 680.

348. Hindson, "Numbers in Prophecy," 247, discusses "symbolic and prophetic" numbers in the book of Revelation, but also comments that there "are also real numbers that point to real events."

349. Valdez, *Historical Interpretations of the "Fifth Empire,"* 21.

350. Introvigne, "Modern Catholic Millenarianism," 550.

351. Introvigne, "Modern Catholic Millenarianism," 564.

352. Vine, *An Expository Dictionary*, 92.

353. LaHaye and Mayhue, "Rapture," 309.

354. LaHaye and Mayhue, "Rapture," 311.

355. LaHaye and Mayhue, "Rapture," 309.

356. Ice and Price, "Tribulation," 385–91.

357. Demy, "Tribulation Saints and Martyrs," 391.

358. Northcott, *An Angel Directs the Storm*, 88.

359. Shuck, "Christian Dispensationalism," 520.

360. Record, *Wanting War*, 47–50.

361. Northcott, *An Angel Directs the Storm*, 89.

362. Court, *Approaching the Apocalypse*, 187.

363. Ice, "Armageddon," 36.

364. Boyer, *When Time Shall Be No More*, 146.

365. Kirsch, *A History of the End of the World*, 233.

366. Court, *Approaching the Apocalypse*, 188.

367. Gallagher, "David Koresh's Christian Millenarianism," 196–97.

368. Gallagher, "David Koresh's Christian Millenarianism," 196.

369. Shuck, "Christian Dispensationalism," 515.

370. McAlister, "Prophecy, Politics, and the Popular," 775.

371. McAlister, "Prophecy, Politics, and the Popular," 773.

372. Byle, "LaHaye," lines 8–9.

373. Boyer, *When Time Shall Be No More*, 107.

374. Boyer, *When Time Shall Be No More*, 107.

375. Northcott, *An Angel Directs the Storm*, 6.

376. Boyer, *When Time Shall Be No More*, 108–9.

377. Lindermayer, "Europe as Antichrist," 42.

378. Lindermayer, "Europe as Antichrist," 42.

379. Boyer, *When Time Shall Be No More*, 277.

380. Showers, "Roman Empire," 344, speculates it might refer to "ten regions."

381. Hathaway, *Babylon in Europe*, 16.

382. McManus, "European Parliament," lines 4–7.

383. See, for example, Grey, *The Seat of the Antichrist*.

384. Whittock, "I Believe in Prophecy."

385. "European Parliament Plenary."

386. Woods and LaHaye, "Babylon," 44.

387. Lindermayer, "Europe as Antichrist," 43.

388. Lindermayer, "Europe as Antichrist," 48–49.

389. See Grey, *The Revived Roman Empire*.

390. Tanner, "Apostate Jerusalem."

391. White, *Mystery Babylon*.

392. Stillwell, *America is Mystery Babylon*.

393. Wiertzema, *The Coming Judgement on Islam*.

394. "CUFI Press Releases," line 2.

395. "CUFI Mission," line 1.

396. "CUFI Press Releases," line 40; Roberts and Whittock, *Trump and the Puritans*, 232.

397. Langton, *Jewish and Christian Perspectives*, 23.

398. Hanegraaff, *Apocalypse Code*, xx–xxii.

399. Mendelsohn Rood and Rood, "Is Christian Zionism Based on Bad Theology?" 52.

400. Mendelsohn Rood and Rood, "Is Christian Zionism Based on Bad Theology?" 46.

401. Korade, Bohn and Burke, "Controversial US Pastors," lines 8–9.

402. Allen, "In the Trump Era," lines 83–84.

403. Roberts and Whittock, *Trump and the Puritans*, 232.

404. "P.M. Netanyahu addresses CUFI."

405. Roberts and Whittock, *Trump and the Puritans*, 248–49.

406. Ravid, "'Til Kingdom Come," 1:06:41.

407. Mantyla, "Scott Lively," lines 5–6 and 11.

Bibliography

Abbott, Wilbur Cortez. *Writings and Speeches of Oliver Cromwell.* 4 vols. Cambridge: Harvard University Press, 1937–47.

Allen, Garrick V. *Manuscripts of the Book of Revelation: New Philology, Paratexts, Reception.* Oxford: Oxford University Press, 2020.

Allen, Jonathan. "In the Trump Era, Evangelicals Take Center Stage on Israel Policy." NBC News, 15 April 2019. https://www.nbcnews.com/politics/white-house/trump-era-evangelicals-take-center-stage-israel-policy-n994326.

Almond, Philip C. *The Antichrist: A New Biography.* Cambridge: Cambridge University Press, 2020.

"America's Changing Religious Landscape." https://www.pewforum.org/2015/05/12/americas-changing-religious-landscape.

Andrew of Caesarea. *Commentary on the Apocalypse.* Translated by Eugenia Scarvelis Constantinou. Washington, DC: Catholic University of America Press, 2011.

Ariel, Yaakov. "Radical Millennial Movements in Contemporary Judaism in Israel." In *The Oxford Handbook of Millennialism,* edited by Catherine Wessinger, 667–87. Oxford: Oxford University Press, 2011.

Baker, David W. *Joel, Obadiah, Malachi.* The NIV Application Commentary. Grand Rapids: Zondervan, 2006.

Bauckham, Richard J. "Apocalyptic." In *New Dictionary of Theology,* edited by Sinclair B. Ferguson and David F. Wright, 33–35, Leicester, UK: InterVarsity Press, 1988.

Bercovitch, Sacvan. *The American Jeremiad.* Madison, WI: University of Wisconsin Press, 1978.

———. *The Puritan Origins of the American Self.* New Haven, CT: Yale University Press, 2011.

Berkey, Jonathan P. *The Formation of Islam: Religion and Society in the Near East, 600–1800.* Cambridge: Cambridge University Press, 2003.

Blythe, Christopher James. *Terrible Revolution: Latter-Day Saints and the American Apocalypse.* Oxford: Oxford University Press, 2020.

Boyer, Paul. *When Time Shall Be No More: Prophecy Belief in Modern American Culture.* Cambridge: Belknap, 1992.

Bradstock, Andrew. *Radical Religion in Cromwell's England.* London: I. B. Tauris, 2011.

Brown, Peter. *The Rise of Western Christendom: Triumph and Diversity AD 200–1000.* 2nd ed. Oxford: Oxford University Press, 2003.

Bryce Ervin, Matthew. *One Thousand Years with Jesus: The Coming Messianic Kingdom*. Eugene, OR: Wipf and Stock, 2017.

Bump, Philip. "Half of Evangelicals Support Israel Because They Believe It Is Important for Fulfilling End-times Prophecy." https://www.washingtonpost.com/news/politics/wp/2018/05/14/half-of-evangelicals-support-israel-because-they-believe-it-is-important-for-fulfilling-end-times-prophecy/?noredirect=on&utm_term=.1e805224984d.

Byle, Ann. "LaHaye, Co-Author of *Left Behind* Series, Leaves a Lasting Impact." https://www.publishersweekly.com/pw/by-topic/industry-news/religion/article/71026-lahaye-co-author-of-left-behind-series-leaves-a-lasting-impact.html.

Capp, Bernard, S. *The Fifth Monarchy Men*. London: Faber and Faber, 1972.

Carlyle, Thomas, ed. *The Letters and Speeches of Oliver Cromwell*. London: Chapman and Hall, 1897.

Cavendish, Richard. "Death of Emperor Frederick II." https://www.historytoday.com/archive/death-emperor-frederick-ii.

Chilton, Bruce D. "Kingdom of God." In *The Oxford Companion to the Bible*, edited by Bruce M. Metzger and Michael D. Coogan, 408–9. Oxford: Oxford University Press, 1993.

Clifford, Paula. *A Brief History of End Time: Prophecy and Apocalypse, Then and Now*. Durham: Sacristy, 2016.

Clouse, Robert G., ed. *The Meaning of the Millennium: Four Views*. Downer's Grove, IL: InterVarsity Press, 1977.

———. "Millennialism in the Seventeenth Century." *Grace Journal*, 6.1 (1965) 3–15.

Cody, David. "Puritanism in New England." http://www.victorianweb.org/religion/puritan2.html.

Coffey, John. "Exile and Return in English Puritanism." In *Early Modern Ethnic and Religious Communities in Exile*, edited by Yosef Kaplan, 289–313. Cambridge: Cambridge Scholars, 2017.

Cohn, Norman. *The Pursuit of the Millennium*. St Albans, UK: Paladin, 1970.

Collins, John J. "Current Issues in the Study of Daniel." In *The Book of Daniel: Composition and Reception, Volume 1*, edited by John J. Collins, Peter W. Flint, 1–15. Leiden: Brill, 2002.

Coulton, George Gordon. *From St Francis to Dante: Translations from the Chronicle of the Franciscan Salimbene, 1221–1288*. Philadelphia: University of Pennsylvania Press, 1972.

Court, John M. *Approaching the Apocalypse: A Short History of Christian Millenarianism*. London: I. B. Taurus, 2008.

———. *Myth and History in the Book of Revelation*. Atlanta: John Knox, 1979.

"CUFI Mission." https://cufi.org/about/mission.

"CUFI Press Releases: On Anniversary of Jerusalem Embassy Dedication, CUFI Reaches Six Million Members." https://cufi.org/press-releases/on-anniversary-of-jerusalem-embassy-dedication-cufi-reaches-six-million-members.

Dass, Nirmal. *The Deeds of the Franks and Other Jerusalem-Bound Pilgrims. The Earliest Chronicle of the First Crusades*. Lanham, MD: Rowman & Littlefield, 2011.

Demy, Timothy. "Tribulation Saints and Martyrs." In *The Popular Encyclopedia of Bible Prophecy*, edited by Tim LaHaye and Ed Hindson, 391–92. Eugene, OR: Harvest House, 2004.

Dockery, David S. *Christian Scripture*. Nashville, TN: Broadman & Holman, 1995.

Doudna, Gregory. "The Sect of the Qumran Texts." In David Stacey and Gregory Doudna, with a contribution by Gideon Avni, *Qumran Revisited: A Reassessment of the Archaeology of the Site and Its Texts*, 75–124. BAR international series, 2520. Oxford: British Archaeological Reports Oxford, 2013.

Drummond, Andy. "A Letter to the Princes of Saxony Concerning the Rebellious Spirit." https://andydrummond.net/muentzer/PDFs/luther_letter_princes.pdf.

Ehrman, Bart D. *Jesus: Apocalyptic Prophet of the New Millennium*. Oxford: Oxford University Press, 1999.

Ekkehard of Aura. *Hierosolymita: De Oppresione, Liberatione ac Restauratione Jerosolymitanae Ecclesiae, Recueil des Historiens des Croisades, Historiens Occidentaux*. Paris France: Imprimerie Royale, 1844, 1895.

Elliott, Emory. "The Legacy of Puritanism." http://nationalhumanitiescenter.org/tserve/eighteen/ekeyinfo/legacy.htm.

Ellis, E. Earle. "Prophecy, Theology of." In *New Dictionary of Theology*, edited by Sinclair B. Ferguson and David F. Wright, 537–38, Leicester, UK: InterVarsity Press, 1988.

"Eschatological Attitudes, 4. The Kingdom of God, Eschatology and the Kingdom of God." http://www.copticchurch.net/topics/patrology/schoolofalex2/chapter20.html

"European Parliament Plenary." http://www. europarl.europa.eu/plenary/en/hemicycle. html.

Faid, Robert W. *Gorbachev! Has the Real Antichrist come?* Tulsa, OK: Victory House, 1988.

Fenton, John C. *Saint Matthew*. The Pelican New Testament Commentaries. Harmondsworth, UK: Penguin, 1963.

Firth, Charles Harding. *Cromwell's Army*. London: Methuen, 1921.

Flannagan, Nate. "Pastor John MacArthur: Covid World 'Perfectly Suited for Coming of the Antichrist.'" https://www.christiantoday.com/article/pastor.john.macarthur.covid.world.perfectly.suited.for.coming.of.antichrist/136051.htm.

Forsyth, Neil. *John Milton: A Biography*. Oxford: Lion Hudson, 2008.

Fraser, Antonia. *Cromwell: Our Chief of Men*. London: Granada, 1973.

Fredriksen, Paula. "Apocalypse and Redemption in Early Christianity: from John of Patmos to Augustine of Hippo." *Vigiliae Christianae*, 45.2 (1991) 151–83.

Fritze, Ronald H., and William B. Robison, eds. *Historical Dictionary of Stuart England, 1603–1689*. Westport, CT: Greenwood, 1996.

Fruchtenbaum, Arnold. "Israel in Prophecy." In *The Popular Encyclopedia of Bible Prophecy*, edited by Tim LaHaye and Ed Hindson, 153–58. Eugene, OR: Harvest House, 2004.

Fukuyama, Francis. *The End of History and the Last Man*. New York: Free, 1992.

Gaebelein, Arno C. "The Attempted Revival of an Unscriptural Theory." *Our Hope*, XLI, July 1934.

Gallagher, Eugene V. "David Koresh's Christian Millenarianism." In *Christian Millenarianism: From the Early Church to Waco*, edited by Stephen Hunt, 196–208. London: Hurst, 2001.

Gilley, Sheridan. "Edward Irving: Prophet of the Millennium." In *Revival and Religion since 1700: Essays for John Walsh*, edited by Jane Garnett and Colin Matthew, 95–110. London: Hambledon, 1993.

Greaves, Richard L. *Glimpses of Glory: John Bunyan and English Dissent*. Stanford, CA: Stanford University Press, 2002.

Grey, Erika. *The Revived Roman Empire: Europe in Bible Prophecy*. Danbury, CT: Pedante Press, 2013.

————. *The Seat of the Antichrist: Bible Prophecy and the European Union*. Danbury, CT: Pedante, 2010.

Grumeza, Ion. *The Roots of Balkanization: Eastern Europe C.E. 500–1500*. Lanham, MD: University Press of America, 2010.

Hadley, Dawn M. *The Vikings in England, Settlement, Society and Culture*. Manchester, UK: Manchester University Press, 2006.

Hanegraaff, Hank. *Apocalypse Code: Find Out What the Bible Really Says about the End Times and Why It Matters Today*. Nashville, TN: Thomas Nelson, 2007.

Hathaway, David. *Babylon in Europe: What Bible Prophecy Reveals about the European Union*. Bognor Regis, UK: New Wine, 2006.

Hill, Christopher. *The World Turned Upside Down: Radical Ideas During the English Revolution*. London: Maurice Temple Smith, 1972.

Hill, Christopher, and Edmund Dell. *The Good Old Cause: The English Revolution of 1640–1660*. New York: Kelly, 1969.

Hindson, Ed. "Numbers in Prophecy." In *The Popular Encyclopedia of Bible Prophecy*, edited by Tim LaHaye and Ed Hindson, 246–48. Eugene, OR: Harvest House, 2004.

Hitchcock, Mark. "Gog and Magog." In *The Popular Encyclopedia of Bible Prophecy*, edited by Tim LaHaye and Ed Hindson, 119–22. Eugene, OR: Harvest House, 2004.

The Holy Bible, New Revised Standard Version (Anglicised Edition). Oxford: Oxford University Press, 1995.

Howe, Thomas A. *Daniel in the Preterists' Den: A Critical Look at Preterist Interpretations of Daniel*. Eugene, OR: Wipf & Stock, 2008.

Hunt, William Chamberlin. *Religious Bodies, 1906. Separate Denominations: History, Description, and Statistics*. Washington, DC: Government Printing Office, 1910.

Ice, Thomas. "Armageddon." In *The Popular Encyclopedia of Bible Prophecy*, edited by Tim LaHaye and Ed Hindson, 36–42. Eugene, OR: Harvest House, 2004.

Ice, Thomas, and James Stitzinger. "Rapture, History of." In *The Popular Encyclopedia of Bible Prophecy*, edited by Tim LaHaye and Ed Hindson, 316–20. Eugene, OR: Harvest House, 2004.

Ice, Thomas, and Randall Price. "Tribulation." In *The Popular Encyclopedia of Bible Prophecy*, edited by Tim LaHaye and Ed Hindson, 385–91. Eugene, OR: Harvest House, 2004.

Ice, Thomas, and Timothy Demy, eds. *The Return: Understanding Christ's Second Coming and the End Times*. Grand Rapids: Kregel Academic, 1999.

Introvigne, Massimo. "Modern Catholic Millenarianism." In *The Oxford Handbook of Millennialism*, edited by Catherine Wessinger, 549–66. Oxford: Oxford University Press, 2011.

Johnson, Paul. *A History of Christianity*. New York: Athenium, 1976.

Jones, Alfred. *Jones' Dictionary of Old Testament Proper Names*. Grand Rapids: Kregel, 1990.

Kaplan, Amy. *Our American Israel: The Story of an Entangled Alliance*. Cambridge: Harvard University Press, 2018.

Kelly, Joseph F. *The Birth of Jesus According to the Gospels*. Collegeville, MN: Liturgical, 2008.

Keynes, Simon. "Apocalypse Then: England A.D. 1000." In *Europe Around the Year 1000*, edited by Przemysław Urbańczyk, 247–70. Warsaw: DiG, 2001.

Kirsch, Jonathan. *A History of the End of the World: How the Most Controversial Book in the Bible Changed the Course of Western Civilization*. New York: HarperCollins, 2006.

Korade, Matt, Kevin Bohn, and Daniel Burke. "Controversial US Pastors Take Part in Jerusalem Embassy Opening." CNN politics, 14 May 2018. https://edition.cnn.com/2018/05/13/politics/hagee-jeffress-us-embassy-jerusalem/index.html.

LaHaye, Tim, and Richard Mayhue. "Rapture." In *The Popular Encyclopedia of Bible Prophecy*, edited by Tim LaHaye and Ed Hindson, 309–16. Eugene, OR: Harvest House, 2004.

Landes, Richard. "Lest the Millennium be Fulfilled: Apocalyptic Expectations and the Pattern of Western Chronography 100–800CE". In *The Use and Abuse of Eschatology in the Middle Ages*, edited by Werner Verbeke et al., 137–211. Leuven, Belgium: Leuven University Press, 1988.

———. "Medieval and Reformation Millennialism." https://www.britannica.com/topic/eschatology/Medieval-and-Reformation-millennialism.

———. "Patristic and Medieval Millennialism." https://www.britannica.com/topic/millennialism/Patristic-and-medieval-millennialism.

———. "The Views of Augustine." https://www.britannica.com/topic/eschatology/Renewed-interest-in-eschatology.

Landman, Isaac, et al. *The Universal Jewish Encyclopedia: An Authoritative and Popular Presentation of Jews and Judaism Since the Earliest Times*, Volume 2. New York: Universal Jewish Encyclopedia, 1939.

Langton, Daniel. *Jewish and Christian Perspectives on the Holy Land*. Cambridge: Woolf Institute of Abrahamic Faiths, 2008.

Leaney, Alfred R. C. *A Commentary on the Gospel According to St Luke*. London: Adam & Charles Black, 1966.

Lindermayer, Orestis. "'Europe as Antichrist': North American Pre-millenarianism." In *Christian Millenarianism: From the Early Church to Waco*, edited by Stephen Hunt, 39–49. London: Hurst, 2001.

Lindsey, Hal, and Carole C. Carlson. *The Late, Great Planet Earth*. Grand Rapids: Zondervan, 1970.

MacLean, Simon. "Apocalypse and Revolution: Europe around the Year 1000." *Early Medieval Europe* 15.1 (2007) 86–106.

Magdalino, Paul. "The History of the Future and Its Uses: Prophecy, Policy and Propaganda." In *The Making of Byzantine History. Studies Dedicated to Donald M. Nicol on his Seventieth Birthday*, edited by Roderick Beaton and Charlotte Roueché, 3–34. Aldershot, UK: Variorum, 1993.

Mantyla, Kyle. "Scott Lively Thinks Kamala Harris May Be the Whore of Babylon and Barack Obama the Antichrist." https://www.rightwingwatch.org/post/scott-lively-thinks-kamala-harris-may-be-the-whore-of-babylon-and-barack-obama-the-antichrist/?fbclid=IwAR2kV1MdA_.

McAlister, Melani. "Prophecy, Politics, and the Popular: The Left Behind Series and Christian Fundamentalism's New World Order." *The South Atlantic Quarterly* 102.4 (2003) 773–98.

McGinn, Bernard. "Forms of Catholic Millenarianism: A Brief Overview." In *Millenarianism and Messianism in Early Modern European Culture, Volume II Catholic Millenarianism: From Savonarola to the Abbé Grégoire*, edited by Karl A. Kottman, 1–13. Dordrecht, Netherlands: Springer, 2001.

———. *Visions of the End: Apocalyptic Traditions in the Middle Ages*. Rev. ed. New York: Columbia University Press, 1998.

McManus, David. "The European Parliament, Strasbourg." https://www.e-architect.com/france/european-parliament-strasbourg.

Mendelsohn Rood, Judith, and Paul Rood. "Is Christian Zionism Based on Bad Theology?" *Cultural Encounters* 7.1 (2011) 41–52.

Miller, Perry. *Errand into the Wilderness.* New York: Harper and Row, 1956.

Moreschini, Claudio, and Enrico Norelli. *Early Christian Greek and Latin Literature, Volume 1.* Grand Rapids: Baker Academic, 2005.

Morris, Leon. *The Gospel According to Matthew.* Grand Rapids: Eerdmans, 1992.

Mounce, Robert H. *The Book of Revelation.* Grand Rapids: Eerdmans, 1998.

Murphy, Frederick J. *Fallen Is Babylon: The Revelation to John.* Harrisburg, PA: Trinity, 1998.

Murray, Iain. *The Puritan Hope: Revival and the Interpretation of Prophecy.* Edinburgh: Banner of Truth, 1975.

"Native Americans and Massachusetts Bay Colony." http://www.womenhistoryblog.com/2007/10/native-americans-and-massachusetts-bay.html

Newcombe, Jerry. *Coming Again.* Colorado Springs, CO: Chariot Victor, 1999.

Newport, Kenneth. "The Heavenly Millennium of Seventh-day Adventism." In *Christian Millenarianism: From the Early Church to Waco*, edited by Stephen Hunt, 131–48. London: Hurst, 2001.

Northcott, Michael. *An Angel Directs the Storm: Apocalyptic Religion & American Empire.* London: SCM, 2007.

Olsen, Henry. "Opinion: America is Becoming Less Religious. That Won't Demolish Conservatism." *The Washington Post*, 2 April 2021. https://www.washingtonpost.com/opinions/2021/04/02/america-is-becoming-more-secular-that-doesnt-mean-conservatives-are-doomed/.

The Oxford Dictionary of Quotations. 3rd ed. Oxford: Oxford University Press, 1979.

Palmer, James. *The Apocalypse in the Early Middle Ages.* Cambridge: Cambridge University Press, 2014.

Patterson, Mark, and Andrew Walker. "Our Unspeakable Comfort: Irving, Albury, and the Origins of the pre-Tribulation Rapture." In *Christian Millenarianism: From the Early Church to Waco*, edited by Stephen Hunt, 98–115. London: Hurst, 2001.

Paxton, Frederick S. "History, Historians, and the Peace of God." In *The Peace of God: Social Violence and Religious Response in France around the Year 1000*, edited by Thomas F. Head, and Richard A. Landes, 21–40. Ithaca, NY: Cornell University Press, 1992.

Percy, Martyn. "Whose Time Is It Anyway? Evangelicals, the Millennium and Millenarianism." In *Christian Millenarianism: From the Early Church to Waco*, edited by Stephen Hunt, 26–38. London: Hurst, 2001.

Pietsch, Brendan M. *Dispensational Modernism.* Oxford: Oxford University Press, 2015.

"P.M. Netanyahu addresses CUFI 2019 Summit in Washington, Arutz Sheva 7, Israel National News." https://www.youtube.com/watch?v=2HuEya5GX1M.

Poole, Kevin. "The Western Apocalypse Commentary Tradition." In *A Companion to the Premodern Apocalypse*, edited by Michael A. Ryan, 103–43. Leiden: Brill, 2016.

Porter, Stanley E. "Millenarian Thought in the First-Century Church." In *Christian Millenarianism: From the Early Church to Waco*, edited by Stephen Hunt, 62–76. London: Hurst, 2001.

Price, Randall. "Temple." In *The Popular Encyclopedia of Bible Prophecy*, edited by Tim LaHaye and Ed Hindson, 371–74. Eugene, OR: Harvest House, 2004.

PRRI. "The 2020 Census of American Religion." https://www.prri.org/research/2020-census-of-american-religion/.

Quasten, Johannes. *Patrology, Volume 2*. Chicago: Thomas More, 1986.

Raedts, Peter. "The Children's Crusade of 1213." *Journal of Medieval History* 3.4 (1977) 279–323.

Ravid, Barak. "'Til Kingdom Come: Trump, Faith and Money." BBC 4, 19 January 2021. https://www.bbc.co.uk/iplayer/episode/mooorgnz/til-kingdom-come-trump-faith-and-money.

Record, Jeffrey. *Wanting War: Why the Bush Administration Invaded Iraq*. Lincoln, NE: Potomac, 2010.

Reinink, Gerrit J. "Political Power and Right Religion." In *The Encounter of Eastern Christianity with Early Islam*, edited by Emmanouela Grypeou et al., 153–70. Leiden, Netherlands: Brill, 2006.

Roach, Levi. *Æthelred the Unready*. New Haven, CT: Yale University Press, 2017.

Roberts, Alexander, et al. *Ante-Nicene Fathers Volume I*. New York: Christian Literature, 1885.

Roberts, James, and Martyn Whittock. *Trump and the Puritans: How the Evangelical Religious Right Put Donald Trump in the White House*. London: Biteback, 2020.

Rose, George. *Tribulation until Translation*. Glendale, CA: Rose, 1943.

Rowland, Christopher. *Christian Origins: An Account of the Setting and Character of the Most Important Messianic Sect of Judaism*. London: SPCK, 1985.

Rubenstein, Jay. *Armies of Heaven: The First Crusade and the Quest for Apocalypse*. New York: Basic, 2011.

———. *Nebuchadnezzar's Dream: The Crusades, Apocalyptic Prophecy, and the End of History*. Oxford: Oxford University Press, 2019.

Sanders, E. P. *Jesus and Judaism*. Philadelphia: Fortress, 1985.

Savory, Roger Mervyn. "Christendom vs. Islam: 14 Centuries of Interaction and Coexistence." In *Introduction to Islamic Civilization*, edited by R. M. Savory, 127–36. Cambridge: Cambridge University Press, 1976.

Schonhorn, Manuel. *Defoe's Politics: Parliament, Power, Kingship and 'Robinson Crusoe'*. Cambridge: Cambridge University Press, 1991.

Schweitzer, Albert. *The Mysticism of Paul the Apostle*. Translated by William Montgomery. London: Black, 1931.

Schweizer, Eduard. *The Good News According to Matthew*. Translated by David E. Green. Louisville, KY: Westminster John Knox, 1975.

Scofield, Cyrus I. *What Do the Prophets Say?* Philadelphia: Philadelphia School of the Bible, 1918.

Shoemaker, Stephen J. *The Apocalypse of Empire: Imperial Eschatology in Late Antiquity and Early Islam*. Philadelphia: University of Pennsylvania Press, 2018.

Showers, Renald. "Roman Empire." In *The Popular Encyclopedia of Bible Prophecy*, edited by Tim LaHaye and Ed Hindson, 341–44. Eugene, OR: Harvest House, 2004.

Shuck, Glenn W. "Christian Dispensationalism." In *The Oxford Handbook of Millennialism*, edited by Catherine Wessinger, 515–28. Oxford: Oxford University Press, 2011.

Sivertsev, Alexei M. *Judaism and Imperial Ideology in Late Antiquity*. Cambridge: Cambridge University Press, 2011.

Slack, Corliss K. *The A to Z of the Crusades*. Lanham, MD: Scarecrow, 2009.

Smith, John Howard. *A Dream of the Judgment Day: American Millennialism and Apocalypticism, 1620–1890*. Oxford: Oxford University Press, 2021.

Smith, Wilbur M. *This Atomic Age and the Word of God.* Boston: Wilde, 1948.

Smolinski, Reiner. "Israel Redividus: The Eschatological Limits to Puritan Typology in New England." *New England Quarterly* 63.3 (1990) 357–95.

Stanton, Gerald. *Kept From the Hour.* Miami Springs, FL: Schoettle, 1991.

Stefon, Matt, ed. *Judaism: History, Belief, and Practice.* New York: Rosen, 2012.

Stillwell, Steven E. *America Is Mystery Babylon: Mystery, Babylon the Great, the Mother of Harlots, and Abominations of the Earth.* Scotts Valley, CA: CreateSpace, 2018.

Swete, Henry Barclay. *The Apocalypse of St John.* London: Macmillan, 1906.

Tabor, James D. "Ancient Jewish and Early Christian Millennialism." In *The Oxford Handbook of Millennialism,* edited by Catherine Wessinger, 252–65. Oxford: Oxford University Press, 2011.

Tanner, J. Paul. "Apostate Jerusalem as Babylon the Great: Another Look at Revelation 17–18." ETS SW Regional Conference, Fort Worth, TX, 31 March 2017.

Theissen, Gerd, and Annette Merz. *The Historical Jesus: A Comprehensive Guide.* London: SCM, 1998.

Tixeront, Joseph. *A Handbook of Patrology.* Translated by S. A. Raemers. St. Louis, MO: Herder, 1920.

Travis, Stephen H. "Eschatology." In *New Dictionary of Theology,* edited by Sinclair B. Ferguson and David F. Wright, 228–31, Leicester, UK: InterVarsity Press, 1988.

Tregelles, Samuel P. *The Hope of Christ's Second Coming.* London: Houlston and Wright, 1864.

Trumbull, Charles G. *Prophecy's Light on Today.* New York: Revell, 1937.

Tuchman, Barbara W. *A Distant Mirror. The Calamitous 14th Century.* Harmondsworth, UK; Penguin, 1979.

Unger, Merrill F., and William White, eds. *Nelson's Expository Dictionary of the Old Testament.* Nashville, TN: Thomas Nelson, 1980.

Valdez, Ana. *Historical Interpretations of the "Fifth Empire": The Dynamics of Periodization from Daniel to António Vieira, S.J.* Leiden: Brill, 2011.

Vine, W. E. *An Expository Dictionary of New Testament Words.* Nashville, TN: Thomas Nelson, 1983.

Walker-Meikle, Kathleen. "The Goose That Went on Crusade." https://www.themedievalmagazine.com/past-issue-features/2020/5/5/the-goose-that-went-on-crusade-by-dr-kathleen-walker-meikle.

Westrem, Scott D. "Against Gog and Magog." In *Text and Territory: Geographical Imagination in the European Middle Ages,* edited by Sylvia Tomasch and Sealy Gilles, 54–78. Philadelphia: University of Pennsylvania Press, 1998.

"When Was the Early Modern Period?" https://www.open.edu/openlearn/history-the-arts/early-modern-europe-introduction/content-section-2.

White, Chris. *Mystery Babylon—When Jerusalem Embraces the Antichrist: An Exposition of Revelation 17 and 18.* Ducktown, TN: CWM, 2013.

Whitelock, Dorothy, ed. *English Historical Documents, Volume I, c.500–1042.* London: Eyre Methuen, 1979.

Whittock, Martyn. "The 1620 Mayflower Voyage and the English Settlement of North America." *The Historian* 145 Spring/Summer (2020) 10–15.

———. "I Believe in Prophecy. But the EU Is Not Babylon the Great." https://www.premierchristianity.com/Blog/I-believe-in-prophecy.-But-the-EU-is-not-Babylon-the-Great.

———. *The Reformation.* Oxford: Heinemann, 1992.

———. "'The Sword Drawne': Christian Dissent and Politics 1649–1666, Particularly in the Fields of Millenarianism and Antinomianism." Undergraduate dissertation, University of Bristol, 1980.

———. "Vikings: When the Hammer Met the Cross." https://www.churchtimes.co.uk/articles/2018/26-october/features/features/vikings-when-the-hammer-met-the-cross.

———. *When God Was King: Rebels and Radicals of the Civil War and Mayflower Generation*. Oxford: Lion Hudson, 2018.

Whittock, Martyn, and Esther Whittock. *Christ: The First 2000 Years*. Oxford: Lion Hudson, 2016.

Whittock, Martyn, and Hannah Whittock. *The Viking Blitzkrieg AD 789–1098*. Stroud, UK: History, 2013.

———. *The Vikings: From Odin to Christ*. Oxford: Lion Hudson, 2018.

Wickham, Christopher. *Framing the Early Middle Ages: Europe and the Mediterranean 400–800*. Oxford: Oxford University Press, 2005.

Wiertzema, John. *The Coming Judgement on Islam: An Exposition of Revelation Chapters 17 and 18*. Maitland, FL: Xulon, 2007.

Woods, Andy, and Tim LaHaye. "Babylon." In *The Popular Encyclopedia of Bible Prophecy*, edited by Tim LaHaye and Ed Hindson, 42–44. Eugene, OR: Harvest House, 2004.

Woolrych, Austin. "Political Theory and Political Practice." In *The Age of Milton: Backgrounds to Seventeenth-century Literature*, edited by C. A. Patrides and Raymond B. Waddington, 34–71. Manchester: Manchester University Press, 1980.

Wright, N. T. *Jesus and the Victory of God*. London: SPCK, 1996.

Zakai, Avihu. *Exile and Kingdom: History and Apocalypse in the Puritan Migration to America*. Cambridge: Cambridge University Press, 1991.

Ziegler, Philip. *The Black Death*. Harmondsworth, UK: Penguin, 1982.